LIBRARIES AND LIBRARIANS OF THE WORLD

LIBRARIES AND LIBRARIANS OF THE WORLD

By:

DR. AMJAD ALI

Deputy Librarian

Aligarh Muslim University, Aligarh

Ess Ess Publications

4837/24, Ansari Road

Darya Ganj

New Delhi-110 002

Ph: 23260807, 41563444

Fax: 41563334

E-mail: info@essessreference.com

url: http://www.essessreference.com

First Published **2006**

ISBN: 81-7000-482-9

Rs.550/-

Published by:
Ess Ess Publications
4837/24, Ansari Road, Darya Ganj, New Delhi-110 002
Tel: 011-23260807, 41563444 Fax: 011-41563334
E-mail: info@essessreference.com
url: www.essessreference.com

Printed in India at:
Printline, New Delhi

CONTENTS

Preface

SECTION - A : LIBRARIES ... 3

SECTION - B : LIBRARIANS ... 135

PREFACE

Libraries are the memory of mankind. They contain knowledge, the most precious creation of man. Libraries existed in all civilizations. The earlier ones rested in the minds of knowledgible persons but with the advent of information technology knowledge expanded enormously.

Librarians are the custodians of knowledge. They have themselves been the most distinguished and knowledgible persons of the society. With the growth of human civilization, knowledge increased in geometrical progression and reached beyond the capacity of man's memory. Hence, ways and means were developed to cope with the unprecedented growth. Librarians expertized in the art of management of knowledge with their specially developed skills.

This book enlists the famous libraries and librarians of the world. It is divided into two sections devoted to libraries and librarians respectively. Entries are arranged in alphabetical order to facilitate an easy consultation.

Information for this volume was collected from various sources of print as well as the electronic media specially the World Wide Web. I feel indebted to some individuals and organizations whose resources have been used in preparation of this volume. Dr. Radhey Shyam, and Mr. Yousuf Siddiqui of the Maulana Azad Library deserve my special thanks for their invaluable assistance in providing useful information on librarians. I also thank the Publisher for bringing out this book.

Dr. Amjad Ali

amjad_alig@yahoo.co.in

SECTION A : LIBRARIES

S. No.	Name	Page No.
1.	Alexandria Library	... 1
2.	Alexandria Digital Library	... 5
3.	Archives of India Labour	... 6
4.	Asa Archives	... 6
5.	Asad National Library	... 8
6.	Asiatic Society Library, Kolkata	... 8
7.	Auckland University of Technology Archive	... 10
8.	Austrian Public Library	... 11
9.	Baker Library	... 12
10.	Bancroft Library	... 12
11.	Beinecke Rare Book and Manuscript Library	... 12
12.	Berkeley Digital Library	... 14
13.	Berlin State Library	... 14
14.	Biblioteca Nazionale Centrale di Roma	... 15
15.	Bibliothèque nationale de France	... 16
16.	Bibliothèque nationale du Québec	... 17
17.	Bodleian Library (Oxford)	... 19
18.	Boston Public Library	... 19
19.	British Library	... 20
20.	Brooklyn Public Library	... 23
21.	California Digital Library	... 23
22.	Cambridge University Library	... 24
23.	Cecil H. Green Library	... 25
24.	Celsus Library	... 26
25.	Central Library, ISI Kolkata	... 26

S. No.	Name	Page No.
26.	Chester Beatty Library	... 27
27.	Chetham's Library	... 27
28.	Connemara Public Library	... 28
29.	Consortium of University Research Libraries	... 28
30.	Delhi Public Library	... 29
31.	Delhi University Library System	... 29
32.	Developing Library Network	... 30
33.	Dhaka University Library	... 32
34.	Die Deutsche Bibliothek	... 33
35.	Digital Library Technology Project	... 34
36.	Digital South Asia Library	... 34
37.	Digitale Bibliothek Information und Medien, Germany	... 34
38.	Dr. Zakir Husain Library	... 35
39.	Dumbarton Oaks Research Library, Washington, DC	... 36
40.	Folger Shakespeare Library	... 36
41.	Free Library of Philadelphia	... 36
42.	Garrison Library	... 37
43.	German Library	... 38
44.	Global Digital Library	... 39
45.	Global Library Services	... 39
46.	Goethals Indian Library & Research Center	... 40
47.	Government Oriental Manuscripts Library, Chennai	... 40
48.	Grand Ayatollah Mar'ashi Najafi Public Library, Qom	... 41
49.	Hakim Mohammed Said Central Library	... 41
50.	Hilandar Research Library	... 42
51.	Huntington Library	... 42

S. No.	Name	Page No.
52.	India Office Library, London	... 42
53.	Indian Digital Library of Engineering Science and Technology	... 43
54.	Indian Institute of Advanced Study Library, Simla	... 43
55.	Indian Institute of Technology Roorkee Archive	... 44
56.	Indira Gandhi National Centre for the Arts Library	... 45
57.	Institute of Asian Studies Library, Chennai	... 46
58.	Institute of Manuscripts Library, Baku	... 47
59.	Institute of Museum and Library Services	... 48
60.	Institute Of Oriental Studies Library	... 48
61.	International Coalition of Library Consortia	... 48
62.	Internet Public Library	... 49
63.	Iraqi House of Manuscripts, Baghdad	... 49
64.	ISI-BC Library Mysore	... 50
65.	J R D Tata Memorial Library	... 50
66.	Jamia Al Azhar Library, Cairo	... 51
67.	Jawaharlal Nehru University Library, New Delhi	... 52
68.	John Rylands University Library, Manchester	... 53
69.	JSTOR, Journals, Digital libraries	... 53
70.	Juma Al Majid Centre for Culture and Heritage, Dubai	... 54
71.	Kedermister Library	... 55
72.	King Faisal Center for Research and Islamic Studies, Riyadh	... 56
73.	Koninklijke Bibliotheek, the National Library of the Netherlands	... 57
74.	Khuda Bakhsh Oriental Public Library, Patna	... 57
75.	LeHigh University Library, United States	... 58
76.	Library and Archives of Canada	... 58

S. No.	Name	Page No.
77.	Library of Ashurbanipal	... 59
78.	Library of Congress	... 61
79.	Library of Sir Thomas Browne	... 63
80.	Library of the British Museum	... 64
81.	Library of Tibetan Works and Archives	... 64
82.	Macmillan Information SuperLibrary	... 66
83.	Maulana Azad Library	... 66
84.	Mohammed VI Library at Al Akhawayn University	... 67
85.	Murdoch University Library	... 68
86.	Mysore University Library, Mysore	... 68
87.	Nalanda Digital Library	... 69
88.	Nalanda University Library	... 69
89.	National Agricultural Library	... 70
90.	National and University Library of Bosnia and Herzegovina	... 71
91.	National Archeological Database "National Archeological Database "	... 72
92.	National Archives and Records Administration	... 72
93.	National Archives and the National Library of Bangladesh	... 74
94.	National Archives of Australia	... 74
95.	National Archives of India	... 75
96.	National Archives of Japan	... 75
97.	National Diet Library	... 75
98.	National Information Standards Organisation	... 76
99.	National Lending Library for Science and Technology	... 76
100.	National Libraries of South Africa	... 77
101.	National Library and Archives of Egypt, Cairo	... 78
102.	National Library of Albania	... 80

S. No.	Name	Page No.
103.	National Library of Australia	... 81
104.	National Library of Bangladesh	... 82
105.	National Library of Bulgaria	... 83
106.	National Library of Canada	... 84
107.	National Library of China	... 84
108.	National Library of Czechoslovakia	... 85
109.	National Library of Denmark	... 87
110.	National Library of Education	... 88
111.	National Library of Greece	... 91
112.	National Library of Guiana	... 92
113.	National Library of India	... 93
114.	National Library of Iran	... 94
115.	National Library of Ireland, Ireland	... 94
116.	National Library of Medicine	... 95
117.	National Library of Nepal	... 96
118.	National Library of New Zealand	... 97
119.	National Library of Norway	... 97
120.	National Library Of Pakistan	... 98
121.	National Library of Russia	... 99
122.	National Library of Scotland	... 99
123.	National Library of Wales	... 101
124.	National Science Library of India NISCAIR	... 101
125.	National Széchényi Library of Hungary	... 102
126.	New York Public Library (NYPL)	... 104
127.	New Zealand Digital Library	... 105
128.	Online Computer Library Center (OCLC)	... 105
129.	Oviatt Library	... 106
130.	Oxford Digital Library	... 106
131.	Pierpont Morgan Library, New York	... 106
132.	Rampur Raza Library	... 107

S. No.	Name	Page No.
133.	Register of Australian Archives and Manuscripts	... 107
134.	RLG's Archival Resources	... 109
135.	Robarts Library	... 109
136.	Rosenbach Museum & Library, Philadelphia	... 110
137.	Royal Asiatic Society Library London	... 110
138.	Royal Asiatic Society Library, Mumbai	... 112
139.	Royal Library of Copenhagen	... 113
140.	Salar Jung Museum and Library, Hyderabad	... 114
141.	Sarasvati Bhavan Library, Benaras	... 115
142.	Saraswati Mahal Library, Tanjore	... 116
143.	Sayajirao Gaekwad Library, Banaras Hindu University	... 117
144.	Scholarly Information Services/Library	... 118
145.	Scholarly Publishing and Academic Resources Coalition	... 118
146.	Seattle Central Library	... 119
147.	State Library of South Africa	... 120
148.	State Library of Victoria	... 121
149.	Suleymania Library	... 122
150.	Suzzallo Library	... 123
151.	Swedish Royal Library	... 124
152.	Swiss National Library	... 125
153.	Topkapi Palace Library, Istanbul	... 125
154.	Troy Public Library	... 126
155.	Turkish National Library	... 127
156.	University of Cambridge Library	... 128
157.	University of Illinois Library	... 129
158.	University of Punjab Library, Lahore	... 130
159.	University of Sydney Library	... 131
160.	Vatican Library	... 132

SECTION B : LIBRARIANS

S. No.	Name	Page No.
1.	Ahmed Rami	... 137
2.	Ainsworth Rand Spofford	... 138
3.	Antoine Alexandre Barbier	... 139
4.	Antonio Genesio Maria Panizzi	... 140
5.	Archibald MacLeish	... 140
6.	Anastasius Bibliothecarius	... 142
7.	Ashurbanipal,	... 144
8.	Bashiruddin, S	... 145
9.	Benjamin Franklin	... 146
10.	Benjamin Peirce	... 148
11.	Berners-Lee, Timothy	... 149
12.	Bonnie Nardi	... 152
13.	Callimachus	... 153
14.	Charles Pickering	... 154
15.	Charles Ammi Cutter	... 155
16.	Charles Wilkins	... 157
17.	Dana, John Cotton	... 159
18.	Daniel J. Boorstin	... 160
19.	David Hume	... 160
20.	Dehkhoda, Ali Akbar	... 162
21.	Demetrius	... 164
22.	Ed Greenwood	... 164
23.	Edmund William Gosse	... 165
24.	Edward Augustussee	... 165
25.	Edward Singleton Holden	... 166

S. No.	Name	Page No.
26.	Eratosthenes of Cyrene	... 167
27.	Francis Hayman	... 170
28.	Friedrich Sylburg	... 170
29.	Fuat Seizgin	... 171
30.	Gabriel Naudé	... 172
31.	Gaius Suetonius Tranquillus	... 173
32.	Gary Price	... 173
33.	George Watterston	... 174
34.	Giacomo Casanova	... 175
35.	Henri Marie La Fontaine	... 176
36.	Herbert Putnam	... 179
37.	Hypatia of Alexandria	... 180
38.	Imtiaz Ali Khan	... 182
39.	Ina Coolbrith	... 183
40.	Issac Casaubon	... 184
41.	James Douglas Pearson	... 187
42.	James Hadley Billington	... 189
43.	Jan Gruter	... 192
44.	Johann Albert Fabricius	... 192
45.	Johann Matthias Gesner	... 194
46.	John Gould Stephenson	... 194
47.	John James Beckley	... 195
48.	John Russell Young	... 195
49.	John Silva Meehan	... 196
50.	Jorge Luis Borges	... 197
51.	Justin Winsor	... 199
52.	Kaul, H.K.	... 199
53.	Kaula, Prithvi Nath	... 201
54.	Kenneth MacLean Glazier, Sr.	... 203

S. No.	Name	Page No.
55.	Khuda Bakhsh Khan	... 203
56.	Larry Page	... 204
57.	Laura Welch Bush.	... 204
58.	Lawrence Quincy Mumford	... 206
59.	Leibniz,Gottfried Wilhelm von	... 206
60.	Li Dazhao	... 208
61.	Ludovico Antonio Muratori	... 209
62.	Ludwig Bechstein	... 209
63.	Luther H. Evans	... 210
64.	Lynne Brindley	... 210
65.	Major Robert Odell Owens	... 210
66.	Mangla, P.B	... 211
67.	Mao Zedong	... 212
68.	Margaret Leiteritz	... 214
69.	Marianne Moore	... 214
70.	Marshal McLuhan	... 215
71.	Melville Dewey	... 217
72.	Michael Lorenzen	... 218
73.	Nancy Pearl	... 219
74.	Newbery, John	... 219
75.	Patrick Magruder	... 220
76.	Paul Otlet	... 220
77.	Philip Larkin	... 221
78.	Pierre François le Courayer	... 223
79.	Raj Reddy	... 224
80.	Ranganathan, Shiyali Ramamrita	... 225
81.	Sanford Berman	... 228
82.	Schumacher Sanford Berman	... 229
83.	Sergey Brin	... 230

S. No.	Name	Page No.
84.	Seymour Lubetzky	... 232
85.	Thomas James	... 232
86.	Thomas Louis Berger	... 233
87.	Wallace Breem	... 233
88.	Wilhelm Lexis	... 233
89.	William Henry Bliss	... 234
90.	William Jones	... 236

SECTION-A : LIBRARIES

Alexandria Library The Royal Library of Alexandria was once the largest in the world. It was founded at the beginning of the 3rd century BC during the reign of Ptolemy II of Egypt after his father had set up the Temple of the Muses or Museum. The initial organization is attributed to Demetrius Phalereus. The Library is estimated to have stored at its peak 400,000 to 700,000 scrolls.

The Library was seeded with Aristotle's own private collection, through one of his students, Demetrius Phalereus. By decree of Ptolemy III of Egypt, all visitors to the city were required to surrender all books and scrolls in their possession; these writings were then swiftly copied by official scribes. The originals were put into the Library, and the copies were delivered to the previous owners. While encroaching on the rights of the traveler or merchant, it also helped to create a reservoir of books in the relatively new city.

The Library's contents were likely distributed over several buildings, with the main library either located directly attached to or close to the oldest building, the Museum, and a daughter library in the younger Serapeum, also a temple dedicated to the God Serapis. The archaeologists claimed to have found thirteen "lecture halls", each with a central podium. The rooms uncovered so far could have seated 5000 students. One of the reasons so little is known about the Library is that it was lost centuries after its creation. All that is left of many of the volumes are tantalizing titles that hint at all the history lost from the building's destruction. Few events in ancient history are as controversial as the destruction of the Library, as the historical record is both contradictory and incomplete. Not surprisingly, the Great Library became a symbol for knowledge itself, and its destruction was attributed to those who were portrayed as ignorant barbarians, often for purely political reasons. Much of the debate rests on a different understanding of what constituted the actual Library.

Large parts of the Library were likely decentralized, so it is appropriate to also speak of the "Alexandrian libraries". Both the Serapeum, a temple and daughter library, and the Museum itself existed until about AD 400. Only if one believes the Museum to be distinct from the Great Library, an event of destruction prior to that point becomes plausible. One account of such an event of destruction concerns Julius Caesar. During his invasion of Alexandria in 47–48 BC, Caesar set the enemy fleet in the harbor on fire. Egert Pöhlmann cites further expansions of the Alexandrian libraries by Caesar Augustus (in the year AD 12) and Claudius (AD 41-54). Even if the most extreme allegations against Caesar were true, this raises the question of what happened to these volumes. The continued existence of the Library is also supported by an ancient inscription found in the early 20th century, dedicated to Tiberius Claudius Balbillus of Rome (d. AD 56).

The idea of reviving the old library dates back to 1974, when a committee set up by the University of Alexandria selected a plot of land for its new library, between the campus and the seafront, close to where the ancient library once stood. The notion of recreating the ancient library was soon enthusiastically adopted by other individuals and agencies. One leading supporter of the project was President Hosni Mubarak of Egypt; UNESCO was also quick to embrace the idea of endowing the Mediterranean region with a center of cultural and scientific excellence. An architectural competition, organized by UNESCO in 1988 to choose a design worthy of the site and its heritage, was won by the Norwegian company Snøhetta from among more than 1,400 entries. At a conference held in 1990 in Aswan, the first pledges of funding for the project were made mostly from the Arab states.

Construction work began in 1995 and the complex was officially inaugurated on October 16, 2002. The dimensions of the project are vast: the library has shelf space for eight million books, with the main reading room covering 70,000 m^2 on eleven cascading levels. The complex also houses a conference center; specialized libraries for the blind, for young people, and for children; three museums; four art galleries; a planetarium; and a manuscript restoration laboratory. The library's architecture is equally striking. The main reading room stands beneath a 32-meter-high glass-panelled roof, tilted out toward the sea like a sundial, and measuring some 160 m in diameter. The walls are of gray Aswan granite, carved with characters from 120 different human scripts. The Library also maintains a copy of the Internet Archive.

Alexandria Digital Library (ADL) The Library started as project in 1994 at the University of California, Santa Barbara (UCSB). At the end of 1998, ADL had an operational Catalog (ca. 2 million metadata records) and Gazetteer (ca. 5 million place name records). The Catalog was constructed mainly from non-MARC metadata, with digital data primarily from U.S. federal and state agencies. The Gazetteer database was constructed from two existing sources: the Geographic Names Information System (GNIS) for U.S. place names and for foreign names the database generated by the U.S. Board on Geographic Names (BGN); these entries were merged and redefined via a locally constructed feature-type thesaurus, using a locally constructed content standard.

In 1999, the UCSB Library assumed ownership of the Catalog and Gazetteer. Since that time, the Catalog emphasizes adding heavy-use digital data of the state of California and is in effect the item-level online catalog for the Map and Imagery Laboratory (MIL) of the UCSB Library, whereas the Gazetteer has become a leader in place name research. It is a consortium of researchers, developers, and educators, spanning the academic, public, and private sectors, exploring a variety of problems related to a distributed digital library for geographically-referenced information. The library's components may be spread across the Internet, as well as coexisting on a single desktop. All the objects in the library will be associated with one or more regions ("footprints") on the surface of the Earth."

Archives of Indian Labour A collaborative project between the National Labour Institute and the Association of Indian Labour Historians, the Archives of Indian Labour are dedicated to preserving and making accessible historic documents on the Indian working class. This library, which is in the English language, contains collections on the All India Trade Union Congress (1928-96), the Commission on Labour (1930-1991), an Oral History of the Labour Movement in India, and special collections on key events in India's labour history. Site: <http://www.indialabourarchives.org/> The Archives of Indian Labour was constituted with the long-term objective to act as a specialised repository of records and voices of the workers, and contain textual, visual and oral records on labour in India.

At present in total 8 special collections comprising 40,000 printed pages, 100 hours of taped interviews are stored in digital form. In addition several special reports and articles on labour history of India are also available on this digital library. This library has been developed using Greenstone open source software at V.V. Giri National Labour Institute, Noida. Registration is required to access the library.

Asa Archives The Asa Archives is a public library of Nepalese Manuscripts named after the late Mr. Asha Man Singha Kansakar. Mr. Kansakar was prominent activist, social worker, educationist and Newar writer who had founded several social, cultural, literary and educational institutions. The nucleus of this was donated by Prem Bahadur Kansakar to Cvasa Pasa, a premier literary association of Newar writers on August 16,1985. To this personal collection were later added the donations of valuable manuscripts and palm leaf documents by several well-wishers and friends. Among them mention should be made of Mr. Ian Alshop, an American student of Kansakar, Dharma Ratna Vajracarya, Guru Sekhar Rajopadhyaya, Rev. Hidonobu Takaoka, Gyan Ratna and Dr. Kamal Prakash Malla. Similarly, more than a dozen other donors have helped this archive with gifts from their personal collections of manuscripts. In this archive there are several valuable collections of palm leaf, loose-leaf pothi and folded manuscripts.

In the Archives, there are more than 6,700 manuscripts and about 1100 palm leaf land grant documents. These manuscripts belong to various sects and genres written in different languages and scripts. Largest among these are the ritual texts, medical texts, manuals of magic and necromancy, astrology/astronomy, Vedic and Puranic texts, and Tantric texts of the êaiva, Bauddha, and êakta sects. A large number also come from the Mahayana and Vajrayana Buddhism. There are technical and symbolical drawings and architectural designs of religious and secular structures, painted covers, and book illustrations of great beauty and delicacy. Perhaps the most important component of the archives is the literary texts, hymns, songs, plays, popular narratives, didactic tales and Buddhist avadanas in the Newar language. One can find specimens of beautiful calligraphy in the collection written in plain black ink, silver and golden letters. The Archives has also a collection of nearly all Nepali books in print, journals, magazines and newspapers in Nepali. There is also a small Nepal collection, consisting of books on Nepal in English and other languages which will be of great interest for study and research on the culture and heritage of the Nepal valley.

Asad National Library The Asad Library was established in 1984 in Damascus to serve as a national library and to house manuscript collections from all over the country. The mid-1990s was an auspicious time for American researchers in Syria because of the establishment of the American Research Institute in Syria (ARIS), a consortium of American universities that has been working for the past several years to establish an institute for research with residential facilities for them in Damascus at par with the European facilities there.

The Asad Library replaced al-Zahiriyah Library. The Asad Library has published annual issues of the Syrian National Bibliography (al-Bibliyuqhrafiya al-Wataniyah al-Suriyah) since 1985. The bibliography is a comprehensive list of Syrian publications. It includes short annotations for some entries and author, title, and subject indexes. A list of all Syrian publishers and a list of newspapers and periodicals are also included. The Asad Library is attempting the publication of a Syrian retrospective bibliography. The first issue was published in 1987. The Asad Library also publishes a quarterly index to Syrian periodicals (al-Kashshaf al-Tahlili lil-Suhuf wa-al-Majallat al-Suriyahi).

The Asad Library is playing a major role in promoting the distribution of Syrian publications outside the country. The library has established exchange programs with many institutions around the world, and willingly continues to do so. The Library of Congress Middle East Cooperative Acquisition Program (MECAP) has established a good relationship with the Asad Library. For the first time in many years MECAP has access to Syrian publications through their representative in Damascus. MECAP provides a blanket order plan that includes Syrian publications. The program's diplomatic connection makes it easy to obtain Syrian publications.

Asiatic Society Library, Kolkata The Asiatic Society is a premier oriental institution of the Asian continent. It was founded in 1784 by Sir William Jones (1746-1794) who dreamt of a centre for Asian studies including almost everything concerning man and nature within the geographical limits of the continent, the history, civil and natural, the antiquities, arts, sciences and literature of Asia.

The Library of the Society is the glory and honour of the Society. Its importance lies not in numerical strength but in its rich and unique contents. The collection has been built up mainly with gifts received from the members, dating back to 25 March 1784, when the Society received with thanks seven Persian manuscripts from Henri Richardson. The next gift came from William Marsden, F.R.S., his book, History of Island of Sumatra (1783) on 10 November, 1984. Since the foundation of the Society, books, manuscripts, drawings, coins, antiquarian and other objects of historical importance were exhibited to the Society's meetings, and kept in the custody of the Secretary. As the Society had no habitat of its own, the risk of loss was serious. After the demise of the founder, the question of a permanent house for the Society was strongly felt for transacting its academic activities and for keeping and preserving for the posterity books, records, art, antiquarian and museum objects.

In 1808 the Library was thrown open to the members and the public. Thus the Society laid the foundation of the first Academic as well as Public Library in India. The books that had been received till then formed the nucleus of the collection. Since then, gifts were pouring in from heads of States (e.g. Emperor of Russia), Institutions, Societies and individuals. Robert Home who was for some time Secretary of the Society and the first Library-in-Charge (1804), donated his small but very valuable collection of works on Art. The first accession of importance was a gift from the Seringapatam Committee (3 February 1808). being a selection from the palace library of Tipoo Sultan. The Collection contains many old and rare works. Special mention may be made of an illuminated manuscript of the Quran an old text of Gulistan, and manuscripts of Padshanamah bearing an autograph of Emperor Shahjahan.

Auckland University of Technology Archive The Archives hold and collect material that reflect the organisational function and history of the Auckland University of Technology, including such areas as AUT Council material, Alumni Association, ASTE records and TIASA records. Memorabilia (i.e. photographs, posters, brochures and promotional material) from Seddon Memorial Technical School in 1895 to the present. Use of material may be restricted subject to conditions of privacy and/or confidentiality. Advice on the appraisal of records and other items for the suitability of transfer to the Archives is available on request. Records of the materials held in the Archives can be accessed through the AUT Library Catalogue. Included in some of these records are digital images of the specific materials.

The University Library Archives is the repository for records of permanent value, which may be used for research purposes by library clients or by the Library for administration purposes. The Archives is responsible for identifying, acquiring, preserving and providing access to these records. The granting of permission to examine and study the records or collections held by the Archives and extract information for research purposes. Those records that are appraised as having continuing value and have been selected for permanent preservation but no longer required for current use.

All the materials in the Library Archives is available for reference unless the Liaison Librarian for the Archives, depositing office, or donor has placed restriction on the records. Records under restriction may be consulted but only with the permission of the donor or depositing office. The Liaison Librarian for the Archives is the person to whom requests to consult records will be made. The Liaison

Librarian for the Archives is responsible to ensure that the rules and regulations governing the access to and the use of material are observed, and to contact donors, when a request is made concerning the use of donated records under restriction. The Archives retains the right to charge for any reproduction or other research service. A schedule of fees is made available regularly. The Archives retains the right to reproduce materials by mechanical, electronic, or photographic means for conservation, security or research purposes.

Austrian National library is the legal successor to the Imperial Royal Court Library of the Austrian Empire. The beginnings of the library go back to the second half of the 14th century when the Habsburgs began to collect manuscripts or to commission them. The splendid baroque library constructed between 1723 and 1726 at Josefsplatz housed all the court library's manuscripts, incunabula, autographs, printed books, maps, globes and copper engravings until the late 19th century. The various special collections were then transferred to buildings adjoining the imperial library.

The library was named the Austrian National Library in 1945 (from 1920 -1945 it was called the National Library). In 1967 central reading areas (catalogues, the main reading room and the periodicals reading room) were moved to the new imperial palace at Heldenplatz. In 1992 the subterranean area with large subterranean depots and additional reading rooms (for large formats and micro forms) was opened. The approx. 6 million items in the ccollections make the Austrian National Library the largest library in Austria. The library holds over 3,086,331 printed books, 1,595,100 picture documents, 386,983 manuscripts and autographs, about 300,000 broadsheets, 258,787 maps, 140,562 papyri and other objects in the papyrus collection as well as 104,403 items in the international esperanto museum.

Baker Library Is the main library at Dartmouth College. The fresco, Baker Library opened in 1928 with a collection of 240,000 volumes. The building was designed by Jens Frederick Larson and funded by a gift to Dartmouth College by George Fisher Baker in memory of his uncle (Fisher Ames Baker, Dartmouth class of 1859). The facility was expanded in 1941 and 1957-1958 and received its one millionth volume in 1970. In 1992, John Berry and the Baker family donated US $30 million for the construction of a new facility adjoining the Baker Library; in 2000, the Berry Library opened. The Dartmouth College libraries presently hold over 2 million volumes in their collections.

Bancroft Library, The Baneroft Library is the rare books and special collections repository of U.C. Berkeley. Specializing in Western Americana and the history of California, its collections include books, printed ephemera, manuscripts, archival collections, and pictorial collections. The library's California Heritage Digital Image Access project makes available over 25,000 images from the collections — primarily photographs, but also drawings, prints, and other images of California

Beinecke Rare Book and Manuscript Library, Yale University's Beinecke Rare Book and Manuscript Library was a 1963 gift of the Beinecke family. The building of this Library is the largest building in the world reserved exclusively for the preservation of rare books and manuscripts. It is built at the center of the University, in Hewitt Quadrangle, which is more commonly referred to as "Beinecke Plaza". A six-story above-ground tower of book stacks is surrounded by a windowless rectangular building with walls made of translucent Vermont marble, which transmit subdued lighting and provide protection from direct light. Three floors of stacks extend under Hewitt Quadrangle.

The library also contains an exhibition hall, study areas, reading rooms, the catalogue room, microfilm room, offices, and the book storage areas. During the 1960s, Claes Oldenburg's sculpture "Lipstick on a Caterpillar Track" was displayed in Beinecke Plaza. In the late 19th century the rarer and more valuable books of the Library of Yale College were placed on special shelving at the Old Library. These were moved to the Rare Book Room collection of Sterling Memorial Library when it opened in 1930. When the Beinecke Rare Book and Manuscript Library opened its doors on October 14, 1963, it had become the home of the volumes from the Sterling Memorial Library Rare Book Room, and three special collections—the Collection of American Literature, the Collection of Western Americana, and the Collection of German Literature. Shortly afterward, they were joined by the James Marshall and Marie-Louise Osborn Collection. Beinecke Library became the repository for books in the Yale collection printed anywhere before 1601, books printed in Latin America before 1751, books printed in North America before 1821, newspapers and broadsides printed in the United States before 1851, European tracts and pamphlets printed before 1801, and Slavic, East European, Near and Middle Eastern books through the eighteenth century, as well as special books outside these categories.

The holdings of the Beinecke Library include American Children's Literature, John James Audubon (including two copies of the double elephant folio of Birds of America), James M. Barrie, John Baskerville, William Thomas Beckford, Sir John Betjeman, John Boswell, Bryher, Cartography, including the "Vinland Map", Ernst Cassirer, Congregationalism, Joseph Conrad, Walter Crane, Dada, Daniel Defoe, Charles Dickens, Norman Douglas, Jonathan Edwards, George Eliot, the Elizabethan Club collection (composed of about 300 volumes of sixteenth- and seventeenth-century literature, including the first four folios of Shakespeare, the Huth Shakespeare quartos, and first or early quartos of all the major dramatists; Erasmus and his contemporaries; Faust, Henry

Fielding, Benjamin Franklin, Goethe, Greek and Latin Literature, Thomas Hardy, Humanism, Incunabula (over 3100 volumes including the Melk copy of the Gutenberg Bible); the James Weldon Johnson Collection; James Joyce, Judaica, Rudyard Kipling, D. H. Lawrence, Doris Lessing, pre-1660 manuscripts (including more than 1,100 medieval and Renaissance codices and several hundred manuscript fragments dating from the fourth century through the Renaissance, as well as the Voynich Manuscript); Thomas Mann, John Masefield, the Mellon Collection of Alchemy and the Occult, George Meredith, Ornithology, the Papyrus Collection, Playing Cards, Polish Literature, Dorothy Richardson, Rilke, Rochambeau Family, Bruce Rogers, the Romanov Family, John Ruskin, Russian Literature, Schiller, Sixteenth-Century Printed Books, Sporting Books, the Gertrude Stein and Alice B. Toklas Collection; Robert Louis Stevenson, Alexis de Tocqueville, Vanderbilt Collection, Rebecca West, the Thornton Wilder papers, and Kurt Wolff.

Berkeley Digital Library SunSITE builds digital collections and services while providing information and support to digital library developers worldwide. It covers information on all aspects of digital library and is specially dedicated to gathering and publishing information about digital library projects and other digital content. It will also provide a platform for digital research and development as well as promote discussions on topics related to digital libraries, museums and archives.

Berlin State Library The Berlin State Library was initially founded in 1661 by the Grand Elector, Friedrich-Wilhelm of Brandenburg. From 1701 to 1918 it served as the Royal Library. Between 1918 and 1945 it was called the Prussian State Library. During World War II the holdings were evacuated into all parts of Germany. After the war they were divided between the German State Library, Unter den Linden, and the State Library - Prussian Cultural Foundation, Potsdamer Strasse. Since the beginning of 1992 the libraries were reunified under the name: Staatsbibliothek zu Berlin - Preussischer Kulturbesitz, (Berlin State Library).

The Staatsbibliothek's Oriental collection is one of the largest in Europe; the scope and importance of the collection of Oriental manuscripts and blockprints means it is held in high esteem the world over. The Oriental Department collects books, periodicals, manuscripts, blockprints, microfilms and an increasing amount of electronic media on countries and peoples, cultures and religions (in particular Hinduism, Islam and Judaism), languages and literature, also in the respective languages, of the following regions: the Early and Christian Orient, Africa, Near and Middle East (including European parts of Turkey, Israel, the Caucasus, Islamic Central Asia), South Asia, Southeast Asia, Oceania as well as what were temporarily Islamic regions of Europe.

Biblioteca Nazionale Centrale di Roma (BNCR) was founded in 1875, in order to provide the new-born Italian Kingdom with a National Archive. The Library, situated in the sixteenth-century Collegio Romano Palace - the former seat of the Jesuitic Bibliotheca Major - was named after King Vittorio Emanuele II. Its first corpus of collections - manuscripts, incunabula and printed books - came from the libraries which had once belonged to the Religious Orders suppressed after the foundation of the Kingdom of Italy in 1860. In 1975 the BNCR moved to a new building situated on the archaeological site of the Castrum Praetorium. It consists of three separated blocks: the readers area, the staff offices and the book storehouse, occupying a total surface of more than 40,000 square metres. A radical change is under way in order to improve reception and services for readers; it will be carried on by an architectural project within the year 2000. In compliance with the provisions regarding the two Italian National Central Libraries (Rome and Florence), the BNCR's main mission consists in preserving the national cultural heritage, developing its own cultural role and providing a strategic plan for services. Its early collections are continuously increased by the legal deposit of all Italian publications. The Library holds and acquires the most important collections of foreign books, in order to document the main aspects of culture and the studies about Italy in the world.

The BNCR collections consist of 5,400,000 monographs and 550,000 serial volumes, more than 84,000 manuscripts, about 2,000 incunabula, 26,000 sixteenth-century books, 9,000 engravings, 22,000 theses, 175,000 microfilms and more than 6,000 long-playing records. Some of the most important and precious ancient collections are the Fondo Sessoriano, the Farfense, the Gesuitico, the Eborense and the Vittorio Emanuele. Special emphasis has been placed cataloguing and automated processing of manuscripts and early printed books. The first result was IGI, Indice Generale degli Incunaboli delle biblioteche d'Italia (General Index of the Incunabula held by Italian Libraries). Recently, automated cataloguing of more than 25,000 sixteenth-century books has been set up. The modern Italian Literature Section (XIX and XX centuries) represents perhaps the richest collection. It includes autographs and manuscripts by outstanding Italian writers, such as Gabriele D'Annunzio, Elsa Morante and Giorgio Vigolo, as well as precious and rare books and editions.

Bibliothèque nationale de France, or BnF, started by King Charles V in 1368, is designed as a repository of all that is published in France. The National Library of France traces its origin to the library of the king founded at the Louvre by Charles V. It expanded under Louis XIV and opened to the public in 1720. Following the series of regime changes in France it became the Imperial National Library and in 1868 was moved to newly constructed buildings on the rue Richelieu designed by Henri Labrouste. In 1988, François Mitterrand announced the construction and the expansion of one of this library, intended to cover all fields of knowledge, and designed to be accessible to all, using the most modern data transfer technologies, which could be consulted from a distance, and which would collaborate with other European libraries.

In *1989*, the services of the architectural firm of *Dominique Perrault* were retained. After the move of the major collections from the rue Richelieu, the National Library of France opened to the public in *1996*. It contains more than ten million volumes. The new building is made of a large esplanade and four L-shaped towers, whose shape recall the shape of an open book. This architecture was controversial; many judged that it was costly, and not very suitable to the storage of book collections. Indeed, wood boards had to be set up at the windows to protect the books from the light. The nearest *Paris Métro station* is *Bibliothèque François Mitterrand.*

The National Library of France is a public establishment under the supervision of the Ministry of Culture. Its mission is to constitute collections, especially the copies of works published in France that must, by law, be deposited there, conserve them, and make them available to the public. It produces a reference catalogue, cooperates with other national and international establishments, and participates in research programs.

Bibliothèque nationale du Québec (BNQ) is the national library of Quebec. Its mission, defined by law is "to assemble, preserve permanently and disseminate Quebec's published documentary heritage together with any related document of cultural interest, and documents relating to Quebec that are published outside Quebec", as well as "to offer democratic access to Quebec's national documentary heritage, culture and knowledge and to act as catalyst in relation to Quebec documentary institutions, thus contributing to the personal development of citizens".

The BNQ receives financing and is obliged by law to

offer free, universal access to all its collections. It was created on 12 August 1967 by the collections and assets of the Saint-Sulpice library, which was originally incorporated in 1910. The general collection of reference works is still located in the historic Beaux-Arts building of the old Saint-Sulpice library, erected in 1915 on Rue Saint-Denis, in the centre of Montreal. However, most of the 240,000 books in the general collection are currently in the new head office and preservation centre, opened in 1997 in the premises of a disused factory, on Rue Holt, in Most of those documents, along with all of the central branch of Montreal's public library's collections, following an agreement between those institutions, are now being relocated in the new Grande bibliothèque du Québec (GBQ) building.

This new library, will hold approximately four millions documents, including one million books, freely available to the general public. The GBQ will be located on Boulevard de Maisonneuve, in the heart of University of Quebec's campus. Among other BNQ's tasks since 1979 is to assign ISBNs prefixes to all French-language publishers in Canada and all non-English publishers in Quebec. As a successful incentive towards the use of ISBN, the government of Quebec has removed provincial sales tax from all monographs bearing an ISBN since 1991. The BNQ has also published a monthly bibliography since 1969, as well as an extensive 26-volume bibliography covering the period between 1821 and 1967, when legal deposit deposit was established. The library catalogue, IRIS (http://www.biblinat.gouv.qc.ca:6611/), has been available online since 1994.

General Biographical Sources include information on all types of famous people from all fields. Specialized Biographical Sources include information for a specific population such as women, or a specific field, such as musicians or scientists

Bodleian Library (Oxford) The Bodleian Library in the University of Oxford is one of the oldest and largest libraries in Europe. It is the main research library of the University of Oxford. It comprises over 30 of the University of Oxford's central and faculty libraries: from the world famous Bodleian Library, established 400 years ago, to the modern digital library ventures. The Bodleian Library (officially Bodley's Library) in Oxford, England known informally to centuries of Oxford scholars as "the Bod" opened in 1602 with a collection of 2,000 books assembled by Thomas Bodley (of Merton College) to replace the library that had been donated to the Divinity School by Humphrey, Duke of Gloucester (and brother of Henry V of England), but dispersed in the 16th century. In 1610 Bodley made an agreement with the Stationers' Company in London to put a copy of every book registered with them in the library.

The Bodleian collection grew so fast that the first expansion of the building was required in 1610–1612, and another in 1634–1637. When John Selden died in 1654, he left the Bodleian his large collection of books and manuscripts. In 1911 the Copyright Act continued the Stationers' agreement by making the Bodleian one of the five libraries in the United Kingdom where a copy of each book copyrighted must be deposited. Two floors of bookstack opened beneath the Radcliffe Camera and Radcliffe Square in 1913, and a large new bookstack and reading room, the New Bodleian building, was built in the 1930s. A tunnel under Broad Street conects the Old and New Bodleians, and contains a pedestrian walkway, a mechanical book conveyor and a pneumatic Lamson tube system for book order. Today, the Bodleian includes several off-site storage areas as well as nine other libraries.

Boston Public Library Boston Public Library was established in 1848. It was the first publicly supported municipal library in America. It was also the first public library to allow people to borrow books and other materials. The library was initially located in a former schoolhouse located on Mason Street, and was opened to the public on March 20, 1854. Later that year, the construction of a new building was authorized by the Library Commission, to be located at the corner of Boylston Street and Dartmouth Street on Copley Square. Charles Follen McKim, of the architectural firm McKim, Mead, and White, was engaged to design the new building, which opened in 1895. The new building included a children's room, the first in the nation. A modernist addition designed by Philip Johnson was completed in 1972; the Johnson Building now houses the circulating collection, while the research library is located in the McKim Building. The main branch is located on Boylston Street in Boston. It is the home of several large collections, including first edition folios by William Shakespeare, and the personal library of John Adams.

British Library Founded in 1753, the British Library was based on the collections of Sir Hans Sloane, physician to King George II and president of the Royal Society; the collections of Sir Robert Cotton and of Edward and Robert Harley, earls of Oxford; and the Royal Library, donated by George II in 1757. Many private collections, including the libraries of King George III (1823) and of Thomas Grenville (1846) continued to expand the collection. The British Museum's library was separated from the British Museum with the British Library Act of 1972 and reorganized as the British Library Reference Division. It is now national library of the United Kingdom and one of the world's largest research libraries, holding over 150 million items and adding some 3 million every year. As of March 2004 the library holds 11.2 million monographs and receives more than 41,500 serials.

As an institution the British Library is surprisingly young compared to equivalent institutions in other countries, having been created in 1973 by the British Library Act 1972. Prior to this, the national library was part of the British Museum, which provided the bulk of the holdings of the new library, alongside various smaller organisations which were folded in (such as the British National Bibliography). For many years its collections were dispersed in various buildings around central London, in places such as Bloomsbury (right next to the British Museum), Chancery Lane, and Holborn. Since 1997, however, the main collection has been housed in a single new building in Euston Road near to St. Pancras and Kings Cross which was designed specially for the purpose by the architect Colin St. John Wilson. It is the largest public building constructed in the United Kingdom in the 20th century. However, newspapers are still held at Colindale and there is also a collection at a site at Boston Spa in Yorkshire. A number of important works are on display to the general public in a gallery called "Treasures of the British Library" which is open to the public seven days a week at no charge. There is an additional exhibition concerned with practical matters connected with the library's collection, such as printing and early sound recording. The library also stages temporary exhibitions on a wide range of subjects which can be illuminated by the items in its collection - which is almost anything, not just literature. There is a charge for these temporary exhibitions. Other items can be accessed in the reading rooms.

In the past the library emphasised its role as a "library of last resort" for people who needed access to deep and specialised collections which they could not find anywhere else. Nowadays it adopts a more welcoming approach and emphasises on its website that anyone who wishes to carry out research is likely to be granted a reader's pass, providing they provide the necessary identification for security purposes. An Act of Parliament in 1911 established the principle of the Legal Deposit, ensuring that the British Library, along with five other libraries in Britain and Ireland, is entitled to receive a free copy of every item published in Britain and The Republic of Ireland. The other five libraries are: the Bodleian Library at Oxford; the University Library at Cambridge; Trinity College Library in Dublin; and the National Libraries of Scotland and Wales.

The British Library is the only one that is entitled to receive a copy of everything within one month of publication; the other five have to wait for up to one year. In 2003, a Private Member's Bill, the Legal Deposit Libraries Act 2003, was passed which extended the Legal Deposit requirements to electronic documents such as CD ROMs and selected websites. The British Library Newspapers section has a similar structure to the main library but runs itself largely independently.

The Library has a more or less complete collection of British and Irish newspapers since 1840, owing in part to legal deposit legislation of 1869 mandating that the library receive a copy of each edition of a newspaper. London editions of national daily and Sunday newspapers are complete back to 1801. In total the collection consists of 660,000 bound volumes and 370,000 reels of microfilm containing tens of millions of newspapers with 52,000 titles on 45km of shelves. Collection of particular interest are the Thomason Tracts containing 7,200 seventeenth century newspapers and the Burney Collection featuring newspaper from the late eighteenth and early nineteenth centuries. The section also has extensive records of non-British Isles newspapers in Roman and Cyrillic alphabets. The collection is less substantive for Middle-Eastern and Oriental alphabets, though some holdings of these are held at the main library in St. Pancras. British Library Newspapers is open to the public and is located in Colindale in North London.

The British Library's secure electronic delivery service started in 2003 at a cost of $6 million brings access to more than one hundred million items (including 280,000 journal titles, 50 million patents, 5 million reports, 476,000 US dissertations and 433,000 conference proceedings) for researchers and library patrons worldwide which were previously unavailable outside the Library due to copyright restrictions. The use of the library's web catalogue also continues to increase. In 2003 more than 9.7 million searches were conducted.

Brooklyn Public Library The Brooklyn Public Library (BPL), founded in 1897, is the public library system of the borough of Brooklyn in New York City and the fifth largest public library system in the nation. The main branch, called the Central Library, is located next to Prospect Park, just off Grand Army Plaza, where Eastern Parkway and Flatbush Avenue intersect. It started construction in 1912 and was completed in 1941. The Central Library was designated a landmark by the New York City Landmarks Preservation Commission in 1997. Another major branch, the Business Library, is located at 280 Cadman Plaza West in downtown Brooklyn. It was opened in 1943. In addition to the Central Library and Business Library, there are 58 more local branches throughout the borough, as well as a bookmobile.

The Brooklyn Public Library system was approved by an Act of Legislature of the State of New York in 1892. The Brooklyn Common Council then passed a resolution for the establishment of the Brooklyn Public Library on November 30, 1896, with Marie E. Craigie as the first director. The Brooklyn Public Library is one of three separate and independent public library systems in New York City. The other two are The New York Public Library and the Queens Borough Public Library.

California Digital Library is the University of California's 11th University library. It was established in 1997 by University of California President Emeritus Richard Atkinson to build the University's digital library, assist campus libraries with sharing their resources and holdings more effectively, and provide leadership in applying technology to the development of library collections and services. Organizationally housed under the UC Office of the President, the CDL operates in close collaboration with all UC campuses and their libraries.

The California Digital Library provides access to scholarly materials, databases of journal article abstracts and citations, electronic journals, publishing tools, and reference databases for the University of California community. It also builds collections and provides public access to digitized materials from cultural heritage organizations such as libraries, museums, and historical societies. CDL collections and services include:

* CaliforniaDigitalLibrary.org: Provides a single point of access for the publicly available digital collections produced or managed by the UC.
* Counting California: Offers "one-stop shopping" for government data and statistics about California.
* Digital Preservation Program: The CDL hosts the UC libraries' digital preservation program to ensure the long-term availability and access to digital content.
* eScholarship Editions: Provides access to nearly 2,000 digital books from academic presses on a range of topics. A significant number of the electronic books are available for free to the public.
* eScholarship Repository: This free, open-access repository infrastructure provides UC departments direct control of publishing scholarly materials such as postprints, journals and peer-reviewed series, and seminar papers.
* Licensed materials: The CDL licenses more than 21,000 journals and 250 article and reference databases on behalf of the UC libraries, saving millions of dollars compared to what would be spent if the campuses acted independently.

Cambridge University Library is the centrally administered library of the University of Cambridge. It comprises 5 separate libraries: the University Library main building, the Medical Library, the Betty and Gordon Moore Library, the Central Science Library (formerly the Scientific Periodicals Library) and the Squire Law Library. It was housed in the 'Old Schools' near the Senate House until it outgrew the space there and a new library in the west of Cambridge was built. The large site on the edge of Cambridge city centre, is now nearly opposite Robinson College. The library was built between 1931 and 1934 under architect Giles Gilbert Scott to match the neighbouring Clare Memorial Court and bears a marked resemblance to his industrial architecture such as the Bankside Power Station. It has been extended several times. The main building houses the Japanese and Chinese collections in the Aoi pavilion, an extension donated by Tadao Aoi and opened in 1998.

There are over 5.5 million books and pamphlets in the library, and more than 1.2 million periodicals. As a legal deposit library, it is entitled to claim without charge a copy of all books, journals, printed maps and music published in Britain and Ireland. The library is open to those with a Cambridge or Oxford degree or a university job. Members of the public can also pay to use it. The library is mainly used for reference since the Cambridge colleges have their own libraries for use by undergraduates. It has a well-used 'Tea room' in which full meals or snacks and beverages are available.

Cecil H. Green Library is the main library on the Stanford University campus and part of Stanford University Libraries and Acedemic Information Resources (SULAIR). It is named for Cecil H. Green. Green Library houses over 2 million volumes, most of which are related to the humanities and social sciences. The building was constructed in the 1910s, and an annex was later added in the 1980s. The original construction is now known as the Bing Wing.

Celsus Library Was two storey building with main reading area located inside the building on a large single floor with a very high ceiling. The statue of Celsus which was found during the excavations are on display in Istanbul Archaeology Museum today. The library was burned down totally approximately in the 3rd century. The front wall was not destroyed totally. It was restored after the disaster and a small pool was constructed right in front of the building. These restorations were done roughly in the 4th century. The sculptured monumental walls dedicated to the memory of the victory gained against the Parts by Marcus Aurelius and Lucius Verius , standing in this pool are on exhibition in the Museum of Vienna today. During the late Roman ages there was an Auditorium used by politicians, artists, public speakers built in front of the library next to the road. There are no remains of this structure today.

Central Library, ISI Kolkata The Library occupies a unique place in academic and research activities of the Institute. It is perhaps the most important central facility provided by the Institute. The Library moved to its present location in 1978.It occupies 4 floors (64000 sq.ft) of a ten storied building at Calcutta with a network of branch libraries at other locations of the Institute. The ISI Library, Calcutta has been functioning also as the Eastern Regional Library of the National Board of Higher Mathematics [NBHM], Department of Atomic Energy, Government of India since 1989. The ISI Library offers following services to the mathematical community in West Bengal, Orissa, and North Eastern States of India: Notification of Recent Additions of Books etc. Inter Library Loan Service. The request for loan should come from the Librarian of the Institute. Access to NBHM Collection and ISI Collection.

Library maintains excellent collection of rarebooks, government publications, data books, occasional papers and other documents/materials. Over the years, the ISI Library has attained the distinction of being one of the richest libraries in India in the areas of mathematics, statistics, and related areas. The Library maintains publication exchange programme of the Institute with regional, international, national, and foreign institutions and organizations. The Library has well equipped facility for reprography and photography. This service is available to all members of the Institute. 1991 Census data is available as Lotus 1-2-3 and dbase3 Plus files. MathSci, a CD-ROM version of Mathematical Reviews, is also available for the users. Remote access to the small electronic collection is possible through Campus Wide Network and shareable CD-Networks.

Chester Beatty Library It houses a large collection of Oriental and Western manuscripts and art. The Library is now located in a new extension to the old "Clock Tower" building in the grounds of Dublin Castle. It moved here in 1999, from its old home in a large house in Shrewsbury Road where it first opened its doors in 1954. The Library is a treasure trove for anyone who is interested in the great religions and cultures of the world, and houses one of the very best collections of its kind. The artefacts and exhibits include ancient manuscripts, prints, miniature paintings, icons, early editions of printed books, and objets d'art from countries and Continents all around the world, such as Asia, the Middle East, Europe, and North Africa. More on these later, but first lets take a look at the man who was responsible for Ireland housing such a magnificent collection. In in 1999 the Library moved to its new custom-built home in the precincts of Dublin Castle. Access is through the Castle's gardens, and there is a lovely glass-roofed entrance hall that links the new exhibition centre with the old 18th century Clock Tower.

Chetham's Library, Manchester was founded in 1653 and claims the distinction of being the oldest public library in the English-speaking world. The library was established in 1653 under the will of Humphrey Chetham (1580-1653) who endowed a 'Hospital' for the maintenance and education of forty poor boys and a Library for the use of scholars. Chetham's Hospital was re-established in 1969 as Chetham's School of Music. The Library has been in use continuously since 1653 and continues as an independent charity, open to readers and visitors free of charge. Chetham's Library holds more than 100,000 volumes of printed books, of which 60,000 were published before 1851. These include especially rich collections of sixteenth and seventeenth-century printed works, periodicals and journals, local history sources, broadsides and ephemera.

Connemara Public Library The Library was found at the turn of the 19th century in 1890 when Lord Connemara the then Governor of Madras State laid the foundation stone for the present Connemara Pubic Library to fulfill the long felt need for a standard library. In 1896 the library named after Lord Connemara and was formally opened. Since then the library had become a part of history as much as a part of our lives continuously functioning till date. Connemara Public Library is open to the public.

Consortium of University Research Libraries (CURL) CURL was established in 1983 to promote co-operation between academic research libraries in Great Britain and Ireland. The rich holdings of the CURL libraries are represented by catalogue records of varying types and quality, and there is a need to take the manual records, which are limited to local use, and make them universally available through electronic databases. This process is known in the library world as retrospective conversion.

The CURL database consists of approximately 18 million machine-readable catalogue records, of which 12 million have been contributed by its member libraries. In 1996 this database became accessible to members of the public through the CURL OPAC (Online Public Access Catalogue) which is available on the World Wide Web. However, the records of many collections within these great academic libraries, particularly those relating to older, scarcer material, remain hidden from view because they are still in manual form, and electronic access to these resources can only be achieved through the provision of machine-readable catalogue records.

Delhi Public Library Delhi Public Library is Owned by the Delhi Government, the Delhi Public Library Network is probably the oldest in town. It was inaugurated on 27th of October, 1951, by Pt. Jawahar Lal Nehru. Today the library has a total of 25 branches, and sends its Mobile Van Library services to every nook and corner of the city, including the Central Jail. Most of them have a section on children's books. Some branches also have the facility of Braille Services for the benefit of visually challenged people.

Delhi University Library System The Delhi University Library began in 1922 with a collection of mere 1380 gift books. During the first decade of its existence it functioned from shifting locales. In 1933 it managed to get a relatively stable space, viz. the ' Dance Hall' of the Old Viceregal Lodge (the present office of the Vice-Chancellor). Sir Maurice Gwyer, Vice-Chancellor of the University from 1938 to 1950 was instrumental in the blossoming of the Library in its new locale. Under his care, it was transformed into "a place as well of beauty as of learning ". One of the early benefactors of the library was Ski G.D. Birla. The Library moved to its present locale in the heart of the Campus on December 01, 1958. The decade of the 1960s was noticeable for a new trend in the growth of the Delhi University Library. Starting with the Faculty of Music and Fine Arts, several Departmental libraries took roots in Faculties of Arts, Mathematics, Social Sciences, Science, and Management Studies.

The 1970s were marked by certain meanderings. At one level, access to the Central Library was closed for the undergraduate students. But at another level, four Zonal Libraries located in the four cardinal directions and spanning over the entire length and breadth of the city of Delhi (but outside the Main Campus) were created for such students. Presently, only the South Zone Library is functioning — the rest were closed between 1998 and 2003. Libraries of the two Law Centres and that of the University of Delhi South Campus were also initiated in the 1970s.

In the last two decades the DULS has also taken initiatives to create a few specialized libraries and focus on newer academic disciplines. A library for the visually challenged scholars (Braille Library) has within it an Audio Book Research Centre with nearly 300 cassettes. During the Platinum Jubilee Year of the Delhi University, a separate Audio-Visual Library was added to the CRL. 450 educational video cassettes of high academic quality covering various academic disciplines were acquired in 1998-99 from agencies such as UGC sponsored Consortium for Educational Communication, IGNOU, Sahitya Academy and Tata Institute of Social Sciences. The Library of the Faculty of Music & Fine Arts treasures 1800 gramophone records in addition to substantive non-book audio-video material. The South Campus Library is taking keen interest in areas of applied sciences such as Plant Molecular Biology, Biochemistry, Biophysics, Microbiology and Operational Research. Similarly, the Central Science Library in the Main Campus is specially sensitive to the needs of the Ambedkar Centre for Biomedical Research, and Departments of Agrochemicals & Pest Management and Environmental Science. Keeping pace with the times, libraries of the Women Studies and Development Centre and the Non-Collegiate Women's Education Board have also grown within the DULS.

Developing Library Network DELNET has been in operation since January 1988 and was registered as a society in 1992. It was initially sponsored by the National Information System for Science and Technology (NISSAT), Department of Scientific and Industrial Research, Government of India and is currently being promoted by the National Informatics Centre, Department of Information Technology, Ministry of Communications and Information Technology, Government of India and India International Centre, New Delhi.

DELNET has been established with the prime objective of promoting resource sharing among the libraries through the development of a network of libraries. It aims to collect, store, and disseminate information besides offering computerised services to users, to coordinate efforts for suitable collection development and also to reduce unnecessary duplication wherever possible.

DELNET has been actively engaged with the compilation of various Union Catalogues of the resources available in member-libraries. It has already created the Union Catalogue of Books,Union List of Current Periodicals, Union Catalogue of Periodicals, CD-ROM Database,Database of Indian Specialists, Database of Periodical Articles, Union List of Video Recordings, Urdu Manuscripts' Database, Database of Theses and Dissertations, DEVINSA Database, sample databases of language publications using GIST technology and several other databases. The data is being updated in each of these databases and is growing rapidly. All the DELNET databases have been resident on DELSIS, an in-house software developed on BASISPlus, an RDBMS, the product of Information Dimensions Inc. of USA which has been provided to DELNET courtesy National Informatics Centre, New Delhi.

DELNET provides an array of facilities including E-mail to its member-libraries including both institutional and associate institutional members. DELNET'S relentless efforts in resource sharing have proved extremely effective. It has indeed been a big leap towards the modernisation of libraries in India. Delnet started as a network of libraries in Delhi in 1988 and was named as Delhi Library Network. It is the first operational library network in India. It was initiated as a project of the India International Centre with the financial and technical assistance by National Information System for Science and Technology (NISSAT), Department of Scientific and Industrial Research, Govt. Of India, It was registered as a society in June 1992 under the Societies Registration Act of 1860 and is currently being promoted by the National Informatics Centre (NIC), Planning Commission, Govt. Of India and India International Centre, New Delhi.

Dhaka University Library, Dhaka The University of Dhaka was established in 1921 under the Govt. of India Act. XVIII of 1920 (Which was based on the recommendations of the Calcutta University Commission presided over by Sir Michael Sadler). It was founded as a unitary teaching and residential University with a constitution similar in many respects to those of the then contemporary English University. Following the creation in 1947 of the province of East Bengal as a part of Pakistan, the East Bengal Educational Ordinance, 1947, was promulgated, by which the University, without prejudice to its original character as a teaching and residential University was entrusted with sole authority to recognise and affiliate all educational institutions in East Bengal above Materict and High Madrasa standard. Accordingly, in 1947, the University of Dhaka affiliated 58 1st, and 2nd grade colleges throughout the whole of East Bengal After independence the Government of the People's Republic of Bangladesh promulgated the adaptation of University Laws by the Bangladesh Ordinance No. 1 of 1972. Afterwards, in pursuance to the Constitution of the People's Republic of Bangladesh, the President Order No. 11 of 1973 which is called the "Dacca University Order, 1973 was Promulgated.

The library service is an integral part of the academic activities of both the faculty members and students. By the size of the collection (over 550,000 estimated), Dhaka University Library is the largest of all academic as well as other libraries of Bangladesh. But it is not the size, but the excellence of its collection, particularly in rare books, ancient manuscripts and collections developed out of special depositories, it is an academician's playground.

The main library houses reading materials including text books, reference materials, rare books, ancient manuscripts (over 30,000 manuscripts on various languages, viz., Sanskrit, Bengali, Arabic, Urdu, Persian, Maithaly, etc.) special collections (including UN collection), current journals and periodicals, Abstracts and Indexes in the Humanities and Social Sciences, old journals and periodicals and many more of interest and requirements of the faculty members and students of the disciplines of arts, social sciences, business studies and law.

Die Deutsche Bibliothek Germany With the re-unification of Germany in October 1990 the Deutsche Bücherei Leipzig (founded 1913) and the Deutsche Bibliothek Frankfurt am Main (founded 1947) - which since 1970 has included the Deutsches Musikarchiv Berlin - have been unified under the name Die Deutsche Bibliothek. Bibliographic records are published in the Deutsche Nationalbibliographie in various series and levels of cumulation in printed as well as in electronic form. Apart from this, Die Deutsche Bibliothek is the producer and supplier of diverse services to public and scientific libraries, the book trade and publishing houses, scientific institutions and foreign national bibliographic centres. The services are offered on a wide range of different media, from conventional title cards to disks, magnetic tapes, CD-ROMs and the Online-database BIBLIODATA.

As the national library, Die Deutsche Bibliothek maintains cooperative relationships at a national as well as at an international level. The main areas of cooperation are: the development and application of common rules and standards at the national and international levels; the production and distribution of bibliographic services in accordance with users requirements; the use of jointly maintained databases, particularly in the area of standardised data; the development and application through international cooperation of modern techniques for the permanent preservation of holdings. On the basis of a historic tradition at the Deutsche Bücherei Leipzig, the Deutsches Buch- und Schriftmuseum is currently under expansion as a documentation centre for the culture of books.

Digital Library Technology Project - Core Technologies for the National Information Infrastructure "The Digital Library Technology (DLT) project and the Public Use of Remote Sensing Data (RSD) project, are two related elements of the Information Infrastructure Technology and Applications component of NASA's High Performance Computing and Communications Program. The DLT Project supports the development of new technologies to facilitate public access to NASA data via computer networks. Of highest priority are those technologies that develop tools, applications, and software and hardware systems that are able to scale upward to accomodate evolving user requirements and order-of-magnitude increases in user access. Although most of the technology is envisioned to be developed in the private sector, an inhouse skill base must be acquired and maintained in key areas of developing technology such as the integration of multimedia data, wide-area networking, resource discovery, and intelligent information retrieval." URL: http://learn.arc.nasa.gov/education/topics/digital.shtml

Digital South Asia Library The Digital South Asia Library provides digital materials for reference and research on South Asia to scholars, public officials, business leaders, and other users. Its collection include reference sources, books and journals, images, maps, statistics, etc.

Digitale Bibliothek Information und Medien, Germany This "Information and Media" digital library created by the University of Applied Sciences, Stuttgart, Germany, includes three collections: a bibliography, full-text documents about digital libraries and related topics, and technical documentation on the Linux operating system. While most digital libraries give every appearance of being unmanned, this one advertises an administrator and helpdesk, both reachable by email. The bibliography collection has full-text-searchable author and title indexes, but does not permit combined searches on multiple metadata fields. However, Greenstone does have a "form search" option that provides the facilities normally available with conventional bibliographic metadata search: a "simple" version that implements an AND operation between one or more fields, and an "advanced" version that provides general Boolean combination (and also allows stemming and case-folding to be controlled individually for each field). Greenstone has "plug-in" import options for numerous metadata formats, including OAI, MARC, BibTex, and Refer. Site: <http://diana.iuk.hdm-stuttgart.de/digbib/gsdl/cgi-bin/library>

Dr Zakir Husain Library named after the President of India Late Dr. Zakir Husain in 1973, is the Central Library of the Jamia Library System, which includes the Faculty and Center libraries. Stocking a rich collection of over 3.00 Lacs learning resources in all major discipline taught in the University and spread over an area of 23,038 sq. feet, the library caters to the academic need of the University students, staff & research scholars. It has spacious reading rooms.

The collection of the Library consists of books, periodicals, pamphlets, manuscripts and photographs. The stack rooms which consist of ground floor plus three upper stories have a carpet area of 9000 sq. feet besides these two halls of same area each house reference and the rare book collection. Periodical section is of 11,125 sq. feet and also has a two-story stack room for bound volumes of periodicals. The library provides open access to readers to the stocks while rare books section; manuscripts and archival sections and text books section observe closed access. The library has fully computerized its most actively used collection, which is searched through OPAC.

Dumbarton Oaks Research Library, Washington, DC The Dumbarton Oaks Research Library and Collection is housed in a nineteenth-century Federal-style house built on the crest of a wooded valley in the Georgetown section of Washington, D.C. The institution now has important research resources in the areas of Byzantine studies, the history of landscape architecture, and Pre-Columbian studies. The collections of Byzantine and Pre-Columbian art and the rare books and prints relating to the gardens are on public display.

Folger Shakespeare Library Henry Clay Folger, an oil company executive, bequeathed his remarkable Shakespeare collection to the American people and provided sufficient funds to house, maintain and expand the collection. It is a well-know research centre in Washington, D.C., for Shakespearean and Elizabeth studies and 16th- and 17th-century literature, and history. The library has an unrivaled collections of Shakespeare's folios and the second largest collection of English books printed prior to 1641. Included in the collections are over 310,000 books and manuscripts; 250,000 playbills; 27,000 paintings, drawings, engravings, and prints; and musical instruments, costumes, and films. In addition to its scholarly mission as a research library, the Folger serves as a museum devoted to Shakespeare.

Free Library of Philadelphia It is the public library system serving Philadelphia, Pennsylvania. In 1890, George S. Pepper, died. At the suggestion of Dr. Pepper, he had earmarked $225,000 of his estate to go towards the foundation of the Free Library of Philadelphia, which was established on February 18, 1891. Lawsuits from private libraries held up the disbursement of the funds until 1894; meanwhile, the city of Philadelphia opened six branches of a separate institution, the Philadelphia Public Library, beginning in 1892.

In 1894 the first branch of the Free Library was opened at City Hall, and later that year the two institutions merged under the Free Library name. By 1898 the Free Library had the largest circulation in the world, at 1,778,387 volumes. The Library's headquarters moved to 12th and Chestnut Streets in 1895. In 1906, it was decided that the Library's permanent headquarters should be along the proposed Benjamin Franklin Parkway and Logan Square was chosen as the site in 1910, the same year the Library moved to 13th and Locust Streets. Ground was broken in 1917 and construction began in 1920. The new building was completed in late 1926, and the Free Library of Philadelphia opened for business at its current location on June 2, 1927.

Garrison Library Founded in 1793 by Colonel John Drinkwater and officially opened in 1804 by the Duke of Kent, the Garrison Library is a prime illustration of how libraries provide a neutral and unpretentious retreat for anyone with a hunger for knowledge and a respect for information. Gibraltar has a history of being a divided nation, the most famous divide being between the British and Spanish residents but also between the political left and right wings and the RAF and Navy. Since its opening two hundred years ago, the Garrison Library has provided a neutral bubble away from political division. The library serves as the head quarters and archive service of the Gibraltar Chronicle, the world's second oldest English language newspaper.

The Garrison is modest-sized but enchanting library of 35, 000 books including many rare volumes. There is an emphasis on the value of culture and travel in the library and boasts an excellent local history collection. Many lithographs and art prints are held here and even the furnishings are said to have interesting historical backgrounds. It is not a government-owned library but rather one funded by a trust. The building is a piece of imposing and impressive architecture and two stories high with a seating capacity of about one hundred patrons.

German Library (German: Deutsche Bücherei) in Leipzig was founded in 1913 to collect all German and foreign language titles published in Germany, Austria and Switzerland. It is now part of Die Deutsche Bibliothek (The German National library). Already in 1848, there had been plans for a German National library. After the restauration, they were not pursued any longer, the stock of books already in existence was stored at the German National Museum in Nürnberg. In 1912, the town of Leipzig, seat of the Leipzig book-fair, the kingdom of Saxony and the "Börsenverein der Deutschen Buchhändler" (society of German book-dealers) agreed to found a German National Library located in Leipzig.

Starting *January 1, 1913*, all publications in the German language were systematically collected (including books from *Austria* and *Switzerland*). The main building of the German Library in *Leipzig* was built 1914-1916 after plans of the architect *Oskar Pusch*. The impressive facade is 160m long and faces the "deutscher Platz". The building was opened on *October 19, 1916*, one day after the monument for the *Battle of the Nations*. Emperor *Wilhelm II* had already left in a huff, as the Leipzig citizens did not conform to Prussian Imperial ideology. The building lot of the library had been donated by the town of Leipzig, while *Friedrich August III*, king of *Saxony* provided the funds for the building. On the facade, the portraits of *Otto von Bismarck*, *Johann Wolfgang von Goethe* and *Johann Gutenberg* are displayed. Statues represent *Technology*, *Justice*, *Philosophy*, *Medicine* etc. The central reading room contains a picture by *Ludwig von Hofmann*, depicting *Arcadia* in *Art Nouveau*-style. The staircase contains a mural showing the founders of the German library. The Library contains a museum for books and letters as well.

Global Digital Library (GDL) Is a proposed international alliance of donor agencies, non-governmental and faith-based organizations, educational institutions, and private corporations in developed nations collaborating with national governments, regional churches, educational institutions, and civil society organizations in developing countries committed to creating a community-owned library system for rural development. At the community level and at the core of the library network are democratically managed independent civil society organizations established for the sole purpose to own, operate, and maintain a proposed system of 10,000 "bricks and mortar" libraries connected to the World Wide Web.

The mission of the Global Digital Library (GDL) is to provide an information services and support network to empower rural communities in developing countries with the requisite technology infrastructure, financial capacity, and human resources to achieve sustainable economic development and permanently alleviate poverty. The goal of the GDL is to develop a network consisting of 10,000 wireless, electronic libraries to improve the lives of 100 million people.

Global Library Services Network GLSN provides remote communities with access to digital libraries for use offline. It implements an architecture and infrastructure to allow large-scale, non-networked digital libraries in remote places to be acquired, installed and updated, on a commercial (but low-cost) basis. GLSN makes arrangements with information providers, both commercial and non-commercial, to populate the collections. There are many freely available demonstration collections, mostly on health topics such as Adolescent Health, Asthma, Chinese medicine, to name just a few. The catalog at the central GLSN site, and a user selecting a particular collection (on

Malaria) to download. GLSN uses Greenstone at its core. GLSN has extended the basic facilities of Greenstone with an interactive web-based interface for selecting

Goethals Indian Library & Research Center The library has a vast collection of 18,663 volumes of books & periodicals. It was originally started by Most Rev. Dr. Paul Goethals, SJ and was handed over to the Jesuits of St. Xavier's College in 1908.The GILRS has extremely rare and precious books. The library is a research center more easily accessible to researchers and students who are most worthy of its inheritance. They are welcome to make use of the library. The library has 61 sections from voyages and travels to Flora and Fauna, lastly to Bibliographies and Dictionaries. The library is a treasure trove of knowledge and information as one can observe by viewing our Homepage. It serves its purpose of disseminating knowledge and providing the information for your needs. This alone makes every effort worthwhile. It is at the service to encourage and support scholarly work.

Government Oriental Manuscripts Library, Chennai The Governemnt Oriental Library Madras is located in the Western Wing of the first floor of the Madras University Library. It is unique in respect of its precious holdings and one of the oldest oriental libraries of the country. The Library possess invaluable printed books and manuscripts of many languages in different scripts specially, Tamil, Telugu, Kannada, Marathi, Malayalam and Persian which provided immense knowledge on the history of South India.

The Library was established out of the efforts of Colonel Mackenzie, an Englishman and an engineer by profession. After his death, these materials were sold by his wife to the Governor General Marquis Hastings which went in possession of the East India company and was later sent to Madras and Kolkatta for the Asiatic society. The collection of the Library increased with the passage of time and the Britishers were the main promoters for it. The Collections of colonel Mackenzie (1754-1821), Dr. Leyden and Mr. C. P. Brown constitute the nucleus of the vast collection of manuscripts preserved in Government Oriental Manuscripts Library, Madras, which consists of manuscripts of works in literature, history, philosophy and science, written in South Indian and Oriental Languages, and of Kaifiyats and inscriptions found in many places belonging to different periods.

Grand Ayatollah Mar'ashi Najafi Public Library, Qom The is world famous for its collection of rare manuscripts. Its historical foundation goes back to the time when Grand Ayatollah Mar'ashi Najafi was studying in the Islamic Seminary of Najaf. That was a time when the importance and value of old manuscripts - Islamic educational and cultural heritage - were not realized. Through great efforts of warding off hunger (after cutting back on food), and working hard in a rice-cleaning factory in Najaf, Ayatollah Mar'ashi saved money to buy old manuscripts and rare books. After coming to Iran, he continued this effort to gather up the precious books, till he had collected an abundant amount of manuscripts and rare books. Thereupon, he founded a small library in a seminary school that he established - The Mar'ashiyyah Seminary School. Later he bought the present building of the library and transferred the books to the newly established library. His great efforts led to the formation of the well-known and precious library of Mar'ashi Najafi.

Hakim Mohammed Said Central Library The Hamdard University library system consists of central library and six faculty libraries—i. faculty of science, ii. faculty of medicine, iii. faculty of pharmacy, iv. faculty of nursing, v. faculty of islamic studies and vi. faculty of management studies and information technology. The central library of the university was named as 'Hakim Mohammed Said Central Library' after the name of younger brother of the founder Hakeem Abdul Hamid. The total library holdings exceed 1.46 lakh including 1,05,000 English, Urdu, Arabic, Persian, Hindi, etc. books. 17,000 bound volumes, 20,000 rare collections and 4500 manuscripts, mostly in Urdu, Arabic and Persian languages.

Hilandar Research Library is the research library of the Research Center for Medieval Slavic Studies at the Ohio State University. It contains the largest collection of medieval Slavic manuscripts on microform. It includes many Cyrillic and Glagolitic manuscripts from 21 countries and from various monasteries on Mount Athos, Greece, including the entire Slavic collection of the Hilandar Monastery

Huntington Library Located in San Marino, California, the Huntington Library is one of the world's leading libraries of Americana and English literature, surpassed only by the British Library and the Bodleian. Its collections include over five million manuscripts, rare books, reference works, and other materials on Anglo-American history, literature and the arts, the history of science, and maritime history. The library includes a conservation center, exhibition hall, art collection, and botanical gardens.

India Office Library, London The East India Company established this library in East India House in 1801 as a public repository for the safe custody of books, manuscripts and works of art placed in its care by its servants in India and by others. The East India Company's Library was systematically developed by the Company and the India Office as a reference library for official administration and as a learned library for scholars, and it served, from 1867, the archival function as the place of legal deposit in Britain for works published in British India. The collection and preservation of the private papers of individuals and organisations connected with India had been carried on by the East India Company and the India Office since early in the nineteenth century, and this activity continues in the Private Papers section of the India Office Records.

The Library holds the documentary archives of the administration in London of the pre-1947 government of India. The 14 kilometres of shelves of volumes, files and boxes of papers, together with 70,000 volumes of official publications and 105,000 manuscript and printed maps, comprise the archives of the East India Company (1600-1858), of the Board of Control or Board of Commissioners for the Affairs of India (1784-1858), of the India Office (1858-1947), of the Burma Office (1937-1948), and of a number of British agencies overseas which were officially linked with one or other of the four main bodies. The India Office Records are part of the Public Records of the United Kingdom, and are open for public consultation under the provisions of the Public Record Acts and in accordance with regulations established by the Lord Chancellor.

Indian Digital Library of Engineering Science and Technology [INDEST] Consortium The Ministry of Human Resource Development (MHRD) has set-up "Consortia-based Subscription to Electronic Resources for Technical Education System in India". This consortia is available in three models. Presently all the IIT's, IISc, NITIE, most of the Regional Engineering colleges and Indian Institute of Management's are its members. The consortium being an open-ended proposition, welcomes institutions to join it on their own for sharing maximum benefits it offers in terms of lower subscription rates and better terms of agreement with the publishers. All electronic resources being subscribed shall be available from the publisher's Website. The membership of the consortium is open to any Private or Government-funded Engineering / Technological / Educational institutions / Universities for one or more electronic resources. The consortium will charge nominal annual fee for its services.

Indian Institute of Advanced Study Library, Simla The Indian Institute of Advanced Study (IIAS) was set up in Simla by the Ministry of Education, Government of India as a society under the Societies Registration Act XXI of 1860 in 1964. The institute started functioning in 1965. The institute aims at free and creative enquiry into the fundamental themes and problems of life and thought. The selected subjects are the humanities, Indian culture, comparative religion, social and natural sciences such other area as the Institute may from time to time decide. It provides facilities for advanced consultation and collaboration besides library and documentation services.

The library collection has been enriched by acquiring private collections of eminent scholars and organizations like British Council, the Asian Foundation and League of Nation's generous gift of hundred of rare pamphlet and books. Later, the Library obtained rare Sanskrit, Arabic and Persian texts and manuscripts containing miniature paintings. The Library has built up a collection of over 1.5 lakh books including about 40,000 back volumes of journals, microfilms and other documents. Presently, it subscribes to about 500 journals. The collection consists of both the primary and secondary sources on information covering the broad area of research in social sciences and humanities. Various facets of Indian History, Culture and Civilization, Post Modernism, Theoretical and Cultural Studies pertaining to Philosophy, Religion, Political Science and Sociology, Gender and Environmental Studies. The main focus of Library has been on filling up major gaps in the collection in the areas of research relating to Central Asia.

Indian Institute of Technology Roorkee Archive The Archives contain more than 12,000 rare and out of print documents published during 18th , 19th and early 20th century. The archival collection has been organized into three sections; namely Thomason College Publications containing all the books published by the College between the years 1847-1947. The copiously produced college calendars, the world famous Roorkee Treaties, Roorkee

Manuals, some class notes in manuscript form by the eminent teachers of the College are important documents in this section, The Ganges Canal Collection containing another important collection of all works concerning the design and construction of the Ganges Canal which is said to be the mother of the Thomason College. and Proby T. Cautley Collection which contains classical works by Col. Sir Cautley on the Design and construction of the Canal such as 'Report on the Ganges Canal Works: From the commencement until the its Opening in 1854'. This report is in three volumes. Notes and Memoranda on the Eastern Jamuna or Doab Canal, on the water courses in Dehradun, sketches of the Doab Canal and 'Ganga Canal: Disquisition on the Heads of the Ganges and Jamuna Canal' are other import documents in this section.

Indira Gandhi National Centre for the Arts Library, New Delhi The Indira Gandhi National Centre for the Arts was established in the memory of Smt. Indira Gandhi, the prime minster of India, It is visualized as a centre encompassing the study and experience of all the arts — each form with its own integrity, yet within a dimension of mutual interdependence, interrelated with nature, social structure and cosmology.

Recognizing the need to encompass and preserve the distributed fragments of Indian art and culture, a pioneering attempt has been made by Indira Gandhi National Centre for the Arts (IGNCA) to serve as a major resource centre for the arts, especially written, oral and visual materials. One of the programmes of this centre, in collaboration with UNDP, is to utilize multimedia computer technology to create a wide variety of software packages that communicate cultural information. Multimedia technology allows the user to interact and explore the subject in a non-linear mode by combining audio, text, graphics, animation and video on a computer.

The IGNCA is a National Information System and a Data Bank of the arts, humanities, cultural heritage with a fully supported reference library of multimedia collections. This information System and Data Bank will serve as a major resource centre for research in humanities, in the arts, in the disciplines of Archaeology, Anthropology, History, Philosophy, Literature, Language, Arts , Crafts etc. It is proposed to have very large library of microfilms / microfisches along with the printed material on Greater India, South Asia, Southeast, Asia and West Asia. Language won't be a barrier in its collection development policy. It is also proposed to have a collection of about half a million works during the next few years.

The reference library of IGNCA has a large collection of primary and secondary material in the broad areas of humanities and the arts. It constitutes books, reprographics of several folios of unpublished Sanskrit, Pali, Persian and Arabic manuscripts in microfilm and microfische, Photographs and slides. The Collection includes books on archaeology; philosophy, religion and ritual studies, history and anthropology, art and literature as well as folk, pastoral and community studies. The library is enriched by many rare collections of illustrious scholars who have made path-breaking contributions in fields related to arts. The library concentrates on encyclopaedias, dictionaries, bibliographies, atlases and catalogues of unpublished manuscripts of Indian and Asian origin. Its holdings and expertize are complemented by those of the other divisions of the Centre.

Institute of Asian Studies Library, Chennai The Institute of Asian Studies in Chennai is a joint venture launched by a few scholars from India and Japan and its main aim is to promote academic research on the cultural facets of Asian countries. One of its main objectives is the quest for perception of Asian literature and culture as a unified and composite whole, transcending geographical, linguistic, and cultural barriers. Many eminent scholars from Western Europe, the former Soviet states, and the

United States have made invaluable contributions to Oriental culture. Similarly, laden with emotional as well as intellectual involvement, few Asian scholars have also devoted themselves hear and soul to Asian Studies. Yet, the area of studies covered so far is not considerable and much more remains to be done. This is brought home to us by the ignorance that prevails in the world of scholarship about the similarities and diversities that exist among the Asian cultures. Only a few Asian works are available in translations in the various languages of the people of Asia. The paucity of reference material is another limitation to scholars who pursue Asiatic researches. Moreover, there are only a few centres of study, which are devoted to the study of Asian cultures in depth.

The Institute of Asian Studies in Chennai has been established with a view to overcoming the existing limitations and to pooling together the scattered resource persons and materials available in various countries so as to enable our academics to carry out research on various aspects of the cultural heritage of the people of Asia in a very systematic way.

Institute of Manuscripts Library, Baku The earliest library in Azerbaijan appeared in the thirteenth century and belonged to the Maruha Observatory. This observatory was created in the second half of the thirteenth century in the city of Meraga of Eastern Azerbaijan in Iran. The library of more than 400,000 volumes was founded by Nasiruddin Tusi, a great scientist, thinker and statesman of that period. In the sixteenth century the biggest library of that time existed at the palace of the Shah Ismail Khatai, a founder of the Safavid dynasty and a famous poet. In the nineteenth century most libraries were private collections. The biggest ones were the personal libraries of Abaskuli bek Bakikhanov and Mirza Fatali Akhundov. Bakikhanov was a prominent Azerbaijani scientist and writer. He is the author of number of works on history, education, philosophy, astronomy and geography. Akhundov was a great Azerbaijani playwright, educator and philosopher. He is considered a founder of Azerbaijani dramatic art and contributed to the development of literary and social thought of the whole Middle East. The first public library was opened in Azerbaijan in 1894.

Institute of Museum and Library Services An independent federal grant-making agency created under the Museum and Library Services Act of 1996 to foster leadership, innovation, and lifelong learning by supporting museums, archives, and libraries of all types, and encouraging partnerships among them. IMLS administers four grant-in-aid programs for libraries, including LSTA grants to state library agencies. IMLS publishes the monthly e-mail newsletter Primary Source.

Institute Of Oriental Studies Library The Institute Of Oriental Studies formerly the Asiatic Museum was founded in 1818. There are many rare or unique religious, historical, and scientific works awaiting their publication. The Institute of Oriental Studies has recently started a project that deals with compiling the manuscripts in the electronic format. The project, which is similar to UNESCO's "Memory of the World" programme, is called: Asiatic Museum. Treasures from St.Petersburg Academic Collection of Oriental Manuscripts (CD-ROM Series). The main library houses reading materials including text books, reference materials, rare books, ancient manuscripts (over 30,000 manuscripts on various languages, viz., Sanskrit, Bengali, Arabic, Urdu, Persian, Maithaly, etc.) special collections (including UN collection), current journals and periodicals, Abstracts and Indexes in the Humanities and Social Sciences, old journals and periodicals and many more of interest and requirements of the faculty members and students of the disciplines of arts, social sciences, business studies and law.

International Coalition of Library Consortia [ICOLC] It is an informal, self-organized group comprising hundreds of library consortia from around the world. The

Coalition serves primarily higher education institutions by facilitating discussion among consortia on issues of common interest. It conducts regular meetings to keep members informed about new electronic information resources, pricing

Internet Public Library The Internet Public Library is a great place to visit. Information is conveniently divided by age groups or research needs. There are interesting hands-on activities for kids, plus an online classroom, an exhibit hall, a reading room with some great tools, and much more. Links to general biographical resources which also includes specialized biography links: Authors & Architects, Authors, Entertainers, Musicians & Composers, Politicians & Rulers, and Scientists & Inventors.

Iraqi House of Manuscripts, Baghdad The Iraqi House of Manuscripts was set up after the 1974 Antiquities Act, which rendered manuscripts part of the national patrimony. The collection was originally housed in the Iraqi National Museum (itself constructed in the 1960's), and then it was provided with its own facilities in the 1980's. It emains administratively part of the Iraqi National Museum but in a separate facility. In the 1990's, after the chaos and dislocations of 1991, the collection was expanded by a campaign to bring together certain regional and private collections. As a result, by 2003 it housed a collection of over 40,000 Arabic, Ottoman, Persian, Kurdish, Hebrew, Syriac, and other manuscripts.

The Iraqi House of Manuscripts was formerly known as Dar Saddam lil Makhtutat/Saddam House of Manuscripts. It had its modest beginning from the foundation of Department of Manuscripts. The department of manuscripts was established in 1962 as part of the Iraqi National Museum in Baghdad. It originally contained 2,526 manuscripts, but expanded throughout the 1970s and 1980s as the government bought manuscripts from collections around the country. In 1988, when the collection had reached 37,083 manuscripts, the state decided to found an autonomous entity, the Saddam House of Manuscripts. Today there are an estimated 50,000 manuscripts of which 7,000 are on loan from other institutions or private collections and there for repair and conservation. The bomb shelter reportedly has 4 sets of doors and is under continuous armed guard. On 3 occasions looters tried and failed to force the doors and loot the shelter. On each occasion the "neighborhood" chased the looters away and burned their vehicles.

ISI-BC Library Mysore Indian Statistical Institute, Bangalore Centre is one among the three important centres of ISI . The ISI Bangalore centre library was established in the year 1976 to meet the academic and research interests of the students, scholar, teachers and others . It has one of the best collection of literature on Statistics, Mathematics, Quality Engineering/ Management and Library & Information Science in India. Presently it subscribes to around 300 international Journals on various subjects. The overall collection of books and reference materials, viz., reports, reprints, directories, encyclopedias, CDs etc., is approximately 23592. At present the library is automated which will enable a better management and easy access of information to users. Very soon the information on library collection will be made available to external users through Internet.

J R D Tata Memorial Library The Library of the Indian Institute of Science (IISc.) Bangalore, was established in 1911 and it is one of the first three departments started in the Institute. It is regarded as one of the best scientific and technical libraries in India. Apart from the main library it has departmental libraries also. The library moved in to the present premises in January 1965, built out of grants provided by University Grants Commission (UGC), in commemoration of the Golden Jubilee Celebrations of the Institute in 1959. In 1995 the library was renamed as "J.R.D Tata Memorial Library".

The National Board for Higher Mathematics (NBHM) has recognised this library as Regional Center for Mathematics for the south region and continued to award a special grant.

It is no exaggeration to state that the IISc library is the largest and finest of its kind in this part of the world. The library has been using the LIBSYS an Integrated Library Management software package with all the modules for the library housekeeping operations. The library Online Catalogue database has more than 1.25 lakh records of books (Bibliographic Information) and information about 22,000 back volumes of periodicals.

Jamia Al Azhar Library, Cairo, Egypt Al-Azhar library was established in the year 1897, A.D., at the time of Imam Mohammed Abdo, when all books related to Islamic Heritage were distributed to a number of Al-Azhar hostels. An independent building, with an Islamic style, is under construction in an area adjacent to Al-Azhar. At the present time it occupies six areas inside Al-Azhar mosque (Aqabghawiah school, Al-Tabrasia school, Al-Abbasy hostel, Hostels libraries (Magharba,Atrak, shawam).The library comprises of 99,062 books consist of 595,668 volumes of the most precious manuscripts and rare books. The library is considered second to " Dar Al-kotob Al-Masriah" in Egypt, as far as the number of books and the rare literatures is concerned.

For centuries, Al-Azhar housed one of the world's largest collections of Islamic manuscripts. There are approximately 3 million ancient manuscripts from various Islamic eras in the Muslim world, 1.3 million of which are located in Egypt. Out of the 1.3 million, 42,164 are housed at Al-Azhar University. It later evolved into a reverend centre for Sunni Islamic learning. In 1897, a central library for Al-Azhar was established, which served as a repository for the vast collection of Islamic works of reference scattered throughout the university's other libraries. Some of the manuscripts date from before 969 AD, when Cairo's founding dynasty, the Fatimids, who ruled Egypt until

1171, entered the country. Because Egypt didn't have printing presses until the early 1800s, many of these old manuscripts are handwritten, in beautiful, surprisingly uniform, Arabic script.

Al-Azhar Library is distinguished from other big libraries in the Islamic world by its rare manuscripts and books written by Al-Azhar scholars and Islamic scholars in general. These manuscripts expound on dozens of subjects, including fiqh [Islamic jurisprudence], medicine and other sciences, literature and history. They're written in Arabic and other languages such as Turkish, Persian and Urdu since students came to Al-Azhar from across the Muslim world.

Jawaharlal Nehru University Library, New Delhi The Library is located at the heart of Academic complex and is accessible easily from all schools on foot. The library has a collection of Books, serials, and Non book material at the tune of 4.6 lakhs approximately. It is subscribing around 1000 serials and is in mailing list of nearly all leading Newspapers of the world. The library is on the mailing list of all publications of Government of India and publications of some very important Intrnational agencies like World Health Organization, Unesco etc. It is also subscribing documents of United Nations. The library has recieved on gratis, valuable life time collection of eminent scholars of India, like Mr. John Mathai, Prof Gyanchand et al. Ambassy of Japan regularly gifts latest books published in Japan to the library. The library has an exchange relations with many Indian and International agencies and National Libraries throughout the world, and through this channel getting their publications in exchange of JNU publications.

A number of projects involve collaboration with partners across the UK and in several other countries. These include universities, colleges and public libraries throughout the UK; the Universities of the Aegean and of Macedonia, Greece; the Microelectronics Applications

Centre, Ireland; Ennis Information Age Town, Ireland; Universiata Oberta de Catalunya, Spain; the Jagiellonian University, Kraków, Poland; Fretwell Downing Informatics Ltd, UK. CERLIM's location in an academic department helps to fuse theory and practice and facilitates the sharing of ideas, techniques and understanding.

John Rylands University Library, Manchester The John Rylands University Library of Manchester (JRULM) is the University of Manchester's library and information service. It is the largest non-legal-deposit academic library in the United Kingdom and supports all subject areas taught by the University.The JRULM provides its members with a large number of services and resources, including the most extensive range of electronic resources of any UK Higher Education library. A range of services is also provided for members of the public, schools and commercial companies. It is an amalgam of two libraries, both founded in the second half of the nineteenth century when Manchester was one of the richest and fastest-growing cities in the world. Manchester University's origins lay in the foundation in 1851 of Owens College, created by a bequest from the local textile magnate John Owens. Its library initially relied heavily on benefactions.

In 1873 the flourishing college moved from makeshift accommodation in the city centre to the fine buildings designed by Alfred Waterhouse, at the heart of the present campus. The Library's greatest benefactor, Richard Copley Christie, funded the University's first separate library building (again designed by Waterhouse) which opened in 1898. By 1903, the year in which Owens College became the Victoria University of Manchester, its library housed around 100,000 volumes.

JSTOR, Journals, Digital libraries JSTOR was founded in 1995 with a broad mission to help the scholarly community take advantage of advances in electronic technologies. Its initial objective has been to build a database comprised of the back volumes of important scholarly research journals. The goal in building this central electronic archive has been to lower the system-wide costs associated with storing and preserving these academic materials while simultaneously increasing their utility. Although originally a grant project of the Andrew W. Mellon Foundation, JSTOR does not rely on the foundation for its ongoing support; rather, it has developed an economic model designed to enable it to achieve financial self-sufficiency and to allow it to operate independently. In its first five years, JSTOR has made remarkable progress. In fact, it has been successful beyond anyone's original expectations.

As of October 2000, the database contains more than six million journal pages from 124 titles in 16 academic disciplines. More than 850 academic institutions in 40 countries have licensed the database, contributing fees to support the preservation and ongoing maintenance of the archive. The organization has delivered on its original promise and is engaged in the process of adding more journals while also reaching out to new types of participating libraries and organizations all over the world. It is fair to assert that there has been a clear endorsement in the scholarly community of JSTOR's goal to serve as a trusted archive of electronic journal literature.

Juma Al Majid Centre for Culture and Heritage, Dubai Juma Al Majid Centre for Culture and Heritage, Dubai is a charitable body for benefit of the public. It was officially established in 1991. The Centre was started by acquiring sources of knowledge in a variety of forms and their preservation, cataloguing and classification. Since that time, preparations were in progress. The Centre was established with full support from its Founder Mr.Juma Al-Majid when he felt that students and researchers, most of them poor, in search of books and references had to spend money travelling and procuring the desired books and copies of manuscripts, often difficult to obtain from Arab and Muslim countries. This was the reason why the library for Islamic, Arabic and humanitarian sciences was established.

The library collection developed gradually into a cultural centre rendering the needed facilities to students and scholars in pursuit of knowledge. It contains a considerable number of copies of manuscripts, university theses and dissertations, printed material, documents, periodicals and other various sources of knowledge.The Centre also publishes books on different subjects as well as a periodical magazine aafaq at-thaqaafa wat turaath (Horizon of Culture and Heritage). It also holds seminars on subjects conducing to its goals. The library contains sources of knowledge: multiple kinds and forms of books, audio and visual material, compact discs, etc., in addition to an assortment of old and new periodicals with over three thousand titles, the periodicals ranging from the extinct to the new and the current. It is to be noted that these sources of knowledge are in a variety of languages like Arabic, Persian, English, French, etc.

Kedermister Library at Langley near Slough in Berkshire is a rare surviving example of an early 17th century parish library, preserved in situ in the decorated cupboards designed for it in 1620 in the parish church of St Mary the Virgin. Founded around 1613 by Sir John Kedermister (d. 1631), it was established to provide for the education of the rector of St. Mary's, and presented to the church in perpetuity by Sir John. A catalogue of the Library listing 307 volumes survives from 1638. A large portion of the library still exists and, with the contemporary catalogue, provides a fascinating insight into scholarship and book collecting in the 17th century. Two of the Library's treasures, the Kedermister Gospels (an 11th century illuminated manuscript) and the Pharmacopolium or a booke of Medicine (a manuscript herbal of 1630) are on permanent deposit in the British Library. Langley, also known as Langley Marish, was formerly in the county of Buckinghamshire, and the Kedermister Library is overseen by Buckinghamshire County Council and governed by a charitable trust. The name Kedermister is the most commonly used, though some sources, including the charity governing the library, use the spelling Kederminster.

King Faisal Center for Research and Islamic Studies, Riyadh The King Faisal Center for Research and Islamic Studies is an operational arm of the King Faisal Foundation. The Center has its own identity and is independently financed. It has its headquarters in Riyadh and was founded in 1983. The Main Library provides accommodation for more than one million books. The collection covers the fields of Islamic Studies and Islamic Civilization. The main reading room houses frequently used reference books in Arabic, English and several other languages. There is a separate reading room for periodicals. At present, these number 3,000 volumes in 16 languages, 35% of which are in Arabic.There is also a collection of rare and out-of-print periodicals. Adopting an unconventional approach, the main library displays few books in the reading rooms. The majority is kept in computerized racks in a special underground storage room, a system that protects the books from unnecessary handling. With its storage capacity of more than one million books and a current inventory of 90,000 titles in 160,000 volumes, as well as 250,000 abstracted articles, this library is a vital resource for scholars.

The children's library, geared toward 5-12 year olds encourages a love of reading and research from an early age and teaches youngsters how to use libraries to full advantage. The library contains more than 18,000 books and magazines and 300 audio-visual cassettes in Arabic, English, and French. A hobby section for drawing, coloring, writing, and games, as well as areas for videos and computers provides further stimulation for the young readers. A separate audio-visual research library has more than 11,000 audio and videocassettes, slides, and films, which contain lectures and documentary material related to the Center's various activities and interests.

Koninklijke Bibliotheek. The National Library of the Netherlands, KB was founded in 1798, based on the private library of the exiled stadhouder Willem V. It was named Koninklijke Bibliotheek in 1806, and was declared as the National Library of the Netherlands in 1982 on the inauguration of its present building. The main mission of the Koninklijke Bibliotheek as the national library of the Netherlands is to preserve the national printed and written heritage. As a depository library the KB collects and preserves all publications that are issued by officially registered Dutch publishers, and in addition a good deal of Dutch grey literature. As a scholarly library the KB serves the academic community and individual scholars.

The KB carries out special tasks relating to the national information infrastructure, library cooperation, library research and the application of technology in information services. Apart from the deposit collection of printed material, the KB has a high level collection of scholarly literature in the humanities and a number of special collections comprising incunabula, medieval and modern manuscripts and early printed books. The KB also has important collections of songbooks, childrens' literature, sportsbooks (e.g. falconry, mountaineering), gamesbooks (e.g. bridge, draughts and chess), books of private presses, and the largest collection of Dutch newspapers, and newspapers from the former Dutch colonies. The coverage of the social sciences is not in depth. Scientific literature is not actively collected. In 1994 the KB had an estimated 2,200,000 bound volumes.

Khuda Bakhsh Oriental Public Library, Patna Khuda Bakhsh Oriental Public Library was founded by Khuda Bakhsh Khan, who donated his entire personal collection to the nation by a deed of trust. It was opened for public in October, 1891 with 4,000 manuscripts, of which he inherited 1,400 from his father Maulvi Mohammed Bakhsh. Acknowledging its rich and rare collection the Govt. of India declared the Library as an Institution of National Importance by an Act of Parliament in 1969. The Library is now fully funded by the Ministry of Culture.

Presently, the Library holds about 2,25,000 books in Urdu, Persian, Arabic and Hindi languages. It subscribes to 527 Journals. There are about 12,000 volumes of serials, which has great value in research. As far as the collection of manuscripts is concerned, the Library holds about 22,000 invaluable manuscripts. Now one of the richest collections of Arabic and Persian manuscripts and Mughal and Central Asian paintings-presently possessing the Khuda Bakhsh Library is fast becoming a centre for preserving and dissemination of knowledge in its special fields of Arabic and Persian learning and Islamic and Medieval Indian Studies.

LeHigh University Library, United States This site contains two collections: one of ancient Chinese vessels, and another called "Bridges of the 19th Century" that contains thirty monographs, manuals, and documents on American bridge engineering from their Special Collections.This collection is noteworthy for the care and attention that has been paid to designing the pages, and the way in which the default Greenstone design has been overridden, as the sample pages show. Site: <http://bridges.lib.lehigh.edu/cgi-bin/library>

Library and Archives Canada Library and Archives Canada is the national library of Canada. Originally founded in 1953, it is a result of a merger between the National Library of Canada and National Archives of Canada in 2003. Its purpose is to preserve the history of Canada through texts, pictures and other documents relevant to the culture of Canada and the politics of Canada. Archival and library material are acquired from government departments, national groups or organizations, private donors, and legal deposit. The maximum fine for not obeying legal deposit is defined by Section 735 of the Canadian Criminal Code as $100,000. The building of Library and Archives Canada was opened on June 20, 1967 by Prime Minister Lester B. Pearson with 400,000 volumes of information which has grown to over 18,000,000.

After the merger there are now slightly more than 1,100 employees in the Library and Archives. The official entrance and the public services are located in Ottawa, Ontario at 395 Wellington Street, near other significant buildings such as Parliament Hill, the Supreme Court of Canada and others. Located at the front of the building is a sculpture named The Secret Bench of Knowledge by Lea Vivot. The building has five floors and covers 52,600 square metres. The administrative units, including the sections responsible for acquisitions (gifts, purchases, and legal deposit), cataloguing, ISBN numbering, conservation and other matters, have long ago overflowed from the main building to several other venues on or around Wellington Street. As of autumn 2004 the 600 or 700 employees in these units will be consolidated in a temporary building in Gatineau, Quebec about 12 km to the North and to the East.

Library of Ashurbanipal The "royal library" of Ashurbanipal was discovered by Austen Henry Layard. It is a remarkable archaeological discovery which consists of thousands of clay tablets and fragments containing texts of all kinds (royal inscriptions, chronicles, mythological and religious texts, contracts, royal grants and decrees, royal letters, assorted administrative documents, etc.) from the 7th century BC. The materials were found in the archeological site of Kuyunjik (then ancient Nineveh, capital of Assyria) in northern Mesopotamia. The site would be found in modern day Iraq. Most texts were taken to England and now belong to the British Museum.

The library actually comprised several smaller collections. A first discovery was made in late 1849 in the so-called South-West Palace, which was the Royal Palace of king Sennacherib (705 - 681 BC). Three years later, Hormuzd Rassam. Layard's assistant, discovered a similar "library" in the palace di Ashurbanipal (668 - 627 BC), on the opposite side of the mound. Unfortunately, no record was taken for the findings, and soon after reaching Europe, the tablets appeared to have been irreparably mixed with each other and with tablets originating from other sites. Thus, it is almost impossible today to reconstruct the original contents of each of the two main "libraries"'.

The whole set is known as "the Library of Ashurbanipal" as it is known that this king was literate and was a passionate collector of texts and tablets. The total number of registered pieces is about 26,000, but we must deduct all smaller fragments that actually belong to the same text, and thus we may submit that the "library" originally included some 10,000 texts in all.

The importance of Ashurbanipal's Library can not be overstated. It was buried by invaders centuries before the famous library at Alexandria was established and gives modern historians much information about the peoples of the Ancient Near East. The ancient Sumerian "Epic of Gilgamesh" and a nearly complete list of ancient Near Eastern rulers among other priceless writings were preserved in Ashurbanipal's palace library at Nineveh. Ashurbanipal's accomplishments are also of great importance to scholars of library history. As a scholar Ashurbanipal reached greatness. Though this library was not the first of its kind, it was one of the largest and the first library modern scholars can document as having most or even all of the attributes one expects to find in a modern library. Like a modern library this collection was spread out into many rooms according to subject matter. Some rooms were devoted to history and government, others to religion and magic and still others to geography, science, poetry, etc, Ashurbanipal's collection even held what could be called classified government materials. The findings of spies and secret affairs of state were held secure from access in deep recesses of the palace much like a modern government archive. Each group of tablets contained a brief citation to identify the contents and each room contained a tablet near the door to classify the general contents of each room in Ashurbanipal's library. The actual cataloging activities under Ashurbanipal's direction would not be seen in Europe for centuries. Partially through military conquests and partially through the employment of numerous scribes there was significant effort placed into what modern librarians would call collection development.

Thus, centuries before the library at Alexandria, a library with many of the characteristics of a modern institution was in existence. Scholars of library history would be well served by further study of Ashurbanipal and his palace library.

Library of Congress Established by Congress in 1800 to function as a research library for the legislative branch of the federal government, the Library of Congress eventually became the unofficial national library of the United States. Located in Washington D.C., LC houses a collection of over 120 million items and administers the U.S. copyright system, serving as the nation's copyright depository. LC is also the primary source of original cataloging in the United States. The machine-readable cataloging (MARC) and cataloging-in-publication (CIP) programs originated at the Library of Congress. Library of Congress is one of four official national libraries of the United States (along with the National Library of Medicine, National Agricultural Library, and National Archives and Records Administration). Originally founded as a research library for the U.S. Congress on April 24, 1800, its original collection was composed of the books of former U.S. President Thomas Jefferson. Later, the Library assumed a role as a legal repository to guarantee copyright protection. All authors seeking American copyright had to submit two copies of the work to the Library. This requirement is no longer enforced, but copies of many books published in the US still arrive at the Library regularly. It contains many important books and collections, such as a Gutenberg Bible.

The Library developed a system of book classification called Library of Congress classification (LC) which is used by most research and university libraries, although most public libraries continue to use the Dewey decimal system. With over 128 million items, it is one of the largest libraries in the history of the world, surpassed only by the British Library, which contains over 150 million items. With over 520 miles of shelves, the Library of Congress certainly is the longest library in the world.

The library is open to the general public for academic research, and runs tours for visitors. Only people with a permit can enter the reading room and access the collection. Permits are available in the Madison building upon presentation of a picture ID. It is estimated that the print holdings of the Library of Congress would, if digitized and stored as plain text, constitute 17 to 20 *terabytes* of information. This leads to the commonly-repeated but misleading equivalence of 20 terabytes to the entire holdings of the Library. Only selected portions of the print holdings have actually been digitized, and the Library currently has no plans for systematic digitization of any significant portion of its books.

The Library makes millions of digital objects, comprising tens of terabytes, available at its American Memory site. American Memory is a source for public domain image resources, as well as audio, video, and archived Web content. The Library of Congress also provides an on-line archive of the proceedings of the U.S. Congress at Thomas (http://thomas.loc.gov), including bill text, Congressional Record text, bill summary and status.

the Congressional Record Index, and the United States Constitution.

Library of Sir Thomas Browne Thomas Browne graduated from the University of Leiden in 1633, having previously studied at the Universities of Montpellier and Padua for his medical degree. Upon his establishment in Norwich as a physician he was able to begin a lifetime's bibliophilia, building a private library, acquiring and no doubt reading many of an estimated 1500 titles. Browne was adept in no less than five contemporary languages (French, Italian, Spanish, Dutch and Danish), Greek and Hebrew these languages as well as the predominant written form of the Renaissance namely Latin are all represented in his Library. The 1711 Sales Auction Catalogue reflects the wide scope of Browne's amateur hobbies and lists the diverse reading material he engaged upon in his lifetime as well as some of the sources for his encyclopaedia Pseudodoxia Epidemica more commonly known as Vulgar Errors. It went through no less than six editions from 1646 to 1672 was translated into French, Latin and Dutch and established Browne's name as one of the leading intellects of seventeenth century Europe.

Browne's erudite learning is reflected in the fact that the Classics of antiquity as well as history, geography, philology, philosophy, anatomy, theology, cartography, embryology, medicine, cosmography, ornithology, mineralogy, zoology, travel, law, mathematics, geometry, literature, both Continental and English, the latest advances in scientific thinking in astronomy, chemistry as well as esoteric topics such as astrology, alchemy, physiognomy and the Kabbalah are all represented in the Catalogue of his library contents. It was however not until 1986 that the Catalogue was first made widely available when the American scholar Jeremiah Stanton Finch, Dean Emeritus at Yale University, completed the indexing of the books of Sir Thomas and his son Edward Browne's libraries, after many years in many libraries. An unknown percentage of books auctioned from the Library of Sir Thomas Browne subsequently formed the foundation for the future British Library.

Library of the British Museum To the library community and the public at large, the best known component of the new national library consisted of the library departments of the British Museum. The Museum's Department of Printed Books was founded in 1753, the year of the foundation of the Museum itself. Over the intervening two hundred years, the library of the British Museum had grown into one of the largest in the world, sustained by its privilege of legal deposit whereby it was entitled to a copy of most items printed in the United Kingdom - not only books and periodicals, but newspapers, maps and printed music. In addition, the Museum's comprehensive holdings of non-legal deposit items had reportedly earned it the accolade from Lenin of possessing (in the 1900s) a more comprehensive collection of Russian books than libraries in Moscow and St Petersburg. Lenin was one of those privileged to use the Museum's spectacular domed reading room.

Designed in the 1850s at the instigation of Sir Anthony Panizzi, then Chief Librarian, the reading room and surrounding bookstacks were constructed in the courtyard of the British Museum providing its library with impressive premises in the heart of what was already an overcrowded building. The Reading Room had been thrown open to all for a short period at the time of its opening in May 1857, thereafter admission was by pass only, giving access to its collections an aura of selectivity and exclusiveness. In addition to Lenin (who used the pseudonym Jacob Richter), the roll call of those holding reader passes included Karl Marx, Charles Dickens, George Bernard Shaw and Virginia Woolf.

Library of Tibetan Works and Archives, Dharamshala Library of Tibetan Works and Archives (TWA) is an autonomous body under direct supervision of

H.H. the Dalai Lama registered with the Government of India under the Registration of Societies Act of 1860 recognised by Himachal Pradesh University as a Centre for Research in 1991 accorded status of National Library, Achieves and Museum by Tibetan Parliament in Exile in 1996

The Library of Tibetan Works and Archives (LTWA) is one of the most important institutions in the world dedicated to the preservation and dissemination of Tibetan culture. The foundation stone for the Library's Tibetan style building was laid on 11th June 1970, in the hill station of Dharamsala, north India. Located within the compound of the Tibetan Government-in-Exile, the Library serves as a repository for Tibetan artefacts and manuscripts and a centre for language and cultural education. Its holdings include more than 80,000 manuscripts, books and documents, hundreds of thangkas, statues and other artefacts, 6,000 photographs, and other materials.

The primary objective of the Library of Tibetan Works and Archives is to provide a comprehensive cultural resource centre and to promote an environment fostering research and an exchange of knowledge between scholars and students.

The Library is home to one of only two Tibetan Oral History projects in the world. Its dynamic thangka painting and woodcarving programmes are indicative of the fact that cultural preservation includes the arts as well as letters. LTWA works in close collaboration with the Central Institute for Higher Tibetan Studies (deemed a university) in Sarnath and the Department of Religion and Culture of the Central Tibetan Administration. With each year of operation increasing numbers of visitors, researchers and students are drawn to this institution which is able to provide them with an educational and cultural experience available nowhere else in the world.

The Library holds 70,000 manuscripts and

documents in Tibetan and 10,000 books in English and foreign languages dealing with Buddhism and Tibet related affairs. Between them, the Tibetan Manuscript Collection and the Foreign Language Reference Library contain more than 80,000 items, ranging from handwritten manuscripts and centuries old documents to contemporary books and periodicals. Parts of the collection are open to the public, while access to others is restricted to accredited scholars and researchers. Study areas are provided in the respective wings housing each collection. Research guidance is available from many resident scholars at the Library. General information about the libraries is available at the reception desk on the ground floor.

Macmillan Information SuperLibrary Is an online World Wide Web database (at mcp.com) to contents of computer books from Que, Sams Publishers, Hayden Press, Que College, NRP, Grady, and Adobe Press. There are other features such as a free online newsletter sent to your email address. The Macmillan USA Information SuperLibrary Newsletter is intended for your own personal use.

Maulana Azad Library The Maulana Azad Library is located at the Aligarh Muslim University at Aligarh in India which is the most respected and important educational centre for Indian Muslims. It was initially founded as Mohammedan Anglo Oriental College at Aligarh in 1875 by Sir Syed Ahmed Khan (1817-1898) and subsequently raised to the status of Aligarh Muslim University (AMU) in 1920.

The Library complex of the University consists of a Central Library and over 80 college/departmental libraries. The Library holds over one million books and a large number of invaluable manuscripts. Libraries of the colleges, institutes and departments, cater to the needs of postgraduates and students of professional courses. The University has established Book Banks for the benefit of students of certain professional courses. The Central

Library was set up in 1875, when this institution was established as Madarsatul Uloom. In 1877, the Madarsa became Mohammadan Anglo-Oriental College. Lord Lytton, the viceroy of India, laid the foundation stone, and the library was named after him as Lytton Library. Eminent scholars like Gardner Brown, Arnold, Releigh, Horowitz, Storey and Auchtelpone functioned as honorary librarians in addition to their teaching responsibilities.

M.A. Library performs the functions of a National Library so far as its collection of Oriental manuscripts are concerned. It is because of these rich collections of immense research value that this Library is reckoned among major libraries of the world. The oldest manuscript owned by the library is more than fourteen hundred years old. It is a fragment of the Holy Quran transcribed by Hazrat Ali, the fourth caliph of Islam and is written on parchment in Kufi script. Another rare collection is the Halnama of Beyazid Ansari, no copy of which is available anywhere else in the world.

Mohammed VI Library at Al Akhawayn University Morocco is a three-storey building that houses a large collection of books and national and international academic journals, magazines and newspapers. The library also provides a campus wide access to a wide variety of electronic resources (full-text electronic books, electronic journals, etc.) The Library subscribes to Document Delivery Services to provide faculty and graduate students with articles not available in the AUI Library collections and databases. Mohammed VI Library at Al Akhawayn University is one of a few open-stacks libraries in Morocco. This system allows free access to all the Library resources and saves students' time. The Library provides a suitable environment for study and research. The library's mission is to further the advancement of learning at AUI and to serve the information and research needs of AUI schools and departments.

Murdoch University Library The Library provides services to the University's staff and students and to members of the wider community. There are two libraries at the Murdoch Campus, on South Street in Murdoch, the Main Library and the Veterinary Library. Another library is located at Rockingham, offering services to staff and students of Murdoch, Challenger TAFE, and Rockingham City public library patrons. Mandurah Senior College (Peel) provides library services for Murdoch University, Challenger TAFE and Mandurah Senior College staff and students. The Library holds collections, and provides access to resources in a number of subject areas, to support the University's teaching and research programmes. Subject areas of particular strength include: libraries have a modern ambience, backed by efficient service and facilities, and supplemented by courteous and competent staff. Apart from providing the best cf reading materials published in the UK, it also provides access to information products online and a wide range of services set to the highest professional standards.

Mysore University Library, Mysore The Mysore University Library was established in the year 1918. The Library is the largest and also oldest among the University Libraries in the State of Karnataka. It has a history of over 78 years. The library was started with 2,311 volumes. It has today a resource collection of nearly 7.5 lakh documents in its system and membership of 5600 users, which include 600 Faculty members, 600 Researchers, 3,500 PG Students, 500 Office Staff, and 400 Graduates of Mysore City. The Library has a rich collection of books relating to "History of Mysore" and administrative reports on the princely State of Mysore, including works on Indian Painting, art and architecture. The Oriental Research Institute (ORI). One of the branches in the system has a collection of Sanskrit , Kannada and Telugu manuscripts . The entire collection constitutes 84000 works in 29000 volumes. 'Mysore Orientalist' the annual publication gives the details of the collection and research activities undertaken by the University.

Nalanda Digital Library Nalanda is the result of the ongoing Digital Library nitiative at National Institute of Technology, Calicut Library. Nalanda Project aims at a full-fledged Digital Library to cater to the increasing demand for information resources from the Campus User Community as well as from Remote Users from rest of the Country. Some resources are open to all, otherwise they are resistricted to NITC campus and their recognised users. At present, it is in evolving stage. The Library was started during 1963, with skeleton staff, inside NITC Campus with books as its major holding.

The holdings of the library increased to double the level of 80's and the area of library also increased with the addition of a new block. The demand on library also increased during this period due to the increase in student strength. The Institute had started a number of part-time programs and short-term training and executive development programs, increasing demand on the services of library. A separate reference reading room for the benefit of the users was started during this period. Similarly a full-fledged D.T.P centre with a graphics studio to meet the publishing needs of the Institute, and a separate Xerox centre were started during this period. A video section with more than 100 titles was started during this period in order to improve the learning resource collection. The services of the library to the weaker sections of the society also increased substantially. The holdings of books reserved separately for the use of students belonging to SC/ST communities had increased during this period.

Nalanda University Library Nalanda came into being in India around 5th century B.C. and was a flourishing town with over 10,000 scholars and an extensive library. Nalanda is sacred to Jains, Buddhists, and Hindus but it has been more famous as one of the places frequented by Lord Buddha preaching his Dharma. He often retired to Nalanda and Rajgir during the rainy season. It was Nalanda that Mahavira the last Jain Tirthankara, had met Goshala.

The International Scholastic Centre at Nalanda described by later Scholars as an International University was founded much earlier than the 5th century A.D. There were scholars from China, Japan, Korea, Mongolia, Tibet, Nepal and Ceylon. At one time there where thousands of scholars at Nalanda and they were lodged in smaller cells which can still be seen in ruins.

Nalanda's library was located in a nine storied building. The subjects taught at Nalanda University covered every field of learning. The courses offered at Nalanda included the study of scriptures of Mahayana and Hinayana Schools of Buddhism, Brahminical vedic texts, Philosophy, logic theology, grammer, astronomy, mathematics and medicine. Over two thousand teachers and ten thousand students crowded its portals. Kings and Emperors built Monasteries here. There was a college of fine arts which was endowed by the Gupta Enperor Kumaragupta. The remains carefully excavated at Nalanda reveals Stupas, a large stairway, decorated panels, lecture halls, dormitories for the monks and students, and metal idols of the Buddha. The main monuments found at Nalanda are the Viharas or Monasteries, chaityas, Stupas, Votive or Commemorative. There are remains of temples with high standard of sculpture depicting household scenes, dancers, and foliage designs.

National Agricultural Library The National Agricultural Library is one of the world's largest and most accessible agricultural research libraries. It serves as a National Library of the United States and as the library of the United States Department of Agriculture. The National Agricultural Library was created as the departmental library for the U.S. Department of Agriculture in 1862 and became a national library in 1962. One of four national libraries of the United States (along with the Library of Congress, the National Library of Medicine, and the National Library of Education), it is also the coordinator for a national network of state land-grant and U.S. Department of Agriculture (USDA) field libraries. In its international role, the National Agricultural Library serves as the U.S. center for the international agricultural information system, coordinating and sharing resources and enhancing global access to agricultural data.

The National Agricultural Library's collection of over 3.3 million items and its leadership role in information services and technology applications combine to make it the foremost agricultural library in the world.It is one of four national libraries of the United States (with the Library of Congress, the National Library of Medicine, and the National Library of Education), it is also the coordinator for a national network of State land-grant and U.S. Department of Agriculture (USDA) field libraries. In its international role, the National Agricultural Library serves as the U.S. center for the international agricultural information system, coordinating and sharing resources and enhancing global access to agricultural data. The National Agricultural Library's collection of over 3.3 million items and its leadership role in information services and technology applications combine to make it the foremost agricultural library in the world.

National and University Library of Bosnia and Herzegovina Was established in October 1945 by the decree of the Ministry of Education of the Federal Bosnia and Herzegovina. Over the time Library has accumulated about 3 million library items including approximately 6.000 titles of periodicals, 3000 manuscripts and old and rare printed books witnessing the multilateral and multiethnic character of the country's history.

Presently the library functions on the basis of the

Law of Librarianship which is, expected eather to be reaffirmed or new law enacted by the Parliamentary Assembly of BiH. According to the present law, the National and University Library is a legal deposit library and the central institution of its kind in Bosnia and Herzegovina. Provisions are made for its central role in establishing and maintaining library and information services throughout the country. It is a member of IFLA and provides home for ISSN and ISBN centers. International cooperation is carried out through staff exchanges, interlibrary loan and book exchanges.

The Library is trying to enhance the joint work with other libraries in Bosnia and Herzegovina, particularly as regards the development and reconstruction of library services and collections. The purpose of the support given to the development of libraries and librarianship as a profession by the National and University Library is to collect and preserve the documentary heritage of Bosnia and Herzegovina. According to the present constitution of Bosnia and Herzegovina, this country consists of two entities, the Federation of Bosnia and Herzegovina and Republic Srpska. This arrangement influences to a certain extant legal, financial and administrative status of libraries in Bosnia and Herzegovina.

National Archeological Database National Archeological Database is a computerized communications network for the archeological and historic preservation community. It is an internationally recognized source of information on public archeology. NADB was established to meet a congressional directive to improve access to information on archeological activities nationwide. NADB is a "database of databases."

National Archives and Records Administration The National Archives of the United States, a federal agency established by Congress in 1934 to oversee the management of all federal records, including the public's right of access to documents and information not specifically exempted under the Freedom of Information Act. NARA's 33 facilities house approximately 21.5 million cubic feet of original textual materials collected from the executive, legislative, and judicial branches. It also includes nonprint materials, such as motion pictures, sound and videorecordings, maps and charts, aerial photographs, architectural drawings, computer data sets, posters, etc.

NARA is administered by an Archivist of the United States appointed by the President with the approval of Congress, and advised by a National Archives Council. It is an independent agency of the U.S. federal government charged with preserving and documenting government and historical records. It also works to increase public access to those documents. NARA is officially responsible for publishing acts of Congress, presidential proclamations and executive orders, and federal regulations. The agency often works closely with scholars to facilitate their studies. Originally, each branch and agency of the U.S. government was responsible for maintaining its own documents, which often resulted in the loss and destruction of records. Congress established the National Archives Establishment in 1934 to centralize federal record keeping, with the archivist of the United States as its chief administrator.

The National Archives was incorporated into the General Services Administration in 1949, but in 1985 it was made an independent agency as NARA. Most of the documents in the care of NARA are in the public domain, as works of the federal government are excluded from copyright protection. However, some documents that have come into the care of NARA from other sources may still be protected by copyright or donor agreements.

The National Archives Building, located immediately north of the National Mall in Washington, DC, opened as its original headquarters in 1935. It houses the original copies of the three main formative documents of the United

States and its government: the Declaration of Independence, the United States Constitution, and the Bill of Rights. These are displayed to the public in the main chamber of the National Archives, which is called the Rotunda for the Charters of Freedom.

The National Archives Building also exhibits other important American historical documents such as the Louisiana Purchase and the Emancipation Proclamation, as well as collections of photography and other historically and culturally significant American artifacts. Due to space constraints, NARA opened a second facility in 1994 at College Park, Maryland, where it is now based. There are now a total of nine regional NARA records facilities across the country, including two major facilities in St. Louis, Missouri which comprise the National Personnel Records Center. The National Archives Building in Washington remains an active NARA office and a major tourist attraction. NARA also maintains the Presidential Library system, a nationwide network of libraries for preserving and making available the documents of U.S. presidents since Herbert Hoover.

National Archives and the National Library of Bangladesh, There are the two most important national institutions in Bangladesh devoted to the cultivation of knowledge and preservation of the country's cultural heritage. The institutions are also the repositories of the country's important historical documents and the nation's creative literary and other works. They work under the guidance of the Ministry of Cultural Affairs, Government of the People's Republic of Bangladesh. The National Archives and the National Library are located in the most picturesque and historical site at the Sher-e-Bangla Nagar of the capital Dhaka.

National Archives of Australia Thiss vast collection is a rich resource for the study of Australian history, Australian society and the Australian people and is accessible to all. It provides a range of databases, guides and leaflets to assist. Its head office is located in Canberra with offices in each State capital and in Darwin. The collection is dispersed in these offices across Australia. In addition to caring for collection, it develops and tours exhibitions, publish books and guides to collection and deliver educational programs. Australian Government agency staff and other recordkeeping professionals are valuable partners for the Archives in ensuring that all Australians can use Commonwealth records. Many records are now created in electronic forms that are harder to preserve and keep accessible over time. It is important to build systems that ensure valuable records survive. The Archives assists agencies by developing policies, standards, guidelines and providing training and advice about modern recordkeeping.

National Archives of India is the repository of the non-current records of the Government of India and is holding them in trust for the use of administrators and scholars. It is an Attached Office of the Department of Culture under Ministry of Tourism & Culture. It was set up in March 1891 in Calcutta (Kolkata) as the Imperial Record Department and subsequent to the transfer of the National Capital from Calcutta to New Delhi in 1911 it was shifted to its present building in 1926.

National Archives of Japan preserves government documents and records of importance as historical materials received by the Prime Minister from various government ministries and agencies, and makes them available to the public with the aim of achieving appropriate preservation and use of such government documents and records that are in the custody of the National Archives or government organs.

National Diet Library Kokuritsu Kokkai Toshokan) is the largest national library of Japan, and is located in Tokyo. The Diet is a Japanese legislature; the library is an equivalent of the U.S. Library of Congress. The library stores copies of all publications published in Japan.

National Information Standards Organisation A nonprofit association accredited by the American National Standards Institute (ANSI) to develop voluntary standards in library science, information science, publishing, and other information services, NISO is designated by ANSI to represent U.S. interests to the Technical Committee on Information and Documentation of the International Organization for Standardization (ISO). NISO Standards cover many aspects of library science, publishing, and information services, and address the application of both traditional and new technologies to information services. It is a non-profit association that identifies, develops, maintains, and publishes technical standards to manage information. An example of a NISO standard is Z39.50, an information retrieval standard that defines the way two computers communicate and share information.

National Lending Library for Science and Technology The third major component of the British Library consisted of the National Central Library or NCL which began operation in 1916 in London and the National Lending Library for Science and Technology (NLLST), in service since 1961 at Boston Spa in Yorkshire. These were amalgamated in 1973 as the British Library Lending Division (BLLD). The function of the Lending Division was to support the library systems of the UK by providing a loan and photocopy service to other libraries throughout the country. The NLLST had a stock specialising in science and technology, containing 25,000 monographs and subscriptions to 1,200 serials; its staff numbered 120. Around 600 tons of the NCL stock, which specialised in humanities and social sciences, was transferred to Yorkshire during the Library's first year of formation. The semi-rural site at Boston Spa occupies around 60 acres of an ex-munitions factory and is well served by road links for easy distribution.

During the 1970s the range of services was expanded and made available to international customers and use of technology became a more integral part of the service. The use of Automated Requesting grew by about 40% in this time and the Lending Division often acted in collaboration with academic and scientific partners in early days of exploring the future of fax transmission and satellite communications. In 1985, the title was changed to the BL Document Supply Centre to reflect the changing emphasis of document supply in which a greater proportion of requests were for copies of articles rather than loans. The stock has grown over the years and now contains over 260,000 journal titles, over 3 million books, almost 500,000 conference proceedings and almost 5 million reports, mostly of a scientific nature.

National Libraries of South Africa It had two national libraries, the South African Library, founded in 1818, in Cape Town, and the State Library, founded in 1887, in Pretoria. In terms of South African legal deposit legislation, each of the national libraries was a legal deposit library, entitled to receive from the publishers a gratis copy of every book, serial, newspaper, government publication or other printed item published in South Africa. In South Africa legal deposit, in some form or another, dates back to 1842. As a result, extensive collections of material of great scholarly value have been built up in the former national libraries.

During the 1990s the Department of Arts, Culture, Science and Technology began a review of all legislation under its jurisdiction, including the National Libraries Act, No 56 of 1985. The Minister of Arts, Culture, Science and Technology in 1996 appointed a Working Group on the National Libraries of South Africa to advise on the future of the two national libraries. The most important recommendation of the Working Group was that the two national libraries be amalgamated to form a dual-site (Cape Town and Pretoria) national library, to be known as the National Library of South Africa. The creation of the new National Library looks ahead to a revitalising and transformation that will align the new institution with the goals of the new democracy. The new institution was constituted on 1 November 1999. On that day the South African Library and the State Library ceased to exist as separate entities and became the Cape Town and Pretoria campusses respectively of the National Library of South Africa.

National Library and Archives of Egypt, Cairo The National Library and Archives of Egypt is a government research and cultural non- profit authority, whose main concern is to render library services throughout Egypt and the Arab World. It was established as an independent legal entity by virtue of the presidential decree in 1993, with an allocated budget including detailed items for each of its activities as specified by the standards of State Master Budget. A 7-storey building over- looking the Nile Corniche in Ramlet Boulac District was allotted from the very beginning to be a large complex for a variety of cultural activities. However, the annex building is now accommodating the National Archives. It is one of several governmental institutions help implementing the Ministry of Culture's responsibilities in the domains of National and Public Libraries, Legacy, Manuscripts, National Archives, Documentation and Information.

The National Library and Archives of Egypt is one of the oldest libraries in the Middle East and its importance lies in having about 55,000 of the most significant collections of manuscripts and microforms in the world which are rendered in Arabic, Turkish and Persian languages.

These rare collections of manuscripts include a wide variety of the Holy Koran (Qur'an), whose early versions are written on paper and parchment, others are in the early undotted Kufi style. Among them are copies written by celebrated calligraphers as Yaquote-al-Mostaasimi. In addition, there is a magnificent collection containing the largest and most richly illuminated versions of the Holy Koran copied in the Mameluke Text-hand, Trilinear and Rayhani writings.

The National Library's collections also include a wide variety of the most valuable manuscripts in various fields of knowledge such as general information, religion, scientific heritage and literature, amongst which is a unique book entitled as (the Message) by Al-Emam-al-Shafi'ai tackling the principles of jurisprudence, and dating back to the third, fourth and fifth centuries, were privately owned by Taymour Pasha, Ahmed Zaki Pasha, Ahmed Tal'at Bey and Mustafa Fadel, then successively acquired and added to the National Library's stock at the end of the nineteenth century.

The collections contain rare Persian manuscripts, some of which are beautifully illustrated by famous Persian painters, like Bostan Sa'adi illustrated in 893 A. H. by Behzad who was entitled as Raphael of the East, also like Shahnama (Book of Kings) by Ferdawsi and Hayder Nama in 416 H.

Ottoman Turkish manuscripts date back to a few centuries ago and represent an important heritage for the Middle East area.

Also, the Arabic papyri collection, discovered at the end of the nineteenth century and amounts to 3.000 papyri, are written in both Arabic and Greek. The majority of such manuscripts are in Arabic and the earliest of which dates back to 22 A. H, and represents invaluable treasure for those who study the development of Arabic calligraphy as they are rich in information about the economic life in Egypt and include deeds of sale and purchase, marriage lines and title-deeds that extend from the Umawi period to Fatimid period.

Similarly, the National Archives has a rare paper historical collection of documents in both Arabic and Turkish languages. The Library's collection include valuable documents' pertaining to the history of Egypt, the earliest of which is the endowment deed of the Fatimid Minister Talae'a bin Ruzeik, dating back to the Ayyubid era (d. 567-648 A. H. / 1058 A.D.). In addition, there are legal documents dating back to the Mameluke era (d. 648-923 A. H. /1250-1517 A.D.), 74 legal documents dating back to the Ottoman era (d. 1517-1805 AD).

National Library of Albania The National Library of Albania was formally founded 1922. However its beginnings go back to 1917. When inaugurated, the National Library had 6000 volumes, books and other library materials and was located within the building of the then Ministry of Education. Among the efforts to enrich its stacks, mention should be made of a Circular of that time by which all publishers were requested to send two copies of each of their publications to this library. When the Second World War came to an end, the National Library with its 15000 volumes in its stacks was located in a separate building. Due to increase of its stacks and growth of its activities, the library facilities increased as well. In 1966 the main part of the National Library was stationed in the new building of the Great Palace of Culture. Today it has both buildings with a surface of 2500 m2 for the stacks, 800m2 for the reading halls and 700m2 for its library staff.

The National Library is the main institution of book preservation and dissemination. It is the center of safeguarding the archives of Albanian publications, serving also as a national bibliographic center and as a professional center of preparing and training librarians. Preservation and conservation of library documents is one of the most important problems for the National Library. The lack of space and the incapability of securing adequate humidity and temperature parameters are a serious risk of damaging library documents. The restoration department founded in 1986 regularly checks the conditions of these documents and carries out their treatment. It restores the most damaged documents cleansing water deacidification, paper and leather restoration, lamination, partial repairing with paper pulp.

The collection of the archives of Albanian publications, specifically created during the first years after the war, in which one copy of every collection is stored, has 61190 book and periodicals titles. In this collection rare and unique works and the first numbers of the Albanian periodicals, etc. are preserved. Albanian publications printed up to 1799, as well as foreign publications of the same period make a special unit that of rare and Antiquary collection.

National Library of Australia The National Library of Australia is located in Canberra, Australia. The library was established in 1960 and grew out of the Federal Parliamentary Library. In that year, it was separated from it by the National Library Act 1960. In 1968, a new building was built for it on the shores of Lake Burley Griffin. The Copyright Act 1968 requires that a copy of every book published in Australia be deposited in the National Library of Australia, and in the appropriate state library.

The library also issues cataloguing-in-publication, ISSNs and ISMNs for Australian publishers. The large National Library building is home various reading rooms and collections. On the ground floor is the Main Reading Room along with private reading rooms. This is where the bulk of the library's Internet access terminals are located. Becuase of the large size of the National Libraries collection of Books, Microfilm and Original documents and Media, the collection is stored at two sites. Behind the scenes of the National Library is over 40KM of shelves. Those items which do not fit there are housed off site at the NLA annex in Hume. In addition to the research facilities available, the National Library offers a Gift shop that includes a large range of Australian books and a cafe and Friends Lounge for members. This and an exhibition hall used for temporary exibits.

National Library of Bangladesh Alter the partition of the Indian subcontinent in 1947 the Government of Pakistan established the National Library of Pakistan in Karachi and a provincial book deposit branch of the Pakistan National Library in Dhaka in 1967, In fact that book deposit branch was the embryo of (lie National library of Bangladesh which came into being after the independence of the country in 1971. After the Liberation War of Bangladesh it was keenly felt by all quarters that a National Library is indispensable for (lie newborn nation. Considering the necessity and importance, the Government of the People's Republic of Bangladesh resolved to set up the National Library of Bangladesh in Dhaka. The Library started functioning with the manpower and resource materials inherited from the Provincial Book Deposit Branch in Dhaka. Later on, in 1973 the two national organizations namely (i) The National Archives of Bangladesh and (ii) The National Library of Bangladesh were merged under the name of the Directorate of Archives & Libraries under the Sports and Culture Division. Ministry of Education, 'the Directorate was first housed in two separate rented places first at 106 Central Road and then at 372 Elephant road, Dhaka. A new building for the National Library of Bangladesh was built in 1985 and the Library was shifted to its new place called The Jutiya Granthi.igur Bliavcin (National Library Building) at 32 Justice S.M.Murshed Sarani, Agargaon, Sher-e-Bangla Nagar. Dhaka-1207. The National Library of Bangladesh is currently run by the Directorate of Archives and Libraries under the Ministry of Cultural Affairs. The National Library is the legal depository of all new books and other printed materials published in the country under the Copy Right Law

The Collection of Bangladesh National Library is the nation's pride. The principal characteristic of its collection is that it covers all major disciplines and branches of human knowledge i.e. Literature. Cultural Heritage, History. Arts. Archaeology, Science and Technology. Medical Science. Engineering, Economics, Agriculture, Library and Information Management, Development Administration. Environment, Woman affairs. HRD, etc and is preserved in scientific manner. In addition to country's all most all publications the library has a large collection of foreign representational publications especially on Asian countries and more specific related to South Asian Studies. The library enriches its collection by various means i.e. acquiring publication under copyright act, purchase, institutional/personal donations, complimentary copies etc. the following are the National Library's collection data up to September 2003. Total number of books and bound volumes in the Library is 5,00,000.

National Library of Bulgaria Bulgaria's National Library was founded in 1878, as Sofia Public Library, based on private donations from Bulgarians and Russians. In 1987 the first legal deposit law was adopted and in 1909 the first law of the National Library was passed. The mission of the St. Cyril and St. Methodius National Library is to preserve the national printed and written heritage. As a deposit library the National Library collects and preserves all publications issued by Bulgarian publishers and in addition a great deal of Bulgarian grey literature. As a scholarly library the National Library serves the academic community and individual scholars, students and citizens.

The National Library is also the archive of the Bulgarian output of printed material and the national bibliographic centre; it holds an archive of 3 million documents from the period of Ottoman domination, feudalism and the Bulgarian Revival. The National Library has a number of special collections comprising incunabula, medieval and modern MSS and early printed books, scores and records, maps, prints and portraits, patents and standards. In 1994 the National Library had an estimated 6,772,330 items, of which 1,515,930 are books and 804,155 bound periodicals.

National Library of Canada Established by the Canadian Parliament in 1953, the National Library of Canada is located in Ottawa, Ontario. Their main role is to acquire, preserve and promote past, present, and future Canadiana. The library offers reference service for a wide variety of enquiries. A location service assists other libraries trying to locate items not in their own holdings. The National Library play a major role in fostering the development of library resources and services throughout the country and facilitating resource sharing among Canadian libraries as outlined in the National Library Act. http://www.nlc-bnc.ca

The NLC electronic collection incorporates formally published Canadian online books and journals. These publications are being acquired, catalogued, and permanently stored at the NLC. Public access is provided on the Internet through the World Wide Web. Catalogue records for Electronic Collection titles, including the Uniform Resource Locators (URLs), are available on NLC's AMICUS system and on resAnet." URL: http://collection.nlc-bnc.ca/e-coll-e/index-e.htm

National Library of China The National Library of China is situated in the West of Beijing. Its predecessor was the Capital Library established in 1909. In 1916 the Library started accepting the legal deposit copies of the national publications. In 1928 the Library got name of the National Beiping Library. After the founding of the People's Republic of China, the Library was renamed Beijing Library. From 1987 the name, National Library of China, has been used in the communication and cooperation with the libraries of other countries. In December 1998, the State Council approved that the Chinese name of the Library is changed to Zhong Guo Guo Jia Tu Shu Guan (the National Library of China). The National Library of China is a comprehensive research library, a national repository of the home publications, a national bibliographic center, a national center of library information networks, and the library research and development center.

The Library serves for central legislature, government, key research institutions, academy, education, business and the general public. The Library is responsible for implementing the official cultural agreements and conducts communication and cooperation with the libraries both at home and abroad. The Library has the total floor area of 170,000 square meters, ranking fifth among the world libraries. By the end of 2003, the Library has a rich collection of 24,1100,000 volumes/items, also ranking fifth among the libraries of the world. In the collection there are 270,000 volumes of rare books, 1,600,000 volumes of general ancient books, 35,000 pieces of the scripted turtle shells and animal bones. The Library not only has the largest collection of Chinese books in the world, but also the biggest collection of materials in foreign languages in the country. It has a strong collection in those materials, such as manuscripts of the notables, revolutionary historical materials, Chinese doctoral dissertations, the UN publications and the increased number of e-publications. The Library opens to the public 365 days a year and its on-line services are available 24 hours a day via its linkage with various multimedia networks and on Internet.

National Library of Czechoslovakia The history of the library is connected with the foundation of the Charles University in 1348. The first written references concerning books are documented in relation to the oldest Charles College, which, having been given a royal gift of manuscripts in 1366. The so-called Old Clementinian Library was founded in 1556 at the coming of the Jesuits and its core was constituted of the Ojvín Monastery Library that had been dissolved. The Jesuit Library, having been enlarged by numerous donations. Another library, called New Carolinian Library, was established in 1638 and it was supposed mostly to meet the needs of the Faculties of Law and of Medicine. In 1777, having been enriched by the Kinsky family and personal libraries, the Imperial and Royal Public and University Library has been founded and supported from that time onwards by the state.

In 1807 a regional government decree made obligatory for all printers to present copies of books they published. In 1918 the newly-formed Czechoslovak state took over the library. The collection of about 420 000 volumes rapidly expanded as donations came from abroad, and different private libraries were bequeathed to the University (e.g. the library of Bernard Bolzano, a papyrus collection).

The Slavonic Library founded in 1920s for the Russian, Ucrainean and Byelorussian emigration is a branch library with very rich holdings from the sphere of history, culture, literature and languages of Slavonic nations.

The main mission of the National Library is twofold: to be the archive library for documents issued on the territory of the Czech lands and to be a public research library especially in the domain of humanities, pure natural sciences, culture, and arts. The close connection between the richness of the historical book collections and the cultural and political development of the country is also manifested in the composition of the collections referring to the content and provenance of the books. The core of the collections is created by Bohemical materials. These works belong to the jewels of Czech culture. Of the total number of old prints in the National Library, that amounts to 500.000 volumes, the selection of the Manuscripts and Old Printed Books Department mostly involves Bohemical documents, unique non-Bohemical prints, a collection of rare bindings, old universisty theses and a collection of pamphlets, such as fair sons, prayers, various leaflets, and obituaries. Private libraries of Czech personalities, such as J. Vlcek, F.X. Salda and Svatopluk Cech, are housed separately.

The most important parts of contemporary collections in the National Library are those connected with the Czech culture and territory, especially those that were published in the Czech lands. Only since 1935 has the National Library been able to built and archive all Czech imprints, due to the second compulsory copy law. Up to 1935, the Library recieved only one such copy which was placed in the publicly accesible cirtulating collection. Therefore, the collection prior to 1935 is encomplete. In order to fill the gaps, we are working on several projects, including supplements to the National Retrospective Bibliography for the early 20th century.

National Library of Denmark . The National Library of Denmark was established in by Frederik III through the appointment of its first librarian. During his reign three prominent Danish libraries were acquired. These and the King's own library became the basic core of the Royal Library. In 1673 the Royal Library moved into its first proper library building - the present National Archives. The first deposit legislation from 1697 required delivery of all printed material from the kingdom to the Royal Library. The present Royal Library building was inaugurated in 1906. The University Library, established in 1482, was divided into the First and Second departments in 1938. The Second Department received the collections in medicine and natural science. In 1989, the First Department of the University Library and the Royal Library were merged into one institution, The Royal Library. The Royal Library is the National Library of Denmark, the national main subject library and the University Library for the University of Copenhagen within the humanities, law, social sciences and theology. It is the National Deposit Library for international organizations, the Danish Museum of Books and Printing, the National

Museum of Photography, and the National Archive for manuscripts and archives of Danes of cultural significance.

The Royal Library serves its users from locations on Slotsholmen (national library division and theology), where a new building opened in September 1999, in Fiolstræde (social sciences and law) and on Amager (humanities). In addition, library services are provided for about 50 institute and centre libraries belonging to the University of Copenhagen. The Library's online information system REX is also host for other institutions and libraries. The Library assumed in earnest the character of a scholarly and national library at the end of the 1700s. A wealth of books was at that time acquired from the vast and comprehensive Danish private book collections of the 18th century. The main emphasis in the older foreign collections is on the historical subjects, but the Library's collections towards the end of the 18th century are generally regarded as among the richest in Europe.

The University Library collection was destroyed in the fire of Copenhagen in 1728, but owing to gifts a new collection was established which form an important part of the University Department's Danish and foreign collection of scholarly literature for circulation within the humanities, theology, social sciences and law. As the National Library of Denmark the Royal Library has a special position with regard to the Danish collections. The various deposit arrangements, which since c. 1700 have directed all publishers or printers to deliver a number of copies of all printed publications to the Royal Library and the University Library, have resulted in the Royal Library becoming the owner of the most complete collection of books published in Denmark and of foreign books about Denmark. Likewise, the Library's Manuscript Department holds Denmark's largest collection of literary archives.

National Library of Education The largest library in the world devoted solely to the collection, preservation, and effective use of research and other information in the field of education. Located in Washington D.C., NLE is funded by the U.S. federal government. It serves the U.S. Department of Education, Congress, and the Office of the President, as well as the general public, and is the center of a national network of libraries, archives, and other information providers in education.

The collections of the Library grew after the reign of King Frederik III, under succeeding kings through the purchase of private libraries, testamentary gifts and spoils of war. The Library assumed in earnest the character of a scholarly and national library at the end of the 1700s. A wealth of books was at that time acquired from the vast and comprehensive Danish private book collections of the 18th century. The main emphasis in the older foreign collections is on the historical subjects, but the Library's collections towards the end of the 18th century are generally regarded as among the richest in Europe. The University Library collection was destroyed in the fire of Copenhagen in 1728, but owing to gifts a new collection was established which form an important part of the University Department's Danish and foreign collection of scholarly literature for circulation within the humanities, theology, social sciences and law.

As the National Library of Denmark the Royal Library has a special position with regard to the Danish collections. The various deposit arrangements, which since c. 1700 have directed all publishers or printers to deliver a number of copies of all printed publications to the Royal Library and the University Library, have resulted in the Royal Library becoming the owner of the most complete collection of books published in Denmark and of foreign books about Denmark. Likewise, the Library's Manuscript Department holds Denmark's largest collection of literary archives.

Presently the The Library includes among its holdings 4,6 mill, books, serials and newspapers. including 4,500 incunabula, 6,303 m manuscripts and archives,

267,774 items of printed music, 344,401 microforms, 5,421 audiovisual documents 10,6 mill, graphic documents, 268,865 cartographic documents and 5,000 m pamphlets etc.

The Libraiy's central collection focuses on the field of education, especially resources published since 1965, as well as related fields such as law, public policy, economics, urban affairs, sociology. history, philosophy, psychology, and information science, in addition to a collection of over 60,000 books, the Library holds more than 800 English-language journals in education and related fields; the complete ERIC (Educational Resources Information Center) microfiche collection; archives of official print and electronic documents published by the U.S. Department of Education; and histories and documentation of education legislation passed by the Congress. The Library also serves as a depository under the Federal Depository Library Program of the U.S. Government Printing Office, making available documents produced by various other federal government agencies.

The Library offers on-site information, statistical and referral services to the public and to representatives of other government agencies and institutions; these services also are available by phone, fax, Internet, and mail. As a participating institution in the U.S. Government Printing Office's Federal Depositor}' Library Program, the Library provides assistance for locating and using government documents. In addition, the Library works with other libraries to support virtual reference services to the public, as well as responds directly to questions from libraries all over the world, submitted on behalf of their customers. In-depth research services are available to the U.S. Department of Education staff and contractors.

The Library circulates its resources to staff and contractors of the U.S. Department of Education. The public may request the Library's resources through their local public, school or academic library; the Library makes its resources available to libraries worldwide.

The Library is located in the U.S. Department of Education's Headquarters Building at 400 Maryland Avenue, SW in Washington, DC, near museums and other federal government buildings along the Mall. The facility is only a few blocks from the Maryland Avenue Exit of the L'Enfant Plaza Metro stop. Public bus service operates within one block of the building. There are several public parking garages within a 2-block radius of the building. If you are planning to visit the Library, you will be required to present a picture ID in order to enter the Headquarters Building.

National Library of Greece Ithe Library was on the island of Aegina, the first capital of Greece, as a part of a big Orphanage in 1829. This Orphanage included a Central School, the National Museum, the National Printing House and a Deposit of books, which developed into a Public Library by decree in 1832. In 1834, the library was moved to Athens and functioned as the first public library of Greece.

In 1838, one year after the foundation of the National University of Athens, its library was founded and enriched by gifts of Greeks and philhellenes. In 1842, the two libraries, the public and the university, joined together administratively and were installed to the new building of the University. In 1866, by royal decree, the two libraries were merged in a single library, the National Library of Greece.

The National Library was hosted to the University of Athens from 1842 to 1903. In 1903, the National Library of Greece was moved to a new building in which is still located. The building of the National Library of Greece, entirely in marble, was designed by the Danish architect Th. Hansen and was realized under the supervision of Ernst Ziller. The building of the National Library of Greece with the ones of the National University of Athens and the Academy of Athens constitute, according, to the expression of their architect Th. Hansen, the Athenian Trilogy. A legal deposit system ensures the fullest possible collection of publications published in Greece. The collections of the National Library of Greece consist of about 1.000.000 titles and more than 1.500.000 volumes of books, newspapers, serials, maps etc. Among the collections of the National Library of Greece, there are 149 incunabula, which is the biggest collection of incunabula in Greece. To the above number must be added a rich collection of 4.500 manuscripts, archives of personalities etc. There is also a collection of microfilms of books, newspapers and manuscripts.

The collection of the National Library of Greece are classified according to an old classification System, Hallische System. Cataloguing is based on the Anglo American Cataloging Rules, 2nd ed. Authority files subject headings, personal names, etc. based on the LC Subject Headings are used. UNIMARC is used as an internal and exchange bibliographic and authorities format. For the needs of the Greek National Bibliography is used Dewey Decimal Classification system.

National Library of Guiana The National Library service operates through a number of service points; the Central Library in Georgetown, Branches, Centres, bookmobile service, Deposit Collection and service to the prisons. The Central Library is the library for Georgetown and is also the administrative headquarters and as such is the policy making body, co-ordinates, monitors and evaluates the entire service. Branches are situated in towns. Rural areas are served by centres which operate on a part time basis and are manned by local library assistants, and the bookmobile service serves sparsely populated areas. A deposit collection is given to a community which is not large enough to support a library centre, or sometimes in special cases it is used to supplement the collection in a small existing library.

National Library of India Located at Kolkata is the largest library in India. It is under the Department of Culture, Ministry of Tourism & Culture, Government of India. The library is designated to collect, disseminate and preserve the printed material produced in India. The library is situated on the scenic 30 acre (120,000 m^2) Belvedere Estate, in Kolkata, formerly Calcutta City. The history of the National Library began with the formation of Calcutta Public Library in 1836. That was a non-governmental institution and was run on a proprietary basis. People contributing Rs. 300/- in subscription became the proprietors. Prince Dwarkanath Tagore was the first proprietor of that Library. Rs. 300/- at that time was a significant amount, so poor students and others were allowed free use the library for some period of time. Lord Metcalf, the Governor General at that time, transferred 4,675 volumes from the library of the College of Fort William, Kolkata to the Calcutta Public Library. This and donations of books from individuals formed the nucleus of the library. Both Indian and foreign books, especially British, were purchased for the library. Donations were regularly made by individuals as well as by the Government.

The Calcutta Public Library had a unique position as the first public library in this part of the world. Such a well-organized and efficiently run library was rare even in Europe during the first half of the 19th century. Because of the efforts of the Calcutta Public Library, the present National Library has many extremely rare books and journals in its collection.

The Imperial Library was formed in 1891 by combining a number of Secretariat libraries in Calcutta. Of those, the most important and interesting was the library of the Home Department, which contained many books formerly belonging to the library of East India College, Fort William and the library of the East India Board in London. But the use of the library was restricted to the superior officers of the Government.

In 1903, Lord Curzon of Kedleston, the Governor General of India, conceived the idea of opening a library for the use of the public. He noticed both the Imperial Library and Calcutta Public Library were under-utilized for the want of facilities or restrictions. He decided to amalgamate the rich collection of both of these libraries. The new amalgamated library, called Imperial Library, was formally opened to the public on January 30, 1903 at Metcalf Hall, Kolkata. The Gazette of India reported, "It is intended that it should be a library of reference, a working place for students and a repository of material for the future historians of India, in which, so far as possible, every work written about India, at any time, can be seen and read." After the independence the Government of India changed the name of the Imperial Library as the National Library, and the collection was shifted from the Esplanade to the present Belvedere Estate. On February 1, 1953 the National Library was opened to the public.

National Library of Iran, The was officially inaugurated in 1937 Prior to this date other libraries existed that performed the same function informally, the first of them being the Library of Dar al-fonun College inaugurated in 1851. In 1899 adjacent to the library of Dar_al-Fonun, another library called the Nation's Library came into existence. Eight years later the two libraries were merged into one under the name of the Public Library of Ma'aref and opened to the users.

National Library of Ireland, Ireland The National Library of Ireland was established in 1877 in Leinster House (the present parliament building) which then belonged to the Royal Dublin Society. The Library of the Royal Society formed the basis of the new National

Library. The present main building opened in 1890. The main aim of the Library is to collect, preserve and make accessible materials relating to Ireland and to provide an accurate record of Ireland's output in manuscript, print and other media. The policy of the Library is to focus on acquiring materials of Irish interest. There are close to one million books and extensive files of newspapers, prints and drawings, maps and photographs. The collection of manuscripts includes the papers of many Irish writers and political personalities. The Library holds world's largest collection of Irish documentary material: books, manuscripts, newspapers, periodicals, drawings, photographs, maps.

The National Library of Ireland is a cultural institution under the aegis of the Department of Arts, Sport and Tourism. Its mission is to collect, preserve and make available books, manuscripts and illustrative material of Irish interest. Users of the Library have a wide variety of interests. They can include those engaged in long-term research with a view to a book or article and those with a specific once off need. The Library has an ongoing programme of exhibitions. Donations of material are always most welcome; in addition, those wishing to make a financial contribution towards the work of the National Library by donation or bequest may do so through the National Library of Ireland Trust. There is also a support group, the National Library of Ireland Society, which is concerned with promoting and publicising the Library. Membership is open to all those with an interest in the Library and the heritage in its care.

National Library of Medicine, The (NLM) is located in Washington, DC, in Bethesda, Maryland. A part of the National Institutes of Health, the NLM is responsible to the Department of Health and Human Services (HHS) and to the Congress, which annually reviews its programs and appropriates funds for its operation. The institution was and continues to be a leader in applying computer technology to the handling of large databanks of medical information. Today, it is the largest library of the health sciences in the world. Extensive information about the programs described here is on the NLM's website at www.nlm.nih.gov.

The National Library of Medicine is independent of the other national libraries. The NLM staff members, however, work closely with their counterparts at the Library of Congress and the National Agricultural Library in a number of areas to ensure, for example, that acquisitions policies are complementary and cataloging practices are consistent. The library's programs are housed in two buildings at the southeast corner of the National Institutes of Health campus. The NLM building, occupied in 1962, contains the collections, technical processing, public services, and administrative offices on five floors (three below ground). All remaining programs are in the adjacent Lister Hill Center Building, a 10-story structure dedicated in 1980. The permanent full-time staffing level of the library in 2000 was about 600.

National Library of Nepal The Library was formally established in the year 1957. The entire collection of Pundit Hem Raj Pandey was purchased by His Majesty's Government of Nepal in 1956 and merged with the collection Central Secretariat Library and named Nepal National in 1957 January 2. The Nepal National Library is a member of the Conference of Directors of National Libraries of Asia and Oceania. For many years the Nepal National Library was administered under the Department of Archaeology of the Ministry of Education. In 1995 the administrative structure was changed, and the Nepal National Library now reports directly to the Minister for Education and Sports. Brief information about NNL can be found on the CDNLAO website, at www.nla.gov.au/cdnlao/nepal.html.

National Library of New Zealand is New Zealand's legal deposit library and a public service department, charged with the obligation to 'enrich the cultural and economic life of New Zealand and its interchanges with other nations' (National Library of New Zealand Act 2003). It is said to be unique in that unlike many other national libraries, it has links to primary and secondary schools through an extensive Schools Programme with 15 service centres and 3 Curriculum Information Service branches around New Zealand. The Legal Deposit Office is also New Zealand's agency for ISBN and ISSN.

National Library of Norway The Library is one of the central cultural institutions in Norway with the ambition to be the best source of documentation on Norway, the country, the people and Norwegian society. The tasks of the Library include the development, preservation, conservation and presentation of the collections of the Library which is based on the Legal Deposit Act. The National Library aims to collect all types of information produced from different types of media. The history of the library dates from 1815 when the national library functions were taken care of by The University of Oslo Library. Since1883 a current national bibliography has been produced.

In 1992 the Norwegian Parliament decided to establish a unified self-contained National Library with its main office located in Oslo. The Office of the National Librarian came into operation in 1994. The Oslo Division was established in 1999 based on the national functions and collections which were at that time separated from the University of Oslo Library. The Library has the most complete collection of books published in Norway and foreign books about Norway. The Library currently receives one copy of each document collected by legal deposit (except motion pictures, videograms, and broadcast material). It purchases foreign language translations of Norwegian literature and documents related to Norway and Norwegians published abroad (Norvegica extranea). The Library holds unique manuscript collections of Norwegian authors, composers, scientists, and politicians.

The Library holds important special collections of music, theatre material, maps, photography, posters, etc. A selective acquisition policy for foreign language materials with the emphasis on materials in Nordic and Western European languages covering selected subject areas is also maintained. The collections comprise all books and serials printed in Norway and books and serials related to Norway printed abroad (Norvegica extranea). Additionally there are specific collections of foreign books and serials supporting the special collections, such as music, drama, geography, and history of institutions, and collections with emphasis on the Nordic countries. The Manuscripts collection includes manuscripts, letters, and archival material from medieval times to the present with a particular emphasis on 18th and 19th century materials from Norwegian scholars and men of letters. The Picture Collection includes about 500,000 objects, mainly portraits and topographical photos. The Map Collection includes about 150,000 objects, comprising all maps printed in Norway, manuscript maps, foreign maps, and printed material on cartography and topography. The Drama Collection includes archival material from Norwegian theatres and printed material focusing on the dramatic arts.

National Library Of Pakistan serves as cultural center of the capital. Library is intended to be a reference library for all purposes, a working place for scholars, Postgraduate students of social sciences and humanities and repository of national published literature for future historians. The concept of a national library is fairly understood, even though national libraries differ in size and scope from country to country. National library of Pakistan was inaugurated in August 24, 1993 by the caretaker prime minister of Pakistan Mr.Moin Ahmad Qureshi. The National library exchanges Government documents with USA; Pakistan National Bibliography with other national libraries of the world; serves as depository for Asian Development Bank publications;and provides information and photocopy service. The National library is a member of the International Federation of Library Associations (IFLA).

National Library of Russia, Moscow The NLR was founded according to the will of Empress Catherine II on May 27, 1795 as the first available Russian Library and national repository. The set-up of the Library took nearly 20 years. A.N.Olenin (1763-1843) the first Director of the Library appointed in 1811 played a significant role in the process. He created the basis of the Library activities which is still topical up to this day. The Library was opened for users on January 14, 1814. In 1828-1834 a new building comprising two large reading rooms designed by C.Rossi and A.F. Shchedrin was added to the old one. The increase in the number of users created the necessity of opening a new reading room. This was opened in a specially erected building in 1862. The building of the former Ekaterininsky Institute on Fontanka Embankment was put at the disposal of the Library in 1950. The expansion of the collection and number of readers, the scattered storage, all these lead to the necessity to construct a new building. The construction started on October 28, 1986. The New Building was opened for readers in the year 1998. The National Library of Russia offers all the various library services, including information, bibliography and cataloguing services, lending-library services and international. book exchange. All the main Library material, including catalogues and the Central Reference Library, are available for the users free of charge.

National Library of Scotland is a legal deposit library in Scotland. It is based in a collection of buildings in Edinburgh city centre, the headquarters being on George

IV Bridge, between the Old Town and the university quarter. There is also a more modern building (1980s) in a residential area on the south side of the town centre, on Causewayside - built to accommodate some of the specialist collections (e.g. map library, science library) and provide large-scale extra storage.

The National Library of Scotland includes some one million books including copies of the Gutenberg Bible and the First Folio of Shakespeare. The National Library of Scotland is a relatively recent body, only formally established by Act of Parliament in 1925. Prior to then, Scotland's national deposit library was the Advocates Library belonging to the Faculty of Advocates. This was opened in 1689 and gained national library status in the 1710 Copyright Act, giving it the legal right to claim a copy of every book published in Britain. In the following centuries, the Library added books and manuscripts to the collections by purchase as well as legal deposit, creating a national library in all but name.

By the 1920s, the upkeep of such a major collection was too much for a private body, and, with an endowment of £100,000 provided by Sir Alexander Grant of Forres, the library's contents weie presented to the nation. The National Library of Scotland was formally constituted by an Act of Parliament in 1925.

Sir Alexander Grant gave a further £100,000 - making his combined donations the equivalent of around £6 million today - for a new Library building to be constructed on George IV Bridge. Government funding was secured which matched Sir Alexander's donation.

Work on the new building was started in 1938, interrupted by the Second World War, and completed in 1956. By the 1970s, room for the ever-expanding collections was running out, and it was obvious that other premises were needed. The Causewayside Building opened in the south-side of Edinburgh in two phases, in 1989 and in 1995, at a total cost of almost £50 million, providing much-needed additional working space and storage facilities.

Since 1999, the Library has been funded by the Scottish Parliament. It remains one of only six legal deposit libraries in the United Kingdom and Ireland, and is governed by a board of trustees.

National Library of Wales (Llyfrgell Genedlaethol Cymru in Welsh) is a legal deposit library in Aberystwyth, Wales. It is entitled to receive a copy of every book published in the United Kingdom and Republic of Ireland and houses over 4 million printed volumes. It includes many rare books including the first book printed in Welsh in 1546 The Library also contains The Welsh Political Archive (http://www.llgc.org.uk/lc/awg_s_awg.htm) and The National Screen and Sound Archive of Wales Many of the most important manuscripts and books have been digitized and made freely available to view on the library's website. The library recently became victim to the theft of several precious maps, assumed to have been sold to private collectors.

The Library is one of the great libraries of the world. Its home is in the seaside town of Aberystwyth in Ceredigion. Since 1911 it has enjoyed the right to collect, free of charge, a copy of every printed work published in Britain and Ireland. In addition it holds a huge collection of works about Wales and the other Celtic countries: books and pamphlets, magazines and newspapers, microforms, ephemera, and a wealth of electronic material. It holds thousands of manuscripts and archives, pictures and photographs, maps, sound recordings and moving images, available for all adults to consult in the building. It also arranges exhibitions throughout the year, as well as lectures and other events.

National Science Library of India NISCAIR It serves as a single window in India for providing all kinds of S & T information. Its role as the national information resource is fulfilled through the National Science Library(NSL) that has a comprehensive collection of S&T publications in the country and is offering services on a national scale. NSL also acts as a referral centre and clearing house for the best utilisation of the existing collection in the country. Thus, it extends its base of operation to the national scale. Set up in 1964, NSL aims at acquiring all important S&T publications published in the country and strengthening its resource base for foreign periodicals by acquiring the journals on CD-ROM or other electronic form as far as possible. NSL has a rich collection of over 1,90,000 books including reference books, reports and standards.

The library has one of the finest collections in the field of information science and technology, reference material/secondary sources, conference/seminar/symposia proceedings in S&T, foreign language dictionaries and medicinal & aromatic plants. It subscribes to almost all worthwhile Indian S&T periodical publications and receives over 5,100 Indian and foreign periodicals. Of these nearly 3500 periodicals are in electronic form including 1,133 full text journals. In addition, full text databases like the U.S. Patents Database and prominent directories are also being obtained on CD-ROM. To provide time bound information services for the corporate and business sector, NISCAIR is acquiring over 800 management and business periodicals on CD-ROM. Information on market intelligence, competitors and global tenders in an area can be provided by scanning international databases.

National Széchényi Library of Hungary The National Széchényi Library of Hungary was founded in 1802. It owes its establishment and name to a highly patriotic Hungarian aristocrat, Count Ferenc Széchényi who at the end of the 18th century sought out Hungarian books in Hungary and abroad, brought them together in a single collection and donated them to the nation in 1802. In the following year a public library, which was open to all, was opened in Pest. Ferenc Széchényi's patriotic deed aroused a nation-wide response. The entire society was mobilised, making donations as personal contributions to help make the nation's library as comprehensive as possible. The National Assembly placed the institution on a broader foundation. In 1808 it set up the Hungarian National Museum to collect the historical, archeological and natural relics of Hungary, and incorporated the library founded earlier by Ferenc Széchényi within this framework.

Aiming at a comprehensive coverage the National Széchényi Library collects publications and prints of any kind produced in Hungary, receiving two deposit copies of each; non-book materials (sound recordings, video materials, electronic documents, etc.); works published abroad in the Hungarian language, written by Hungarian authors, translated from Hungarian or related to Hungary; as well as manuscripts in Hungarian or pertaining to Hungary. In addition to the material listed above which is termed "Hungarica" material, the Library also collects literature connected with the Finno-Ugrian peoples and also literature relative to the neighbouring peoples and countries. At present the library has holdings of over 7 million units: 2.3 million books, 335 000 volumes of serial publications (newspapers and periodicals), 270 000 written and audio music documents, and over 1 million units of manuscripts. The number of maps totals ca. 200 000 and the number of pictures and engravings is ca. 310 000. There are nearly 3 million posters and small prints. The library has microfilm copies of more than 270 000 documents.

The collection of books includes such rarities as the first book printed in Hungary, the Chronica Hungarorum which was printed and published in 1473. With its 8,600 copies of works published before 1711, the Collection of Early Books is the richest collection of old Hungarian books in the country. It has 1,700 incunabula dating from the first century of book printing. The most complete collection of the various editions of works by Hungarian writers can be found here which includes about 600 editions of works by Sándor Petôfi and more than 3,000 editions of works by Mór Jókai. The libraries of famous historical figures such as Lajos Kossuth and Imre Madách form a valuable part of the collection.

New York Public Library (NYPL) is one of the United States of America's leading libraries, and one of three public library systems serving New York City. Its main building on Fifth Avenue (illustration, right) is the crowning achievement of the Beaux-Arts architectural firm of Carrere and Hastings. The library consolidated with The New York Free Circulating Library in February, 1901.

The main Research Library was built on Fifth Avenue in Manhattan between 40th and 42nd Streets, and was dedicated on May 23, 1911, opening the next day. The famous lions guarding the entrance were sculpted by Edward Clark Potter. In the 1980s the library added more than 125,000 square feet (12,000 m^2) of space to its storage capacity. This expansion required a major construction project in which Bryant Park, directly west of the library, was closed to the public and excavated.

The new library facilities were built below ground level. The park was then restored on top of the underground facilities and re-opened to the public. The NYPL maintains eighty-five Branch Libraries throughout The Bronx, Manhattan, and Staten Island. Branch locations offer popular fiction and basic research materials, and NYPL's four specialized Research Libraries offer world-renowned collections on a wide variety of topics. The research libraries include The Humanities and Social Sciences Library.

The New York Public Library for the Performing Arts, Schomburg Center for Research in Black Culture and the Science, Industry and Business Library. The NYPL has frequently appeared in feature films, most often as backdrop or a brief meeting place for characters. It serves as the backdrop for a central plot development in the 2002 film Spider-Man and a major location in the 2004 apocalyptic science fiction film The Day After Tomorrow.

New Zealand Digital Library The New Zealand Digital Library project is a research programme at The University of Waikato whose aim is to develop the underlying technology for digital libraries and make it available publicly so that others can use it to create their own collections. They have developed a 'Greenstone' Software for the development of digital library. It is available for download.

The Library website shows several dozen demonstration collections built by project staff. Some highlight particularly unusual capabilities such as the Musical Digital Library and First Aid in Pictures. The Musical Digital Library subsection offers several innovative collections that involve music retrieval by singing or humming a snatch of the desired tune. In some collections, text search can be combined with melody matching to yield a more comprehensive search technique. First Aid in Pictures is a collection designed for illiterate users: it presents purely pictorial, diagrammatic, information on basic First Aid. All the indexing mechanisms are also purely visually based. Explanatory text can be displayed at the bottom of each page, and spoken by a voice synthesizer. Site: <http://nzdl.org/>

Online Computer Library Center (OCLC) Founded in 1967, OCLC is a nonprofit, membership, computer library service and research organization dedicated to the public purposes of furthering access to the world's information and reducing information costs. More than 45,000 libraries in 84 countries and territories around the world use OCLC services to locate, acquire, catalog, lend and preserve library materials. Researchers, students, faculty, scholars, professional librarians and other information seekers use OCLC services to obtain bibliographic, abstract and full-text information when and where they need it. OCLC and its member libraries cooperatively produce and maintain WorldCat—the OCLC Online Union Catalog. It is a computerized library service and research organization based in Ohio. The Center operates an international network that libraries use to acquire and catalog books, order custom-printed catalog cards, arrange interlibrary loans, and maintain location information on library materials. Formerly called Ohio College Library Center. CSUL is a member and uses their database for cataloging.

Oviatt Library (Delmar T. Oviatt Library) serves the California State University, Northridge (CSUN) campus. The library is named for Delmar T. Oviatt who was instrumental in the founding of CSUN. Today it features over 1.2 million volumes in its collection. Construction on the library was done in two parts. The first phase finished on October 24, 1973 and the second nearly doubled the size in 1991 by the addition of east and west wings. The 1994 Northridge earthquake badly damaged the building forcing the library to close. The core (phase 1) re-opened later that year, but the wings were demolished and reconstructed. The wings re-opened in 2000.

Oxford Digital Library (ODL (http://www.odl.ox.ac.uk)) is a key-component of the e-strategy of Oxford University Library Services (OULS). It has been established to develop the technical infrastructure for an enhanced service, providing online access to the collections. The Bodleian Library has also offered its support (http://www.ox.ac.uk/blueprint/2001-02/2102/13.shtml) to the establishment of the JournalServer open-access digital library and allocated resources on the Oxford Digital Library Servers.

Pierpont Morgan Library, New York The Morgan Library is both a museum and a center for scholarly research, the Morgan Library is an extraordinary complex of buildings in the heart of New York City. Changing exhibitions are drawn from the permanent collections and from other museums and libraries providing access to some of the Western world's most significant cultural artifacts.

Rampur Raza Library Rampur was a small state in the Northern part of India but it was very rich in many respects. It contributed a lot to the intellectual and literary world. Such contributions could not be received from larger states as far as the field of knowledge specially music, poetry and education is concerned. The Raza Library of Rampur is the manifestation of such contributions by the rulers of the state. The Central Government took over the library with effect from 1st July, 1975 under Rampur Raza Library Act (Act No.22 of 1975). The affairs of the library are managed by the Rampur Raza Library Board which has been set up under Section 4 (2) of the Act. It is the governing body with His Excellency, the Hon'ble Governor of Uttar Pradesh as the Chairman. There is a provision of twelve other members including one descendant of the erstwhile ruling Nawab family of Rampur, distinguished historians, scholars in Arabic, Persian and Urdu literature besides officials concerned with the affairs of the library in the Central and State Governments.

Housed in two magnificent buildings in the fort of Rampur, the library has a remarkable collection of 15,000 manuscripts, including 150 illustrated ones with 4,413 graphics in them. Besides, there are 205 manuscripts on palm leaves, 1,000 miniature paintings and 1,000 specimens of Islamic calligraphy. The library has more than 50,000 volumes of printed books. It also possesses vast collection of art objects and ancient astronomical instruments. Another feature of the library collection is manuscripts belonging to the libraries of Halb, Makkah, Madinah, Egypt, Iran, Afghanistan and royal libraries of emperors and noblemen.

Register of Australian Archives and Manuscripts (RAAM) is a guide to collections of personal papers and non-governmental organisational records held by Australian libraries and archives. R A A M is a successor to the Guide to collections of manuscripts relating to Australia which was published by the National Library of Australia from 1965 to 1995. The project to convert the Guide to a web-accessible database was a cooperative venture initiated by the National Library with the assistance of a grant from the Towards Federation 2001 Working Group on High Priority Cross-Sectoral Projects. New records were added to the existing 6,000 entries in the Guide to create a database of 29,000 records at the time of release in October 1997. This had grown to 37,000 records by December 2000.

RAAM provides researchers with a convenient, centralised register of locations for primary research material. It does not provide detailed descriptions of the collections themselves; rather, it alerts researchers to the existence of collections and enables them to pursue further enquiries about the material, either online or through direct contact with repositories.

RAAM is a research tool which offers Register of Australian Archives and Manuscripts flexibility in searching. A user can search the database using a name, an occupation or any other indexed term. The repositories whose holdings are listed in RAAM can also be browsed by name or by State or Territory location. Some entries include links to detailed lists for the content of the collection described. A help page assists users to construct their search. There is a database description and a set of sample records to assist users to interpret their search results.

Links are provided from RAAM entries to the repository entries in the *Directory of Archives in Australia* maintained by the Australian Science Archives Project for the Australian Society of Archivists, so researchers can obtain more detailed information about the repository and its collections.

Entries in the RAAM database vary in detail, depending on the source of the entry. However, mandatory description is limited to essential information to ensure ease of contribution and more comprehensive coverage. Repositories with records in RAAM include the National Library of Australia's Manuscript Collection, the La Trobe Library, the Mortlock Library, the Australian War Memorial and personal papers held by the Australian Archives. RAAM covers a large number of significant collections not previously listed in the Guide or in the National Bibliographic Database. Further development of RAAM to ensure that it fulfills its valuable research role relies on the continuing cooperation and commitment of Australian libraries and archives to contribute records to the database, either directly or via Kinetica. Options for updating RAAM include an online form, electronic transfer of records or, in some instances, submission of written records.

RLG's Archival Resources Provide centralized access for searching and retrieval of archival finding aids that have been encoded using SGML [Standard General Markup Language] and the emerging standard for Encoded Archival Description (EAD). The finding aids are indexed centrally at RLG but are supported in a distributed environment. Some reside on a server at RLG, others are located on other servers around the world. Archival Resources also includes access to RLG's AMC (Archival and Mixed Collections) file. AMC provides researchers with timely and comprehensive access to brief, high-level information for nearly half a million collections of manuscripts and archives, and has greatly enhanced the dissemination of information about the holdings in repositories around the world.

Robarts Library is the main humanities and social sciences library of the University of Toronto. It is the third-largest university library in North America, after Harvard and Yale. The library is named after former Ontario Premier John Robarts. The library's main building is a large brutalist/futurist concrete structure designed to look like a peacock. The library is designed to look like a giant peacock when viewed from the south with the small tower in front designed to be the peacock's neck and beak, while the library stacks in the background are meant to be its extended tail. It is considered by some to be a great architectural achievement, but others consider it to be hideous. It has many nicknames including Fort Book, the Bunker, and the Turkey. Its design was conceived in the 1960s by Toronto architects Mathers and Haldenby, in collaboration with the New York architecture firm Warner Burns Toan & Lunde, who specialize in precast concrete buildings. Construction of the 14-story library was completed in 1973.

The library was initially designed for graduate students only, but following massive student protests, undergraduate students were also granted access. The library's initial design was for the shelving system to revolve, to allow for faster collection by library staff, who would then send books downstairs for pickup. After Robarts was opened to all students, the rotating system was mothballed, although the tracks used by the revolving shelving system are still visible. Robarts Library is home to the Thomas Fisher Rare Books Library, which contains a priceless collection of manuscripts and first editions.

Rosenbach Museum & Library, Philadelphia Housed in an 1865 townhouse off Rittenhouse Square, this museum contains over 330,000 rare books and maunscripts collected by the world renowned rare book dealer, Dr. A.S.W. Rosenbach. Among the museum's treasures are the manuscript of James Joyce's"Ulysses", the first book published by in North America, and Modernist poet Marianne Moore's living room.

Royal Asiatic Society Library London The Society has a long and distinguished history. It was founded in 1823 by a group of people led by the Sanskrit scholar Henry Colebrooke, who had worked in South Asia and wished to pursue the objectives set out in the Society's

Royal Charter of 1824 relating to investigation connected with, and for the encouragement of, science, literature and the arts in relation to Asia. During the Nineteenth Century the Royal Asiatic Society was the main centre in Britain for scholarly work on Asia and had many distinguished Fellows including the Duke of Wellington, Rabindranath Tagore, Sir Henry Rawlinson and Sir Richard Burton. Over the years a number of societies with similar purposes and programmes have been established in South Asia, Hong Kong, Japan, Korea, Malaysia and Thailand, and have been recognised as associates of the Royal Asiatic Society. Members of these societies are entitled to attend lectures and use the Library while in London temporarily, and to join as subscribing Fellows without other sponsorship.

The Library is primarily for the use of the members of the Society, both Fellows and Library Associates. Other readers may be admitted, by prior appointment, for a limited period of time. The geographical scope of the library includes all of Asia from Turkey in the West to Japan in the East, from Siberia in the North to Sri Lanka and Indonesia in the South. There is also a certain amount of material on Islamic North Africa. The time coverage of the collections is very roughly that of the last two thousand years with a few important exceptions. Firstly the Society does not concern itself with Current Events, that is to say roughly the last fifty years. Secondly where there are major continuous civilizations such as in India or China material relating to the origins and ancient history of those civilizations is included, whereas ancient Middle Eastern history is largely excluded. The subject coverage of the library is, broadly speaking, that of the Humanities i.e. History and Politics, Religion and Philosophy, Languages, Linguistics and Literature (classical rather than modern), Art, and Geography. The natural sciences such as mathematics and astronomy are covered in general works on the histories of various civilizations.

Royal Asiatic Society Library, Mumbai Society's genesis is traced to 1804 when the literary Society of Bombay was established by a great savant, Sir James Mackintosh, The Recorder of Bombay, with the objective of "promoting useful knowledge particularly such as is more immediately connected with India" .Amongst those who attended the first meeting were Jonathan Duncan , then Governer of Bombay, the noted historian William Erskine, Sir Charles Forbes, and the two friends, the artist Henry alt and Viscount Valentina whose journals of travels in the East, published in 1809, with sixty engravings after painting by Salt, have become collector's tem today.

In 1829 the Literary Society, thereafter known as the Bombay Branch of Royal Asiatic Society was normally to become an integral part of the Royal Asiatic Society of Great Britain. In 1830, the BBRAS moved into the north wing of the newly constructed Town Hall, on payment of the princely sum of Rs. 10,000. In 1873, the Bombay Geographical Society and in 1896 the Anthropological Society , donated their libraries and museums, and merged heir activities with those of the BBRAS.

The Library of the Asiatic Society is one of the well known Libraries in India. It has a collection of nearly 2.5 lacs books, receives nearly 150 current periodicals and has 80,000 bound volumes of periodicals, and maps. Most of the collection is very rare and therefore valuable. At present, the library is used by 2,900 members on all the week days, except on Sundays and Bank Holidays, from 10.30 a.m. to 7.30 p.m. The catalogue has been computerized so also the Library operations. The members are provided borrowing facilities. In addition, they are provided an access to internet. Some of the rare collection is microfilmed and can be accessed through the microfilm reader and reader printer. The Library has a bindery of its own. To provide more space to the books, the Library has introduced the Mobile Racks System.

It has a special room where the rare books are preserved. To enhance the collection of the library, the Society has established 'Gift and Exchange Scheme' and executed it successfully. This scheme has been introduced for receiving gift of books from scholars and bibliophiles. However, the library is interested in receiving only those books which come within the purview of its activities viz. books of a scholarly nature on subjects like Indology, the Social Sciences, Asian Studies, the Arts, Literature and Culture. Others are donated to those libraries in the city which are likely to be interested in them.

Royal Library in Copenhagen is the national library of Denmark and the largest and most important library of Scandinavia. It contains many historical treasures; all works that have been printed in Denmark since the 17th century are deposited there. The library was founded around 1648 by King Frederik III who seeded it with a comprehensive collection of European works. It was opened to the public in 1793. In 1989 it was merged with the prestigious University Library. Today it has three sites: one at Fiolstræde specializing in the social sciences, one at Amager specializing in the humanities, and the main library at Slotsholmen covering all subjects.

The old building of the Slotsholmen site was built in 1906 and is a copy of Charlemagne's Palace chapel in the Aachen Cathedral.

In 1999, a new building was opened at Slotsholmen, known as the "Black Diamond" (Den sorte diamant). Named for its outside cover of black marble and glass, it houses a concert hall in addition to the library. Between 1968 and 1978, the library saw one of the largest book thefts ever. Someone had managed to steal some 3200 historical books worth more than $50 million, including manuscripts by Martin Luther and first editions by Immanuel Kant, Thomas More and John Milton. The theft remained undetected until 1975. Between 1998 and 2002, the thief succeeded in selling books worth some $2 million at various auctions. The case was finally solved in September 2003, after a stolen book had surfaced at Christie's auction house in London. The thief, an employee of the library's oriental department named Moeller-Kristensen, had died in February 2003. His family then became careless in selling the remaining books. At a raid of the family's home in November 2003, some 1500 books were recovered. In June 2004, his wife, son, daughter in law and a friend were sentenced to prison terms ranging from 18 months to 3 years. The verdict is being appealed. The friend was today found not guilty of all charges and acquitted.

Salar Jung Museum and Library, Hyderabad

The Salar Jung Museum of Hyderabad is the repository of the artistic achievements of diverse European, Asian and Far Eastern countries of the world. The major portion of this collection was acquired by Mir Yousuf Ali Khan popularly known as Salar Jung III, but quite a few items were inherited by him from his father Nawab Mir Laiq Ali Khan Salar Jung II and his grand father Nawab Mir Turab Ali Khan, Sir Salar Jung I.

The museum is home to 43,000 art exhibits and 50,000 books collected from all over the world. Old timers believe that the present collection constitutes only half of the original art wealth amassed by Salar Jung III. His employees siphoned off part of it, since Salar Jung was a bachelor and depended upon his staff to keep a vigil. Some more art pieces were lost or stolen during the shifting of the museum from Dewan Devdi to the present site. The museum, declared an institution of national importance by an Act of Parliament in 1961, overlooks another landmark, the languid Musi, of the four hundred-year-old city founded by Mohammed Quli Qutub Shah. This great treasure trove is a tribute to man's eternal quest for beauty and elegance, particularly India's remarkable cultural diversity and heritage.

The library collection is very rich in histories, biographies ornate prose and official letters and documents which through light on the political and cultural life of the Deccan from the 17th to the 19th centuries. Some of the works are very rare indeed. Other attractions are a gallery exclusively devoted to the celebrated family of the Salar Jungs, a children's section, a reference library and a section devoted to rare and ancient Arabic Urdu and Persian manuscripts, including a handwritten miniature Qoran. On display are unique mementos like the panegyric in Urdu presented to Sir Salar Jung and Nizam VI in memory of their visit to Delhi to witness the Imperial Proclamation of Queen Victoria in 1877. The first room houses the personal items of the Salar Jung household such as various mementoes received by the Salar Jungs, embroidered sherwanis and a commodious and arresting masnad (ceremonial throne-like chair used by Salar Jung III). In the room, one can also see a large portrait of Mir Yousuf Khan, the clothes of the nobility, their books and furniture and bric-a-brac.

Sarasvati Bhavan Library, Benaras The Library has been named after the Goddess of learning i.e. Sarasvati. It is located at the Sampurnanada Sanskrit University campus in Benaras. The genesis of the Sarasvati-Bhavana Library and its manuscripts collection can be traced back to 1791 and after its long journey, it has grown from the 5852 manuscripts to 1,11,132 from purchase, gifts and donations, etc. The first landmark took place in the year 1791 when the Banaras Government Sanskrit College was established. At the same time, the establishment of Sarasvati-Bhavana Library was sought keeping in view the use and proper preservation and conservation of the manuscript collections of the Institute although there was no independent building of Sarasvati Bhavana Library or the Institute at that time.

The manuscript collections in Sarasvati Bhavana Library grew from 5852 to 50000 in the year 1948. The year 1963 may be taken as the most crucial year because in this year basic reorganization schemes were undertaken keeping in view the proper utilization of the Library materials acquired in Sarasvati Bhavana Library by the scholars and the users. As a result, a second annexe building was built in the name of Sarasvati Bhavana Library under the UGC aid in which all the printed books of the main building of Sarasvati Bhavana were shifted. Apart from this, the administration, microfilming and binding sections were established in this new building.

Saraswati Mahal Library, Tanjore The Library has been named after Maharaja Serfoji's. It is located at the palace of the Maharaja. The Library contains paper manuscripts on different subjects such as science, medicine, engineering, astronomy, painting, dancing, etc. in various languages such as Sanskrit, Tamil, Telugu, Marathi and some European languages. Around 8,000 of these are on palm leaves. This is the result of the efforts of the Nayak and Maratha rulers for over 300 years. This palace library was originally developed by the Nayak rulers. The Maratha rulers especially Raja Serfoji made a major contribution, organising a massive collection of good books. The Library has been enriched with several very fine collections of manuscripts every one of them rare, valuable and very interesting manuscripts.

Now, the Library has a rich collection of manuscripts numbering 40,000 in Sanskrit, Marathi, Telugu, Tamil and other languages. Besides manuscripts, it has a collection of over 23,000 books in the Indian and European languages covering various disciplines. There is a large number of illustrated manuscripts in Saraswati Mahal Library, Tanjavur, Tamil Nadu. Long before the illustrated story telling began in the modern era, multi-colour paintings, drawings and sketches have embellished manuscripts. While such illustrated manuscripts, several centuries old, are available throughout India, the Archives of IGNCA has a collection of about 800 slides from select illustrated manuscripts in the Saraswati Mahal Library. The slides are from four manuscripts selected from the list.

Sayajirao Gaekwad Library, Banaras Hindu University The Banaras Hindu University Library system, the largest University Library System in the country, germinated from a small but precious collection donated by Prof. P.K. Telang in the memory of his father Justice K.T. Telang in 1917 and housed in the Telang Hall of the Central Hindu College, Kamachha. It was nurtured in its infancy by the renowned historian Sir Jadunath Sarkar. With the University taking shape at its present premises, the library was also shifted in 1921 to the Central Hall of the Arts College(now Faculty of Arts) and then in 1941 to its present majestic building built with the munificent donation from Maharaja Sayajirao Gaekwad of Baroda, on the pattern of the great library British Museum in London on the suggestion of Pandit Madan Mohan Malaviya, the founder of university, after his return from the Round Table Conference, London in 1931. Its majestic circular Central Hall has been furnished with elegant furniture's made of famous and rare variety of Burma Teak woods. Beginning with a small but precious donated collection, its grew by leaps and bounds with magnificent donations of personal and family collections from many eminent personalities and families like Lala Sri Ram of Delhi, Jamnalal Bajaj of Wardha, Roormal Goenka, Batuk Nath Sharma, Tagore Family collection, Nehru Family collection, etc. amongst a score of others and purchase of books and journals out of the regular fund with the result that it has a collection of around 60,000 volumes in 1931 itself.

The trend of donation of personal and family collection to the library continued as late as forties with the result that it has unique pieces of rarities of books and journals dating back to 18th century. With this sound footings and background, the library took long strides during sixties and seventies in its development and metamorphosed in a system of libraries with the establishment of institute, faculty and departmental libraries during the period. Presently the Banaras Hindu University Library System consists of Central Library at apex and 3 Institute Libraries, 8 Faculty Libraries, 25 Departmental Libraries, with a total collection of over 13 lakh volumes to serve the students, faculty members, researchers, technical staff of fourteen faculties consisting of 126 subject departments of the university.

Scholarly Information Services/Library, It is part of the Division of Information of The Australian National University, one of the world's major research universities. The mission of the Library is to achieve excellence in the provision and promotion of information services to meet the research, teaching and learning needs of the University. To meet these needs the Library provides access to an extensive range of information resources both electronically and in print.

Scholarly Publishing and Academic Resources Coalition (SPARC) It was founded as an initiative of the Association of Research Libraries (ARL) in 1997. Throughout the 1990s, ARL directors at major North American research libraries had identified the high and fast-rising cost of scientific journals as one of the most critical issues facing academe. Data showed that the cost of these journals threatened the future of scholarly communication by forcing libraries into major journal cancellation programs and cutbacks in monograph purchases to accommodate price hikes, thus limiting availability of scholarly information. Publishers were almost uniformly unresponsive to requests from libraries to curb price hikes. Meanwhile, the pace of acquisitions and consolidation among commercial publishers was increasing, and, therefore, market power was concentrated in the hands of just a few very large journal publishers. As a result, competition among commercial journal publishers was extremely limited. SPARC was founded to foster increased competition in the scholarly communications marketplace as a means of moderating and driving down prices and counterbalancing growing commercial dominance. Through partnerships with scientific societies and independent publishers, which introduce high-quality, low-cost competitors to commercial journals, as well as far-reaching solutions such as BioOne (an online aggregation of bioscience research journals), SPARC fulfills a mandate to return science to scientists.

Seattle Central Library is an 11-story glass and steel building in downtown Seattle, Washington. The 362,987 square foot (34,000 m^2) public library can hold about 1.45 million books and other materials, features underground public parking for 143 vehicles, and is expected to draw about 8,000 visitors each day. It is the third Seattle Central Library building to be located on the same site at 1000 Fourth Avenue, the block bounded by Fourth and Fifth Avenues and Madison and Spring Streets. Just 56 meters (185 ft) high, the Seattle Central Library is remarkable for its architecture rather than its height. Seattle's tallest building, is 285 meters (937 ft), and the iconic Space Needle is 184 meters (605 ft) tall.

The library has a unique, striking appearance, consisting of several discrete "floating platforms" seemingly wrapped in a large steel net around glass skin. Herbert Muschamp, an architecture critic for The New York Times, described it as "a blazing chandelier to swing your dreams upon" and a "big rock candy mountain of a building." The Seattle Central Library opened to the public on Sunday, May 23, 2004.

The architects conceived the new Central Library building as a celebration of books, deciding after some research that despite the arrival of the 21st century and the "digital age," people still respond to books printed on paper. The architects also worked to make the library inviting to the public, rather than stuffy, which they discovered was the popular perception of libraries as a whole.

Although the library is an unusual shape from the outside, the architects' philosophy was to let the building's required functions dictate what it should look like, rather than imposing a structure making the functions conform to that. For example, a major section of the building is the "Books Spiral," designed to display the library's nonfiction collection without breaking up the Dewey Decimal System classification onto different floors or sections. The collection spirals up through four stories on a continuous series of shelves, allowing patrons to peruse the entire collection without using stairs or traveling to a different part of the building. Other internal features include the Microsoft Auditorium on the ground floor; the "Living Room" on the third floor, designed as a space for patrons to read; the Charles Simonyi Mixing Chamber, a version of a reference desk that provides interdisciplinary staff help for patrons who want to have questions answered or do research.

State Library of South Africa The "Staats-Bibliotheek der Zuid-Afrikaansche Republiek" (State Library of the South African Republic) came into being from a donation of books from the Maatschappij der Nederlandsche Letterkunde. These books consisted of a complete library of of Dutch works, mainly Dutch literature and language, to the Transvaal Republic's government. The first consignment of eight chests of books arrived in 1883, including a chest from the Dutch Bible Society. On 21 September 1887 the Transvaal government approved the constitution of the Staats-Bibliotheek. As Pretoria began to grow in size, there arose a need for a public library.

The first Pretoria Public Library had opened its doors in 1878, but because of ongoing financial problems was closed down in 1890. In 1893 strong public support saw another public library arise, this time under the wing of the Staats-Bibliotheek and with the bookstock of the former Public Library. From that time onward until 1964, the State Library performed a dual role as public library and national library. The first national librarian, the Afrikaans poet Jan Celliers, saw exchange agreements as a means of enriching the State Library's collections. The first exchange agreement was entered into in 1898 with the Smithsonian Institution of Washington in the United States. In terms of the agreement the State Library would receive all American official publications in exchange for two copies of each official publication of the South African republic. From the early thirties under the guidance of the visionary national librarian Matthew Stirling, the State Library began to develop the character of a central library for South Africa, taking on functions such as striving for a national library lending system and a centre for bibliographical information.

State Library of Victoria is the central library of the state of Victoria, Australia, located in the city of Melbourne. It is sited on the block bounded by Swanston, LaTrobe, Russell, and Little Lonsdale Streets, in the northern centre of the central business district. The Library's combined collections contain over 1.5 million books and 16,000 serials, including the diaries of the city's founders, John Batman and John Pascoe Fawkner, as well as the folios of Captain James Cook. In 1853 the decision to build a state library was made at the instigation of Lieutenant-Governor Charles La Trobe and Sir Redmond Barry. A competition was held to decide who would design the new building. Local architect, Joseph Reed (who later designed the Melbourne Town Hall and the Royal Exhibition Building) won the commission. On 3 July 1854, the recently inaugurated Governor Sir Charles Hotham laid the foundation stone of both the new Library and the University of Melbourne.

The Library opened in 1856, with a collection of 3,800 books chosen by Sir Barry, the President of Trustees. Augustus H. Tulk, the first Librarian, was appointed three months after the opening. The Library complex also held the State's Gallery and Museum, until the National Gallery of Victoria moved to St Kilda Road in the 1960s, and the current Melbourne Museum was built in the Carlton Gardens in the 1990s.

Temporary buildings built in 1866 for the Intercolonial Exhibition remained in use by the Library until 1909, when work began on a new annexe building to mark the Library's Jubilee. This new building was the landmark Domed Reading Room, which opened in 1913, and was designed by Norman G. Peebles. Its octagonal space was designed to hold over a million books and up to 500 readers at a time. It is 34 3/4 m in both diameter and height, and the dome's annulus is nearly 5m wide. The dome was the largest of its type in the world on completion, and its original skylights were covered in copper sheets in 1959 due to water leakage. The Room was closed in 1999 to allow for rennovation, during which natural light was returned. The now renamed La Trobe Reading Room reopened in 2003. In 1965, the La Trobe Building annexe was opened to house the Library's Australiana collection, which has since moved to the La Trobe Reading Room.

Suleymania Library, Istanbul The Süleymania Complex was built by the chief architect at the royal court, Mimar Sinan (Koca Sinan) for Sultan Süleyman the Magnificent, and was completed in 1557. Today, the Süleymania Library occupies the First and Second Madrasas (colleges or seminaries, especially ones connected with a mosque) of the original complex. Each room in the Medrese has a rectangular window that looks out on the Mosque. In the back yard there are a number of rooms surrounding a garden, each having a door opening to the underside of the portico and with a fireplace inside. On both sides there are six rooms facing one another. On the west side, there is a classroom in the middle above the portico. Both Madrasas have the same architectural characteristics. Each of them has a classroom, a corridor stretching beneath three domes, a large room with its entry from the corridor, and twenty more rooms. The classroom of the Second Medrese is the reading room of the present

Library. The rooms are used today as stacks, with illumination and humidity regulators, for storing the Library's collections, and from where material is served to the reader on request.

In 1918, books in the library were moved to the Second Medrese of the Süleymania complex. Several foundation libraries like Asir Efendi, Besir Aga, Çelebi Abdullah Efendi, Hafiz Ahmet Pasa, Kiliç Ali Pasa, Laleli, Merih Pasa, Molla Çelebi were added to the main library which was then named Süleymania Umumi Kütüphanesi (the Süleymania General Library). It has continued to grow with the addition of many other foundation libraries, including a very important one, the Ayasofya Library.

This rich library, founded in Ayasofya (St Sophia) by Sultan Mahmud I in 1739-1740, was joined to the Süleymaniye Library in 1967. The Süleymaniye has now five affiliate libraries: Atif Efendi Library, Haci Selim Aga Library, Köprülü Library, Nuruosmania Library, and Ragup Pacha Library. Apart from the manuscripts, the library includes printed books, books in foreign languages, and Turkish books in Latin script under the title of contemporary works.

Suzzallo Library is the central library of the University of Washington in Seattle, and perhaps the most recognizable building on campus. It is named for Henry Suzzallo, who stepped down as president of the University of Washington in 1926, the same year the first phase of the library's construction was completed. The library's original architects, Charles H. Bebb and Carl F. Gould, called for three structures built in Collegiate Gothic style and arranged in a roughly equilateral triangle with a bell tower in the center.

The first phase, which dominates the eastern side of Central Plaza, better known as Red Square, forms the west face of this triangle. The south face of the triangle was completed in 1936 in the second phase of construction. The original plans were abandoned with the third wing of the library, completed in 1963. By this time the University had largely moved away from its earlier architectural style adopting instead modernist concrete and glass forms. A final addition was completed in 1990 with the Kenneth S. Allen Library wing, named for Microsoft co-founder Paul Allen's father, an associate director of the University library system from 1960 to 1982. The bell tower called for in the original plans was never built. Adorning the exterior of the early wings are terra cotta sculptures of influential thinkers and artists selected by the faculty. They include Moses, Louis Pasteur, Dante Alighieri, Shakespeare, Plato, Benjamin Franklin, Justinian I, Isaac Newton, Leonardo da Vinci, Galileo Galilei, Johann Wolfgang von Goethe, Herodotus, Adam Smith, Homer, Johann Gutenberg, Ludwig van Beethoven, Charles Darwin and Hugo Grotius. Three figures representing "Mastery", "Inspiration", and "Thought" additionally appear above the main entrance. A noted highlight of the library is the Graduate Reading Room. It features cathedral ceilings and tall stained glass windows and spans the entire third floor of the west face of the library. Its distinctive look is said to have been inspired by Henry Suzzallo's openly-stated belief that universities should be "cathedrals of learning."

Swedish Royal Library The Royal Library, or Kungl. Biblioteket (KB), is the national library of Sweden. As such it collects, describes, preserves and makes available all domestic printed materials in Swedish and other languages, as well as publications with Swedish association published abroad. This obligation was laid down in 1661 in an ordinance from the Swedish Privy Council Chancery. The ordinance (legal deposit) ordered all printers in the Realm of Sweden to send two copies of every publication printed to the Chancery before the material was distributed. One copy was to go to His Majesty's Archives (Riksarkivet), the other to the Royal Library. The motive for this provision stemmed not from a desire to preserve publications for posterity but from a desire to monitor their contents. Since 1997 the Royal Library also archives the Swedish part of the World Wide Web as part of a project called kulturarw3 (a play on words; kulturarv is Swedish for cultural heritage). Initially, the contents was not available to the public due to issues of copyrights, but as of 2004 visitors to the library can access the archive from dedicated terminals. The institution is also a Government Agency charged with the responsibility of coordinating Sweden's research libraries and for the Library Information System, LIBRIS.

Swiss National Library Founded in 1894, the Swiss National Library is an institution which is part of the Federal Office of Cultural Affairs. Under the terms of the law by which it is regulated, it is charged with collecting, cataloguing, and conserving information in all fields and disciplines, and in any medium, connected with Switzerland, as well as with ensuring the widest possible accessibility to and dissemination of such data. A more recently created institution than most other national libraries or our own national leading university, cantonal and municipal libraries, the National Library is intended to be open to all, and, by the breadth and scope of its collections, it aims to reflect the plurality and diversity of Swiss culture. Since 1911, the date of the first federal law to govern it, the Swiss National Library has been collecting, conserving and making available to the public the Helvetica Collection. Helvetica means not only the entire literary and information output published in Switzerland, but also any work either ancient or modern published abroad relating to Switzerland and its people. It also includes works, and their translation in any language, by Swiss or other nationals living in Switzerland. The new law of 1992 has enabled the scope of Helvetica to be extended to include the new media.

Topkapi Palace Library, Istanbul The present Topkap Palace, the home of the Ottoman sultans and the administrative center of the Ottoman Empire for four hundred years, was turned into a museum in 1924, the manuscripts, found in many pavilions and rooms, were gathered together to form the New Library. Today, the Islamic manuscripts preserved in this new library have been sorted out into categories of Arabic, Persian and Turkish. A complete catalogue was compiled and published by F.E. Karatay in 1960. The first of the Arabic catalogues contains Korans and works of Koranic commentary. These Korans and Commentaries, which have been gathered from the various pavilions, buildings and rooms of the Palace and are classified by the name of the location where they were found, number more than two thousand. The collection of Korans, the richest to be found anywhere in the world, comprises texts of the Koran inscribed during the 7th - 19th centuries in Arabia, Ian, India, Maghrib (North Africa) and the lands dominated by the Seljuks and Ottomans. Almost all have been prepared by famous calligraphers, gilded by master gilders, and bound by the most capable bookbinders of the times. The 1600 or more Korans found in the first volume of the Arabic catalogue are preserved in the Palace Library as rare books. Among these are seven believed to be inscribed by Caliph Osman, nine accredited to Caliph Ali, two ascribed to Hasan and Hussein as well as many translations. There are twenty-one Turkish translations, thirty-nine Farsi translations, twenty-one Chagatay translations and one Uygur translation.

Troy Public Library Citizens of Troy became interested in establishing a public library. The library's search for a permanent home spans 96 years. For many years the library moved to and from offices and homes of those who had been designated librarian. In 1820, when it was housed above the River Street Drug Store of that year's librarian, Ira Wells, 190 of its 687 volumes were destroyed by fire. By 1835, soon after the incorporation of the Troy Young Men's Association, the library and that organization joined forces in an effort to seek a more permanent location for a public library. In 1845, the Troy Library voted to disband and turn its property over to the Troy Young Men's Association. In 1846, the collection was moved to its first somewhat more permanent home in the Athenaeum Building, which the Young Men's Association rented from the Troy Savings Bank.

The Troy Public Library was an expensive building, produced with the finest materials and the best construction techniques available. The building opened on May 12, 1897, with appropriate ceremony and fanfare. Unfortunately, needed operating support did not match the grandeur of the new library. The Troy Public Library celebrated its 100th Anniversary in the Hart Memorial Building in 1997. As the Trustees and Friends look forward to one hundred more years of service, the Troy Public Library remains a vital institution, committed to serving the diverse needs of the citizens of Troy.

Turkish National Library (TNL) The Turkish National Library is one of the youngest national libraries in the world. Planning for it began on April 2, 1946, in a small room of the Directorate of Publications at the Ministry of Education. A collection of 8,000 books accumulated in a very short time. The TNL Preparation Office temporarily moved into a five-room building on April 1, 1947, and remained there for eight months. During this period 60,000 items were stored in the building. To house the collection, a new building was provided. After two years of preparation, the TNL was opened to the public on August 16, 1948. Because the first library building proved inadequate to meet the demands of growth, a proposal was made in 1965 to plan a new building. Plans were developed during the years 1965-1973, and the building was constructed between 1973 and 1982. The library moved there in 1983, and services to users started on August 5, 1983.

The TNL collection consists of 1,414,108 works including books,periodicals and non-book materials.There are 943,964 books and 356,340 volumes of periodicals containing newspapers, magazines, bulletins, annuals etc. in the TNL collection. The collection of non-book materials consist of 92,099 works including posters, maps, musical scores, sound recordings (disc or cassette), paintings etc. stored in special conditions. According to the Legal Deposit Act dated 1934, a single copy of all publications printed in Turkey must be sent to the TNL.However, efforts are being made to update this Law, because it does not cover all types of material and lacks sufficient sanction. Collection development activities of the TNL includes the purchasing of foreign publications on Turkey, accepting donations and exchanging of works with other libraries and organizations abroad within the framework of international exchange programs. The number of Turkish books printed in Arabic script in TNL exceeds 50,000. This collection includes books printed between 1729 and 1928, the period between the dates when the first printing house in Turkey starded to operate and the Latin alphabet was adopted. There is also a collection of about 21,705 manuscripts and rare books gathered through purchasing and donations. Efforts to develop both collections are still under way.

University of Cambridge Library The University of Cambridge is one of the oldest universities in the world and one of the largest in the United Kingdom. Its reputation for outstanding academic achievement is known worldwide and reflects the intellectual achievement of its students, as well as the world-class original research carried out by the faculty members of the University and the Colleges. Its famous Colleges and University buildings attract visitors from all over the world. The University's museums and library collections hold many treasures which give an exciting insight into some of the scholarly activities, both past and present.

The University Library was originally founded in the 14th century but there were no oriental books in the Library's earliest collections apart from Bibles. From the 1630's and for the next two centuries many books from individual oriental scholars (from both Britain and Europe) were added to the Library's collections. Other early bequests to the Library from Britain and Europe also contained some oriental items. The Library also acquired the libraries of many Cambridge oriental scholars, some of whom collected extensively abroad. The end of the 19th the oriental collections began to be developed more extensively and during the 20th century purchasing from abroad increased with the aim of forming a more consistent coverage of the areas and subjects involved.

Library houses extensive oriental collections which relate to and derive from all areas of the Middle East, South and Southeast Asia and East Asia. Not all areas are covered in equal depth and some particular areas and subjects are covered more thoroughly than others. The scope of the holdings embraces all periods from pre-history to the present day. The collection aims at extensive coverage of works which are important contributions to scholarship in the areas of the humanities and social sciences. It also collects representative collections of literature written in Asian languages. The collection is primarily a book collection but serials also form an important part of the provision. There are also significant holdings of manuscripts, archives and rare books, many of immense value and significance.

University of Illinois Library Urbana-Champaign, also known as UIUC and the U of I is the largest campus in the University of Illinois system. It is highly ranked in library and information science, engineering, computer science, physical sciences, advertising, psychology, agriculture, and accounting. The campus is divided almost exactly between the cities of Urbana and Champaign. The university is composed of 18 colleges and institutes that offer more than 150 programs of study. There are approximately 29,000 undergraduates and 10,000 graduate students at Urbana-Champaign. A nationally acclaimed research center, UIUC is the site of the National Center for Supercomputing Applications, which created the first graphical Web browser, Mosaic and Telnet.

The University has the third largest academic library, and the largest public engineering library (Grainger Engineering Library) in the country. The Daily Illini is the (unofficial) student newspaper. In 1952 the University built the ILLIAC (Illinois Automatic Computer), the first computer built and owned entirely by an educational institution. UIUC is also the site of the Department of Energy's Center for the Simulation of Advanced Rockets, an institute which has employed graduate and faculty researchers in the physical sciences and mathematics in some of the most advanced research in the field. This history of excellence is continued in the 21st century, most recently with the opening of the Siebel Center for Computer Science, the most technologically advanced academic facility to date. The mascot for the University is a Native American figure, Chief Illiniwek, which has sparked significant controversy. Critics of the mascot claim that it is a racist stereotype, while supporters claim that it is unoffensive and is a source of pride for many students. The University is deeply divided on this issue; while the faculty have unanimously condemned the mascot, the administration is largely supportive of it.

University of Punjab Library, Lahore The University of the Punjab was formally established with the convening of the first meeting of its Senate on October 14, 1882 at Simla. It was the fourth University to be established by the British colonial authorities on the Indian Subcontinent. The first three universities were established by the British rulers at their initial strongholds of Bombay, Madras and Calcutta. The University of the Punjab came into existence as a result of a long drawn struggle of the people of Punjab after the war of independence in 1857. Contrary to the three previously established universities, which were only examining institutions, the University of the Punjab was both teaching as well as examining body right from the beginning.

Until independence in 1947 the University of the Punjab fulfilled the educational needs of a vast region of the Subcontinent. Partition of the Subcontinent somewhat reduced the geographical limits of the jurisdiction of the University. However, for many years after independence it still ranged over vast areas including Punjab, NWFP, Baluchistan and Azad Jammu & Kashmir. New universities were set up later in the country to share responsibility for imparting higher education with the University of the Punjab.

The strength of the University *Faculty* was greatly reduced because of the migration of non-Muslim teachers and scholars at the time of independence. The University functioning was restored, mainly due to the efforts of the eminent educationist like Dr. Umar Hayat Malik, who became the first Vice Chancellor after the independence. Academic programs were initiated soon after the independence under many new departments.

University of Sydney Library is the largest library in the southern hemisphere, with a collection of over 5.1 million items (circa 2004). The Library itself is composed of 20 libraries across 9 campuses. The main building, Fisher Library, is named after Thomas Fisher, an early benefactor. Amongst the collection are many rare items such as one of the two extant copies of the Gospel of Barnabas, and a first edition of Philosophiae Naturalis Principia Mathematica by Sir Isaac Newton. Fisher Library, located on Eastern Avenue in the Darlington/Camperdown campus of University of Sydney and adjacent to Victoria Park, is the main building. It actually consists of two conjoined libraries, which were built separately due to funding issues in the early days of the university. Fisher Undergraduate library (Building F03), holds multiple copies of texts commonly used by undergraduate students of the university. Fisher Research library (Building F04), is an accessible stack library with a larger and more historical collection. There is additional space in the F04 building which is used by the School of Psychology. The basement of the building also houses the Fishery Café, a location largely unknown to most of the student population probably because it is unable to be accessed from the front of the building nor from within the library itself. Most of the other libraries of the University of Sydney Library are associated with particular Schools and Faculties.

Vatican Library (Latin: Bibliotheca Apostolica Vaticana) is the library of the Holy See, located in Vatican City. It is one of the oldest and most significant libraries of historical texts. Pope Nicholas V established the library in 1448 by combining some 350 Greek, Latin and Hebrew codices inherited from his predecessors with his own collection and extensive acquisitions, among them manuscripts from the imperial library of Constantinople. When its first librarian, Bartolomeo Platina, produced a listing in 1481, the library held over 3500 items, making it by far the largest in the Western world. Around 1587, Pope Sixtus V commissioned the architect Domenico Fontana to construct a new building for the library; it is still in use today. Books were displayed on benches to which they were chained.

The library was enriched by several bequests and acquisitions over the centuries. In 1623, the hereditary Palatine Library of Heidelberg containing about 3500 manuscripts, was given to the Vatican by Maximilian I, Duke of Bavaria in thanks for the adroit political maneuvers of Pope Gregory XV that had sustained him in his contests with Protestant candidates for the electoral seat. A token 39 of the Heidelberg manuscripts were sent to Paris in 1797 and were returned to Heidelberg at the

Peace of Paris in 1815, and a gift from Pope Pius VII of 852 others was made in 1816. Aside from that, the Palatine Library remains in the Vatican Library to this day.

In 1657, the manuscripts of the Dukes of Urbino were acquired. In 1661 the Greek scholar Leo Allatius was made librarian. Christina of Sweden saw to it that her library, which was for all practical purposes the entire royal library of Sweden of the time, became part of the Vatican Library on her death in 1689. Today, the library holds some 75,000 manuscripts and over 1.1 million printed books, which include some 8,500 incunabula. The Secret Vatican Archives were separated from the library at the beginning of the 17th century; they contain another 150,000 items. Among the most famous holdings of the library is the Codex Vaticanus, the oldest known manuscript of the Bible. The Secret History of Procopius was discovered in the library and published in 1623. A commonly repeated urban legend has it that the Vatican Library holds the largest collection of pornography in the world. There are also a few mildly erotic works of art, but very little since the Renaissance. The Vatican Library is a research library for history, law, philology, science and theology, open to anyone who can document their qualifications and their research needs to view the collection.

SECTION-B : LIBRARIANS

Ahmed Rami Ahmed Mohammed Rami was born in Cairo on August 9th, 1892. In 1914, Rami graduated from the Higher Teachers School and was appointed teacher of geography and English language at Cairo Private School. Six years later, he was appointed a librarian at the Higher Teachers Library. This post offered him a unique opportunity to read Arabic, English and French poetry and literature. In 1924, he left for Paris for a year-long scholarship to study the latest techniques of librarianship. In Paris he studied Persian language at the Oriental Language Institute. The Persian language diploma helped him translate the famous Omar Al-Khayyam Quatrain from the original Persian version to Arabic. His translation was so adequate that it reflected Al-Khayyam's philosophy. In 1925, he worked as a librarian at the Egyptian National Book House, known as Darul Kotob. He applied the modern techniques he learned in France to organise Darul Kotob.

After working in Darul Kotob for 13 years, he joined the League of Nations as a librarian. In 1945, he returned to Egypt where he worked as an advisor to the Egyptian Broadcast House. Three years later he returned to Darul Kotob as a Deputy President. During his career, Ahmed Rami won a large number of awards and orders of merit. In 1965, he was granted Intellectual Excellence Order by King Hassan II of Morocco.

Rami also won the State Order of Merit in literature in 1967. He was also granted a prestigious Lebanese order of merit and the Paris based Composers Association gave him a memorial plaque with his name engraved on it in recognition of his contributions. When he was 15 years old, he wrote his first patriotic poem. In 1910, Al-Rewaiat Al-Gadida magazine published another poem which was his first poem to be published. In 1918, Rami published his first diwan. It was a literary event at that time. He introduced to Arabic readers a new type of poetry. In 1927, he was given a two-year scholarship to Paris, where he had the happiest memories of his youth at the Sorbon. He wrote in three types of literature on love, emotional and patriotic poetry. As for dramatic literature, he translated about 15 of Shakespeare's immortal plays such as "Hamlet", "Julios Caesar", "The Tempest" and others which were performed at Yussif Wahbi and Fatma Roshdi theatres.

In the last years of his life, he was so famous for writing lyrics that people were about to forget his classical poems and plays and only remember his lyrics. Om kulthoom sang an ode written by Ahmed Rami and composed by Sheikh Abu Al-Ala Muhammad which was a great success. Rami wrote the songs of Muhammad Abdel Wahab's films such as "The White Rose" and " Tears of Love" and some other famous songs as "Why Did You Keep Silent My Tonge" and "On the Ben Tree's Leaves".

Ahmed Rami practised three sorts of literary activities; in poetry, he wrote in several themes ranging from emotional to patriotic poetry and wrote six collections of poetry, in drama, Rami translated around 15 foreign plays, such as Shakespeare's Hamlet, Julius Ceasar and the Tempest. Moreover, he wrote one play entitled "Love of Poets". He also translated the famous quatrains of the Persian poet Omar El-Khayyam. This translation is one of the most fascinating masterpieces of the modern Arabic literature and in song writing, he wrote more than 500 songs, including 200 for the legendary singer Om Kolthoum. Their co-operation started in 1915 and their last masterpiece was presented in 1972. His first collection captured the attention of his contemporary poets like Khalil Motran, Ahmed Shawqi, Hafez Ibrahim and El-Mazni. They said that his poetry expressed the various conditions of the human spirit. He died on June 4th, 1981.

Ainsworth Rand Spofford (September 12, 1825-August 11, 1908) was the sixth United States Librarian of Congress, serving from 1864 to 1897. Spofford was born in Gilmanton, New Hampshire. Ill health prevented him from attending Amherst College. He instead, at age 19, moved to Cincinnati, Ohio, where he became a bookseller, publisher, and newspaper man. In 1859 he became associate editor of the Cincinnati Commercial. He was also active in Republican party politics and was a delegate to the nominating convention of John Charles Frémont in 1856. In Washington D.C. in 1861, shortly after reporting on the Battle of Bull Run for his newspaper, he accepted the appointment of Chief Assistant Librarian from Librarian of Congress John G. Stephenson.

After Stephenson's resignation, President Abraham Lincoln appointed Spofford to the post of Librarian of Congress. Spofford is generally credited with overseeing the expansion of the Library from a Congressional resource into a national institution. During Spofford's tenure, the Library expanded from over 60,000 items to more than one million. Spofford presided over the move of the Library from the Congressional Reading Room in the US Capitol to its own building, now called the Thomas Jefferson Building, in 1897, a building which Spofford campaigned for. Spofford stepped aside in favour of a younger administrator, John Russell Young, and returned to his old post of Chief Assistant Librarian, where he remained until his death. He was a prolific author and editor and his publications include A Book for All Readers (3d ed. 1909); The Library of Choice Literature (10 vol., 1888), and the annual American Almanac (1878-89).

Antoine Alexandre Barbier (January 11, 1765 - December 5, 1825) was a French librarian and bibliographer. Born in Coulommiers (Seine-et-Marne) he took priest's orders, from which, however, he was finally released by the pope in 1801. In 1794 he became a member of the temporary commission of the arts, and was charged with the duty of distributing among the various libraries of Paris the books that had been confiscated during the French Revolution. In the execution of this task he discovered the letters of Huet, bishop of Avranches, and the manuscripts of the works of Fénelon. He became librarian successively to the French Directory, to the

Conseil d'Etat, and in 1807 to Napoleon, from whom he carried out a number of commissions. He produced a standard work in his Dictionnaire des ouvrages anonymes et pseudonymes (4 vols., 1806—1809). Only the first part of his Examen critique des dictionnaires historiques (1820) was published. He had a share in the foundation of the libraries of the Louvre, of Fontainebleau, of Compiègne and Saint-Cloud; under Louis XVIII he became administrator of the king's private libraries, but in 1822 he was deprived of all his offices. Barbier died in Paris on December 5, 1825.

Antonio Genesio Maria Panizzi (1797 - 1879), better known as Anthony Panizzi, was a British librarian of Italian birth. He was born in the province of Modena, Italy, but moved to England in 1823, becoming a British citizen in 1832. He had a string of posts at the British Museum library: first Assistant Librarian (1831-37), then Keeper of Printed Books (1837-56) and finally Chief Librarian (1856-67). The British Museum library was, in fact, the National library of the United Kingdom in all but name. With over a million books it was, at the time, the largest library in the world. Its famous circular Reading Room was designed by Sydney Smirke on a suggestion by Panizzi. While there, he undertook the creation of a new catalogue, based on the Ninety-One Cataloguing Rules which he devised, with his assistants. These rules served as the basis for all subsequent catalog rules of the 19th and 20th centuries, and are at the origins of the ISBD of the 21st century and of digital cataloguing elements such as Dublin Core. Panizzi also made editions of Matteo Maria Boiardo's Orlando Innamorato and Ludovico Ariosto's Orlando Furioso. He was knighted in 1869.

Archibald MacLeish Archibald MacLeish was born in Glencoe, Illinois, on May 7, 1892. First educated at Hotchkiss School, MacLeish later studied at Yale and Harvard Law School, where he was first in his class. Although he focused his studies on law, he also began writing poetry during this time. In 1916 he married Ada Hitchcock.

At the onset of World War I, MacLeish volunteered as an ambulance driver, and later became a captain of field artillery. Upon returning home, he worked in Boston as a lawyer but found that the position distracted him from his poetry. He resigned in 1923, on the day that he was promoted to partner in the firm. MacLeish then moved his family tc France and began to focus on writing. There he was to befriend fellow writers such as Kay Boyle, Ernest Hemingway, and Ezra Pound. During the next four years he published four books of poetry, including The Happy Marriage (1924) and The Poet of Earth (1925). In 1928 MacLeish returned to America, where he began research for his epic poem Conquistador by travelling the steps and mule-ride of Cortez's army through Mexico. MacLeish won the Pulitzer Prize for his efforts in 1932.

From 1930 to 1938, MacLeish worked as an editor at *Fortune* magazine. During that period, he wrote two radio dramas to increase patriotism and warn Americans against fascism. MacLeish also displayed increasing passion for this cause in his poems and articles. In 1939, President Franklin D. Roosevelt persuaded him to accept an appointment as Librarian of Congress, a position he kept for five years. MacLeish thoroughly reorganized the Library's administrative offices and established the Library's series of poetry readings. At the same time, MacLeish served as director of the War Department's Office of Facts and Figures and assistant director of the Office of War Information, specializing in propaganda. In 1944 he was appointed assistant Secretary of State for cultural affairs. After World War II, MacLeish became the first American member of the governing body of UNESCO, and chaired the first UNESCO conference in Paris.

In 1949 Archibald Macleish retired from his political activism to become Harvard's Boylston Professor of Rhetoric and Oratory, a position he held until 1962. From

1963 to 1967 he was Simpson Lecturer at Amherst College. Macleish continued to write poetry, criticism, and stage- and screenplays, to great acclaim. His Collected Poems (1952) won him a second Pulitzer Prize, as well as the National Book Award and the Bollingen Prize. J.B. (1958), a verse play based on the book of Job, earned him a third Pulitzer, this time for drama. And in 1965 he received an Academy Award for his work on the screenplay of The Eleanor Roosevelt Story. Archibald MacLeish died in April 1982 in Boston, Massachusetts.

Anastasius Bibliothecarius, librarian of the Roman Catholic Church, b. about 810; d. 879. He was a nephew of Bishop Arsenius of Orta, who executed important commissions as papal legate. Anastasius learned Greek from Greek monks, and obtained an unusual education for his era, such that he appears to be the most learned ecclesiastic of Rome in the barbaric period of the ninth century. During the reign of Nicholas I (855-67) Anastasius was abbot of the monastery of the Virgin Mary on the farther side of the Tiber (in Trastevere), and was employed by the pope in various matters. He was also active as an author, and translated Greek works into Latin, one of these being the biography of St. John the Almsgiver, which he dedicated to Nicholas I. The successor of Nicholas, Adrian II (867-72), appointed Anastasius librarian of the Roman Church, an important office which gave him much influence at the papal Court. In 869 he was sent by Emperor Louis II as envoy to Constantinople, with two men of high rank in the Frankish Empire, to negotiate a marriage between the oldest son of the Byzantine emperor and the daughter of the emperor in the West. When the envoys arrived at Constantinople, the Eighth Oecumenical Council was still in session, and Anastasius, who attended the last session (February, 870), zealously defended the papal cause and was of much service to the papal legates. On their way home the papal legates were robbed, and the "Acts" of the council were carried off. However, they had given most of the declarations of obedience of the Greek bishops to Anastasius, who also had a copy of the "Acts", and was thus able to bring these documents to the pope. At the pope's order, he translated the "Acts" into Latin. The succeeding pope, John VIII (872-82), also esteemed Anastasius, confirmed him in the office of librarian, entrusted important affairs to him, and encouraged him to further literary work. Anastasius was in correspondence with the deposed Byzantine patriarch, Photius, and sought to mediate between the patriarch and the pope and also to assuage the controversy over the Holy Ghost by assuming that the Latins understood the procession (processio) of the Holy Ghost from the Son in the sense of transmission (missio

During the pontificate of Adrian II, Anastasius became involved in serious difficulties: in 868 a near relative of his named Eleutherius forcibly carried off the daughter of the pope, and soon after killed both her and her mother. The murderer was executed and Anastasius, who was regarded as the instigator of the murder, was punished by excommunication and deposition. He lived at the imperial Court, and sought by the intervention of the emperor to exculpate himself before the pope. Hergenröther (Photius, II, 230-240) maintains, with good reason, that the librarian and the presbyter Anastasius (the antipope) were one and the same person, and weaves all the statements concerning the latter into the biography of Anastasius, while Langen (Geschichte der römischen Kirche, III, 270 sqq.) considers them different persons.

In August, 879, Zacharias of Anagni appears as librarian of the Roman Church, so that Anastasius must have died shortly before this date. Anastasius translated from Greek into Latin the "Acts" of the Seventh and Eighth Ecumenical Councils, as well as several legends of saints, along with other writings. He also compiled a historical work, "Chronographia tripartita", from the Greek writings of Theophanes, Nicephorus, and Syncellus, and made a collection of documents concerning the affairs of Pope Honorius. Several important letters written by him have been preserved.

Ashurbanipal, or Assurbanipal, (reigned 668 - 627 BCE), the son of Esarhaddon and Naqi'a-Zakutu, was the last great king of ancient Assyria. He is famous as one of the few kings who could himself read and write. Assyrian sculpture reached its apogee under his rule (Northern palace and south-western palace at Nineveh, battle of Ulai). The Greeks knew him as Sardanapal; Latin and other medieval texts refer to him as Sardanapalus. During his rule the Assyrian splendour was not only due to its military power but also to the culture and art. Ashurbanipal created a library at Nineveh in which he gathered all cuneiform literature available by that time.

Ashurbanipal assembled "the first systematically collected library" at Nineveh. A library, in Oppenheim's view, apparently, was distinct from an archive: earlier repositories of documents had accumulated passively, in the course of administrative routine. Tablets from the library of Nineveh preserve the most complete source for the Sumerian/Babylonian Epic of Gilgamesh. Other sets of tablets offer what is essentially a Sumerian/Akkadian dictionary. There are arcane astronomical/astrological texts. By far the largest group of tablets (almost all of which are in the British Museum, London) however, are 'omen' texts that taught the scribes how to recognize the significance of portents. Assurbanipal only became crown prince in 672, when Esarhaddon's oldest son Sin-iddina-apla died.

Assurbanipal was very unpopular with the court and the priesthood. Contracts were made with leading Assyrians, members of the Royal family and foreign rulers to assure their loyalty to the crown prince. But it was only the energy of his mother Naqi'a-Zakutu that assured his ascent to the throne when Esarhaddon suddenly died during his Egyptian campaign. Ashurbanipal's reign, like that of most Assyrian kings was marked by incessant warfare. He began by making war on his brother Shamash-shum-ukin, who had been installed as king in Babylon; Ashurbanipal conquered Babylon and destroyed it. Assurbanipal ruled with an iron hand, crushing Egyptian insurrections as well as the one his own brother led against him in Babylon. He also conquered Elam, Phoenicia, Armenia and a great part of the Arab territories, and overcame the city of Susa. Oppenheim's dates for Ashurbanipal are drawn from references in the inscription of the mother of Nabonidus. Oppenheim notes the curious break in all documentation during the final decade of his rule. The date of his death is not known with certainty, the last tablet to mention his name is a private contract from Nippur dated to 631, the 38th year of his rule. Other texts say that he ruled 42 years, that is, till 627/626).

Bashiruddin, S Professor Syed Bashiruddin was a famous librarian from India. He was born in the year 1902. Since childhood, Bashiruddin was a bright student but his family conditions did not allow him to continue studies after matriculation which he passed in first division. In 1919, young Bashiruddin left his home in Orissa for a famous educational institution of Indian Muslims in the Northern part of the country. He continued his studies and passed examinations in higher studies andf also worked in the Lytton Library of the Mohammadan Anglo Oriental College side by side.

Hardly a year after starting his service career, the College was recognized as University and the Librarian Mr. Khan Bahadur Abdullah left Aligarh for the Imperial Library (now National Library of India) leaving enough scope for him to prove his worth as librarian of a growing insitution. He obtained Certificate in Library Science from London College in London in 1931. While abroad, he had a chance to visit many prominent libraries of the world. Coming back to his parent institution at Aligarh he adopted similar techniques for management of the Library. The

Aligarh Muslim University introduced a certificate course in Library science in 1951 which was enhanced to a bachelors degree in the subject after a short period of five years and it was due to the untiring efforts of Syed Bashiruddin.

Bashiruddin was an excellent librarian and his services were recognized in academic circles of the institution and abroad. His services were recognized by the Government of India and he was awarded Padamshri for his contribution to the academic world. He died in 1984 at the age of 82.

Benjamin Franklin (, 1706–April 17, 1790) was an American journalist, publisher, author, philanthropist, abolitionist, public servant, scientist, librarian, diplomat, and inventor. One of the leaders of the American Revolution, he was well known also for his many quotations and his experiments with electricity. Franklin was a member of the Freemasons, corresponded with members of the Lunar Society and was also elected a Fellow of the Royal Society. In 1775, Franklin became the first U.S. Postmaster General. Franklin's inventions include the Franklin stove, bifocals, the medical catheter, lightning rod, swimfins, and the odometer.

Franklin began the first public library in Philadelphia. The newly founded Library Company ordered its first books in 1732, mostly theological and educational tomes, but by 1741 the library also included works on history, geography, poetry, exploration and science. The success of this library encouraged the opening of libraries in other American cities, and Franklin felt that this enlightenment partly contributed to the American colonies' struggle to maintain their privileges.

In recognition of his work with electricity, Franklin was elected a Fellow of the Royal Society and received its Copley Medal in 1753. The cgs unit of electric charge has been named after him: one franklin (Fr) is equal to one statcoulomb. Franklin established two major fields of physical science, electricity and meteorology. In his classic work (A History of The Theories of Electricity & Aether), Sir Edmund Whittaker (p. 46) refers to Franklin's inference that electric charge is not created by rubbing substances, but only transferred, so that "the total quantity in any insulated system is invariable". This assertion is known as the "principle of conservation of charge". As a printer and a publisher of a newspaper, Franklin frequented the farmers' markets in Philadelphia to gather news. One day Franklin inferred that reports of a storm elsewhere in Pennsylvania must be the storm that visited the Philadelphia area in recent days. This initiated the notion that some storms travel, eventually leading to the synoptic charts of dynamic meteorology, replacing sole dependence upon the charts of climatology. Franklin established the first American academy, The Academy and College of Philadelphia, in 1749.

In 1751 Franklin and Dr. Thomas Bond obtained a charter from the Pennsylvania legislature to establish a hospital. Pennsylvania Hospital was the first hospital in what was to become the United States of America. In politics he proved very able both as an administrator and as a controversialist; but his record as an office-holder is stained by the use he made of his position to advance his relatives. His most notable service in domestic politics was his reform of the postal system, but his fame as a statesman rests chiefly on his diplomatic services in connection with the relations of the colonies with Great Britain, and later with France. He was also involved in the creation of the first volunteer fire department, free public library, and many other civic enterprises. In 1754 he headed the Pennsylvania delegation to the Albany Congress. This meeting of several colonies had been requested by the Board of Trade in England to improve relations with the Indians and defence against the French. Franklin proposed a broad Plan of Union for the colonies. While the plan was not adopted, elements of it found their way into the Articles of Confederation and the Constitution. In 1757 he was sent to England to protest against the influence of the Penn family in the government of Pennsylvania, and for five years he remained there, striving to enlighten the people and the ministry of the United Kingdom as to colonial conditions.

At Oxford University Franklin was awarded an honorary doctorate for his scientific accomplishments and from then on went by "Doctor Franklin." On his return to America, he played an honorable part in the Paxton affair, through which he lost his seat in the Assembly, but in 1764 he was again dispatched to England as agent for the colony, this time to petition the King to resume the government from the hands of the proprietors. In London he actively opposed the proposed Stamp Act, but lost the credit for this and much of his popularity because he secured for a friend the office of stamp agent in America. Even his effective work in helping to obtain the repeal of the act did not regain his popularity, but he continued his efforts to present the case for the Colonies as the troubles thickened toward the crisis of the Revolution. This also led to an irreconcilable conflict with his son, who remained ardently loyal to the British Government. In 1767 he crossed to France, where he was received with honor; but before his return home in 1775 he lost his position as postmaster through his share in divulging to Massachusetts the famous letter of Hutchinson and Oliver. On his arrival in Philadelphia he was chosen as a member of the Continental Congress and assisted in editing the Declaration of Independence.

Benjamin Peirce (April 4, 1809 – October 6, 1880) was an American mathematician who taught at Harvard University for forty years. He made contributions in celestial mechanics, number theory, algebra, and philosophy of mathematics. After graduating from Harvard, he became a tutor there (1829), then was appointed professor of mathematics in 1831. He added astronomy to his portfolio in 1842, and remained as Harvard professor until his death. In addition, he was instrumental in the development of Harvard's science curriculum, served as the school's librarian, and was director of the U.S. Coast Survey from 1867 from 1874. In number theory, he proved there is no odd perfect number with fewer than four prime factors. In algebra, he was notable for the study of associative algebras. He first introduced the terms idempotent and nilpotent to describe elements of these algebras.

In the philosophy of mathematics, he became known for the statement that "Mathematics is the science that draws necessary conclusions", and believed, along with George Boole, that mathematics could be used to analyze logic. This was in opposition to the program of Gottlob Frege and Bertrand Russell to base mathematics on logic. He was an expert witness in the Howland Will forgery trial. His analysis of the signature in question showed that it resembled another particular handwriting example so closely that the chances of such a match were tatistically extremely remote. His son Charles Peirce was also an accomplished scientist and scholar.

Berners Lee, Timothy Timothy Berners_Lee was born in London, England on 8 June 1955, and graduated from the Queen's College at Oxford University, England, 1976. Whilst there he built his first computer with a soldering iron, TTL gates, an M6800 processor and an old television. He spent two years with Plessey Telecommunications Ltd (Poole, Dorset, UK) a major UK Telecom equipment manufacturer, working on distributed transaction systems, message relays, and bar code technology. In 1978 Tim left Plessey to join D.G Nash Ltd (Ferndown, Dorset, UK), where he wrote among other things typesetting software for intelligent printers, and a multitasking operating system.

A year and a half spent as an independent consultant

included a six month stint (Jun-Dec 1980)as consultant software engineer at CERN, the European Particle Physics Laboratory in Geneva, Switzerland. Whilst there, he wrote for his own private use his first program for storing information including using random associations. Named "Enquire", and never published, this program formed the conceptual basis for the future development of the World Wide Web.

From 1981 until 1984, Tim worked at John Poole's *Image Computer Systems Ltd,* with technical design responsibility. Work here included real time control firmware, graphics and communications software, and a generic macro language. In 1984, he took up a fellowship at CERN, to work on distributed real-time systems for scientific data acquisition and system control. Among other things, he worked on FASTBUS system software and designed a heterogeneous remote procedure call system.

In 1989, he proposed a global hypertext project, to be known as the World Wide Web. Based on the earlier "Enquire" work, it was designed to allow people to work together by combining their knowledge in a web of hypertext documents. He wrote the first World Wide Web server, *"httpd"* and the first client, *"WorldWideWeb"* a what-you-see-is-what-you-get hypertext browser/editor which ran in the NeXTStep environment. This work was started in October 1999, and the program "WorldWideWeb" first made available within CERN in December, and on the Internet at large in the summer of 1991.

Through 1991 and 1993, Tim continued working on the design of the Web, coordinating feedback from users across the Internet. His initial specifications of URIs, HTTP and HTML were refined and discussed in larger circles as the Web technology spread.

In 1994, Tim founded the World Wide Web Consortium at the Laboratory for Computer Science (LCS) at the Massachusetts Institute of Technology (MIT). Since that time he has served as the Director of the World Wide Web Consortium which coordinates Web development worldwide, with teams at MIT, at INRIA in France, and at Keio University in Japan. The Consortium takes as its goal to lead the Web to its full potential, ensuring its stability through rapid evolution and revolutionary transformations of its usage. The Consortium may be found at http:// www.w3.org/.

In 1999, he became the first holder of the 3Com Founders chair at LCS, and is now a Senior Research Scientist within the Lab. The Lab merged with the AI lab to became "CSAIL", the Computer Science and Artificial Intelligence Laboratory at MIT. He is the author of "Weaving the Web", on the the past present and future of the Web.

In 1995, Tina Berners-Lee received the Kilby Foundation's "Young Innovator of the Year" Award, and an honorary *Prix Ars Electronica,* and was corecipient of the ACM Software Systems Award. In 1997 he was awarded the IEEE Koji Kobayashi Computers and Communications Award, the Duddell Medal of the Institute of Physics, the Interactive Services Association's Distinguished Service Award, the MCI Computerworld/Smithsonian Award for Leadership in Innovation, The International Communication Institute's Columbus Prize, and an OBE. In 1998, he received the Charles Babbage award, the Mountbatten Medal of the National Electronics Council, the Lord Lloyd of Kilgerran Prize from the Foundation for Science and Technology, PC Magazine Lifetime Achievement Award in Technical Excellence, a MacArthur Fellowship and The Eduard Rhein technology award. In 1999, Time magazine dubbed him one of the 100 greatest minds of the century and he received a World Technology Award for Communication Technology, and an Honorary Fellowship to the Society for Technical Communications. In 2000, he received the Paul Evan Peters Award of ARL, Educause and CNI, the Electronic Freedom Foundation's pioneer award, and the George R Stibitz Computer Pioneer award at the American Computer Museum, and the Special Award for Outstanding Contribution of the World Television Forum. In 2001 he received the Sir Frank Whittle Medal from the Royal Academy of Engineering. In 2002 he was the recipient of the Japan Prize from the Science and Technology Foundation of Japan. He shared the Prince of Asturias Foundation Prize for Scientific and Technical Research with with Larry Roberts, Rob Kahn and Vint Cerf; became a Fellow of the Guglielmo Marconi Foundation, and received the Albert Medal of the Royal Society for the encouragement of Art, Manufactures and Commerce (RSA). In 2004 Tim was listed in the new year's honours list for a knighthood (KBE) for services to the global development of the Internet and was knighted by H.M. the Queen on 16th July, 2004. Also in 2004 he was awarded the first Millennium Technology Prize and the Special Award of the American Society for Information Science and Technology. In 2005 he received the Common Wealth Award for Distinguished Service for Mass Communications the Die Quadriga Award, the Institute of Physics President's Medal, and the Financial Times Lifetime Achievement Award.

He has honorary degrees from the a number of institutions of USA, UK, Australia and the rest of the World

Bonnie Nardi is best known as the lead author of Information Ecologies: Using Technology with Heart, Nardi & O'Day, (MIT Press, 1998). She is widely known among librarians especially research, reference and digital librarians for Chapter 7 of Information Ecologies, which focused on librarians as keystone species in information ecologies. Bonnie Nardi is currently a member of the faculty of the School of Information & Computer Science (*http://www.ics.uci.edu*) at University of California, Irvine. She had written Information Ecologies while a researcher at ATT Labs Research (*http://www.research.att.com/*). Nardi's self-described theoretical orientation is "activity theory, a philosophical framework developed by the Russian psychologists Vygotsky, Luria, Leontiev, and their students. My interests are user interface design, collaborative work, computer-mediated communication, and theoretical approaches to technology design and evaluation." She is currently conducting a study of blogging.

Callimachus Callimachus was a great librarian, bio-bibliographer, and cataloger at the Alexandrian Library in the third century B.C.E. He has been referred to by many as the "Founding Father" of librarians. His work was not only important in the field of library science, as he was also the author of a great deal of poetry and kept extensive records of important Greek Literature.

Ptolemy II of Egypt employed Callimachus to work in the Alexandrian Library. At that point of time Callimachus was known as a poet and scholar, not as a librarian. His employment at the Library is explained by the fact that the librarians of the time were usually scribes or scholars. Callimachus wrote a great deal of poetry before working in the Library and while he was working there. His most famous poetical work was the Aetia, written around 270 B.C.E. This work is evidence of his interest in the antiquities, an interest that becomes more apparent in his works done for the Library. Other poetical works by Callimachus include Iambi, Hecale, Hymns, Ibis, and the Epigrams.

Callimachus opened a school in the suburbs of Alexandria, and some of the most distinguished grammarians and poets were his pupils, among them was Apollonius of Rhodes. He was subsequently appointed by Ptolemy Philadelphus chief librarian of the Alexandrian library, which office he held till his death (about 240). His Pinakes (tablets), in 120 books, a critical and chronologically arranged catalogue of the library, laid the foundation of a history of Greek literature. According to the Suda, he wrote about 800 works, in verse and prose; of these only six hymns, sixty-four epigrams and some fragments are extant; a considerable fragment of the Hecale, an idyllic epic, has also been discovered in the Rainer papyri. His Coma Berenices is only known from the celebrated imitation of Catullus (the latter's 66th poem). His Aitia (causes) was a collection of elegiac poems in four books, dealing with the foundation of cities, religious ceremonies and other customs. According to Quintilian (Inst it. x. 1. 58) he was the chief of the elegiac poets; his elegies were highly esteemed by the Romans, and imitated by Ovid, Catullus and especially Propertius. The extant hymns are extremely learned, and written in a laboured and artificial style. The epigrams, some of the best specimens of their kind, have been incorporated in the Greek Anthology.

In spite of his extensive work in poetry it is for his prose work that Callimachus gains his importance in librarianship. This work is known as the *Pinakes*, which was an early chronlogical subject catalog. This catalog not only contained information about the text, but also had information about the author and if there were any doubts about the authenticity of the work. This catalog not only cataloged the works of the Library, it gives important information about what works were being used at that time in the ancient world. The *Pinakes* itself consisted of 120 books that contained critical and biographical information on all the works, and their authors, held by the library. This is most likely the first time that such a large cataloging project was attempted and the results were very impressive. Not only were the collections of the most impressive library in the ancient world cataloged, but it also created what was at the timethe most complete record of Greek literature. It is no wonder that Callimachus is described as the founding Father of librarians. If he is not that, then he is at least the founding father of catalogers.

Charles Pickering (November 10, 1805 - March 17, 1878) was an American naturalist. Born in Susquehanna

County, Pennsylvania, the grandson of Colonel Thomas Pickering, he grew up in Wenham, Massachusetts and received a medical degree from Harvard University in 1823. A practicing physician in Philadelphia, he became active as librarian and curator at the city's Academy of Natural Sciences. Pickering went with the United States Exploring Expedition of 1838-1842 as one of its naturalists, then upon his return was appointed to a post at the Patent Office. This did not last long; in 1843 he traveled to Africa and India to research native races. He later moved to Boston, where he resumed his medical practice.

Charles Ammi Cutter Charles Ammi Cutter was born in Boston, Massachusetts on March 14, 1837. His early, classical education prepared him for entry into the clergy. He studied at Harvard College from 1851 to 1855 and then spent a year tutoring applicants for college entrance exams. Subsequently, he entered the Harvard Divinity School in autumn, 1856 (Immroth 380). Even before his graduation, in 1858, Cutter was appointed assistant librarian of the School and he unwittingly began what would become his life's work. His first job was to prepare a new catalog of the Divinity school library in response to a major accession that doubled the size of the collection.

In December of 1868, Cutter was chosen as librarian of the Boston Anthenaeum and he began the arduous task of preparing a published catalog of the holdings. This appeared in five volumes, published in stages between 1874 and 1882. Writing in 1931, Cutter's nephew and biographer William Parker Cutter notes that "It has been the model for many other dictionary catalogs; and even now is in frequent usage by catalogers in search of full names and similar information"

Because of the pragmatic approach taken - one of the stated goals was to make the catalog easy for the public to use - "it began to be used at a number of libraries. Rules for a Dictionary Catalog eventually went through four editions, the last (1904) being published after Cutter's death. It was "recognized immediately as the treatise on cataloguing. and remains classic".

In 1876, the American Library Association was established. Charles Cutter was one of the approximately one hundred founding members. He served as president in 1888 and 1889 and he served on the ALA council from 1889 until 1902. It is reported that at the time of his death, he had attended more annual meetings than any other member. Cutter was also active on various ALA committees and with the Massachusetts Library Club. He also attended both of the 'International' Library Conferences, in London, respectively in 1877 and 1897, serving as honorary vice-president of the latter. Finally, from 1881 until 1893, Cutter served as General Editor of the ALA publication Library Journal.

Another of Charles Cutter's significant contributions to the world of library science was his Expansive Classification system. The name comes from the fact that it is developed in seven stages: the first, being very simple, for the smallest library. and, finally, the seventh, designed for the largest library. Each level was of increasing complexity. Cutter's aim was very ambitious. His stated goal was "to prepare a scheme applicable to collections of every size, from the village library in its earliest stages to the national library with a million volumes" (qtd. in Tauber and Wise 109). As the library grew in size, each section of the classification would be further sub-divided and increased in specificity.

Cutter's system was never widely adopted for several reasons. Most significant is the fact that the seventh (i.e. final) level of classification was never completed. It was in progress at the time of Cutter's death in 1903 and several sections were published posthumously but significant elements, especially the technology classes, were never completed. Henry Bliss has argued that the Seventh Classification had become unworkably complex and unbalanced. Too many categories were allocated to obscure scientific topics but other areas such as Sociology, Social Psychology, and Business were allocated much too little space.

While Cutter's Expansive Classification was not successful, it later formed the basis for the widely adopted Library of Congress classification system. It was "used to develop the first class of the Library of Congress classification, `Class Z: Bibliography and Library Science', and was a basis for a general outline of all the classes.

One aspect of Charles Cutter's work remains with us today. As part of his work on Expansive Classification, he developed a system of alphabetic tables used to abbreviate the names of authors. He first developed and published the two-figure tables between 1891 and '93. As these tables were put into regular use, Cutter "began adding a third figure in exceptional instances as the need arose (in such cases as fiction or biography)". Three-figure tables were systematically worked out and published from 1899 to 1901 (Immroth 382).

Charles Ammi Cutter died on September 6, 1903 at Walpole, New Hampshire. He was survived by his wife and two adult sons. Ironically, Cutter's most significant contribution to the field of Library and Information Studies was his system of Expansive Classification. Despite the fact that it was never widely adopted, it strongly influenced the development of the Library of Congress classification system. Also, the system of author numbers he devised continues in wide use and still bears his name.

Charles Wilkins (1749? - 1836), Sir Charles Wilkins was an English Orientalist. He was born at Frome in Somerset, probably in 1749, and in 1770 he went to India as a writer in the East India Company's service. Becoming attracted to the study of Oriental languages, particularly Sanskrit, he did important work towards facilitating such study by founding a printing press for these languages, taking a large personal share in the practical work of preparing the type. He returned to England in 1786, but continued his study of Sanskrit, and afterwards became librarian to the East India Company, and examiner at Haileybury when a college was established there in 1805. Wilkins was knighted in 1833 in recognition of his services to Oriental scholarship, and died in London. He was a pioneer in Oriental studies, being the first Englishman to acquire mastery of Sanskrit and to make a thorough study of Indian inscriptions in that script.

Wilkins compiled a Sanskrit grammar and published several translations from the sacred books of the East, besides preparing a new edition of John Wilkins Richardson's Persian and Arabic dictionary, and a catalogue of the manuscripts collected by Sir William Jones, who acknowledged his indebtedness to Wilkins, and whom Wilkins assisted in founding the Asiatic Society of Bengal. The eldest son of Peter George Patmore, himself an author, Coventry was born at Woodford in Essex. He was privately educated, his father's intimate and constant companion, and inherited from him his early literary enthusiasm. It was his ambition to become an artist, and he showed much promise, being awarded the silver palette of the Society of Arts in 1838. In the following year he was sent to school in France for six months, where he began to write poetry. On his return his father planned to publish some of these youthful poems; but meanwhile Coventry had become interested in science and the poetry was set aside.

In 1847 he married Emily, daughter of Dr. Andrews of Camberwell. At the Museum he was instrumental in 1852 in starting the Volunteer movement. He wrote an important letter to *The Times* upon the subject, and stirred up much martial enthusiasm among his colleagues. In the next year he republished, in *Tamerton Church Tower*, the more successful pieces from the *Poems* of 1844, adding several new poems which showed distinct advance, both in conception and treatment; and in the following year

(1854) appeared the first part of his best known poem, "The Angel in the House," which was continued in "The Espousals" (1856), "Faithful for Ever" (1860), and "The Victories of Love" (1862). In 1862 he lost his wife. In later years he lived at Lymington, where he died. A collected edition of his poems appeared in two volumes in 1886, with a characteristic preface which might serve as the author's epitaph. "I have written little," it runs; "but it is all my best; I have never spoken when I had nothing to say, nor spared time or labour to make my words true. I have respected posterity; and should there be a posterity which cares for letters, I dare to hope that it will respect me." The obvious sincerity which underlies this statement, combined with a certain lack of humour which peers through its naïveté, points to two of the principal characteristics of Patmore's earlier poetry; characteristics which came to be almost unconsciously merged and harmonized as his style and his intention drew together into unity.

His best work is found in the volume of odes called *The Unknown Eros*, which is full not only of passages but of entire poems in which exalted thought is expressed in poetry of the richest and most dignified melody. Spirituality informs his inspiration; the poetry is glowing and alive. The magnificent piece in praise of winter, the solemn and beautiful cadences of "Departure," and the homely but elevated pathos of "The Toys," are in their various manners unsurpassed in English poetry. Patmore is one of the best-regarded Victorian poets. His son, Henry John Patmore (1860-1883), was also a poet.

Dana, John Cotton, 1856-1929 A public librarian for over forty years, John Cotton Dana began his career in 1889 as head of the Denver Public Library, moved to the City Library of Springfield in 1898, and ended his career at the Free Public Library in Newark, New Jersey. A leader in the library profession, he served as president of the American Library Association from 1895-96, as a member of its council from 1896-1902, and as president of the Special Libraries Association from 1909-10, an organization he helped establish. His philosophical approach to librarianship is best expressed in his book Suggestions, published in 1921 by F. W. Faxon.

Daniel J. Boorstin (October 1, 1914 - February 28, 2004), an American historian and writer, was the Librarian of Congress from 1975 until 1987. Boorstin wrote more than 20 books, including a trilogy on the American experience and one on world intellectual history. The Americans: The Democratic Experience, the final book in the first trilogy, received the 1973 Pulitzer Prize in history. Boorstin also wrote the books The Discoverers and The Creators, a pair of books that attempt to survey the scientific and artistic histories of humanity respectively. He studied at Balliol College, Oxford, was a lawyer and university professor. He also served as director of the National Museum of History and Technology of the Smithsonian Institution. When President Gerald Ford nominated Boorstin to be Librarian of Congress, the nomination was supported by the Authors League of America but opposed by the American Library Association because Boorstin "was not a library administrator." The Senate confirmed the nomination without debate. During his term as Librarian of Congress, Boorstin established the Center for the Book to encourage reading and literacy. In addition, he spearheaded what became a 10-year project to completely renovate the Thomas Jefferson Building of the Library of Congress, restoring the main building to its original 1897 condition. He became Librarian of Congress Emeritus on August 4, 1987. Boorstin was born in Atlanta, Georgia and died in Washington, D.C.

David Hume (April 26, 1711 – August 25, 1776) was Scottish philosopher and historian and, with Adam Smith and Thomas Reid among others, one of the most important figures in the Scottish Enlightenment. Many regard Hume as the third and most radical of the so-called British

Empiricists, after the English John Locke and the Anglo-Irish George Berkeley; this bracketing of Hume, Locke, and Berkeley, though traditional, ignores the major influence on Hume of various Francophone writers such as Pierre Bayle and various other figures on the Anglophone intellectual landscape such as Isaac Newton, Samuel Clarke, Francis Hutcheson, and Joseph Butler. Historians most famously see Humean philosophy as a thoroughgoing form of Scepticism, but many commentators have argued that the element of Naturalism has no less importance.

Hume scholarship has tended to oscillate over time between those who emphasize the sceptical side of Hume (such as Reid, Greene, and the logical positivists), and those who emphasize the naturalist side (such as Norman Kemp Smith, Stroud, and Galen Strawson). Hume was born in Edinburgh and attended Edinburgh University. At first he considered a career in law, but came to have, in his words, "an insurmountable aversion to everything but the pursuits of philosophy and general learning". He did some self-study in France, where he also completed A Treatise of Human Nature at the age of twenty-six. Although many scholars today consider the Treatise to be Hume's most important work and one of the most important books in the history of philosophy, the public in England did not at first agree. Hume himself described the (lack of) public reaction to the publication of the Treatise in 1739–40 by writing that the book "fell dead-born from the press". After a few years of service to various political and military figures, Hume returned to his studies.

After deciding that the Treatise had problems of style rather than of content, he reworked some of the material for more popular consumption in An Enquiry Concerning Human Understanding. It did not prove extremely successful either, but more so than the Treatise. Hume failed to gain chairs of philosophy in Edinburgh and in Glasgow, probably due to charges of atheism, and to the opposition of one of his chief critics, Thomas Reid. However, between philosophical pursuits, Hume did achieve literary fame as an essayist and historian. Attention to his works grew after no less a philosopher than Immanuel Kant credited Hume with awakening him from "dogmatic slumber". Though Hume wrote in the 18th century, his work seems still uncommonly relevant in the philosophical disputes of today compared to that of his contemporaries.

Dehkhoda, Ali Akbar Ali Akbar Dehkhoda was born in Tehran at about the year 1297. His father, called Khanbaba Khan, was one of the small landowners of Ghazvin city who had emigrated to Tehran before Ali Akbar's birth. Ali Akbar was only ten years old when his father passed away. He continued his schooling under the guardianship of his mother from that time on.

After his father's death, one of the great scholars of the time named Sheikh Gholam Hossein Broojerdi, was assigned to educate Dehkhoda. When The School of Political Science was founded in Tehran some years later, Dehkhoda began studying there. He soon started to learn the French language too. After closing down of the newly born Parliament (Majlis) in the reign of Mohamad Ail Shah (king), Dehkhoda was exiled to Europe along with a number of other freedom fighters. He then went to the city of Iverdon in Sweden and published three issues of his newspaper, Soor Esrafeel .

After that, Dehkhoda went to Istanbul and with the cooperation of a number of Iranians residing in Turkey; he published another newspaper in Farsi called Soroosh [a messenger-angel, Gabriel, who is invisible but whose voice is heard] which fifteen issues of this newspaper had been published. After the conquest of Tehran by the revolutionary army and the overthrow of Mohammad Ali Shah Ghajar, Dehkhoda was elected to the National Legislative Assembly by both the people of Tehran and of Kerman.Upon the insistence of the revolutionary movement leaders, he left the territory of the Ottoman

Empire and returned to Iran. During the First World War, Dehkhoda went into seclusion for various reasons and took refuge in one of the villages of Chahar Mahal Bakhtiari (in the south-central parts of Iran); and when the war was over, he returned to Tehran. He, however, retired himself from political activities and began working on scientific, literary and cultural questions.

Dehkhuda's contribution to knowledge is immence. After the end of the First World War and his return to Tehran from Chahr Mahal va Bakhftiari, in 1918, Mr. Dehkhoda began a far and wide study of the proverbs used by common people, the people in the street, as well as all the ones he could find in the precious treasures of Persian poetry and prose collections. He then began to make his own collection by classifying the material he had gathered and finding the roots of every item and its current variations. This led to the compilation of the four-volume "Amsal va Hekam" which was published in Tehran during the years 1929-1932. A selection of these proverbs and wise sayings were published along with some notes written by Mr. Dehkhoda about the Preface of the four-volume text, in the form of a new book (entitled" Bargozideh Amsal va Hekam".

After he had completed his work on "Amsal va Hekam" (as mentioned above), Dehkhoda continued his studies on Farsi words and on the poetry and prose texts that he had collected during the past several years, and worked on the meanings of the material he had gathered up to then. He soon had in his possession some three million file cards based on very credible texts written by masters of Persian and Arabic poetry and prose, as well as printed texts and manuscripts of books on history, geography, medicine, astrology, astronomy, mathematics, philosophy, religion, jurisprudence, etc. These file cards formed the basis of what later became Dehkhoda's great lexicon.

Another part of Dehkhoda's works is related to the

corrections he made on the collections of poetry written by celebrated Iranian poets. Some of these have been published, but some have not, as yet. Among these are: Marginal notes to the Collection of Poetry of: Nasser Khosro, Seyed Hassan Ghazvini, Hafiz, Manoochehri Farrokhi, Masood Saad, Soozani; Corrections made to the Collection of Poetry of Ibn Yamin, and the corrections of Yousef and Zoleikha. In addition to these, he translated two books in his youth, neither of which was ever published. These are: The Rise and Fall of the Roman Empire, and Montesquieu's The Spirit of Laws. Among other works by Dehkhoda, one may mention French-Farsi Dictionary, Corrections made to Asadi's Farsi Lexicon, Corrections Made to 'Sahah al Fors (The second Farsi Lexicon). None of these have been published either.

Demetrius Demetrius of Phalerum the Greek put together the central collection for the Library of Alexandria while he was in Greece. He might be considered the originator of the library idea, although this honor should also belong to the first and second kings of the Ptolemaic period. Ptolemy the First Soter ordered the establishment and organization of the library at his expense, while Ptolemy the Second Philadelphus completed his work. The foundation of the library was the joint achievement of all three; Soter, Philadelphus, and Demetrius.

Ed Greenwood (born 1959) is a Canadian librarian who invented the Forgotten Realms Dungeons & Dragons campaign setting. Ed Greenwood and Jeff Grubb together penned the Forgotten Realms Campaign Boxed Set in 1987, for TSR - though Greenwood had used the Forgotten Realms for his home Dungeons & Dragons campaign since 1975. The spawned campaign world was a success, and he has been involved with all subsequent incarnations of the Forgotten Realms in D&D. Probably Greenwood's most lasting character from the setting is the wizard Elminster. Since the release of the Forgotten Realms, Greenwood has published many Forgotten Realms novels. He retains certain rights of his setting, but is essentially a freelance author.

Ed has published over two hundred articles in Dragon magazine and Polyhedron newszine, is a lifetime charter member of the Role Playing Game Associaton (RPGA) network, has written over thirty books and modules for TSR, and been Gen Con Game Fair guest of honor several times. He has also contributed to most Forgotten Realms gaming accessories, and authored many more - including the detailed Volo's Guide series. He writes regular Realsmlore columns for the Wizards of the Coast website (http://www.wizards.com/forgottenrealms), and frequents the Candlekeep (http://www.candlekeep.com) web forums. In addition to all these activities, Ed works as a library clerk and has edited over a dozen small press magazines.

Edmund William Gosse (September 21, 1849 - May 16, 1928) was an English poet, author and critic, the son of Philip Henry Gosse. He worked as assistant librarian at the British Museum from 1867, and in 1875 became a translator at the Board of Trade, a post which he held until 1904. In the meantime, he published his first volume of poetry, On Viol and Flute (1873) and a work of criticism, Studies in the Literature of Northern Europe (1879). He became acquainted with the pre-Raphaelites and Algernon Swinburne. From 1904, Gosse was librarian of the House of Lords, where he exercised considerable influence. He wrote for the Sunday Times, and was an expert on Thomas Gray, William Congreve, John Donne, Jeremy Taylor, and Coventry Patmore. He can also take credit for introducing Ibsen's work to the British public. His most famous book is the autobiographical Father and Son, about his troubled relationship with his father, Philip. In later life, he became a formative influence on Siegfried Sassoon, whose mother was a friend of Gosse's wife, Ellen.

Edward Augustussee Bond (31 December 1815-2 January 1898) Was an English librarian. He was born at

Hanwell, the son of a schoolmaster. He was educatod at Merchant Taylors school, and in 1832 obtained a post in the public record office. In 1838 he became an assistant in the manuscript department of the British Museum, where he attracted the notice of his chief, Sir Frederick Madden, the most eminent palaeographer of his day, and in 1852 he was made Egerton librarian. In 1856 he became assistant keeper of manuscripts, and in 1867 was promoted to the post of keeper. His work in reorganizing the manuscript department was of lasting value, and tc him is due the classified catalogue of MSS., and the improved efficiency and punctuality of publication of the department. In 1878 he was appointed principal librarian. Under his supervision were erected the new buildings of the White Wing, which provide accommodation for prints, drawings, manuscripts and newspapers, and the purchase of the Stowe manuscripts was concluded while he remained in office. He founded, in conjunction with Sir E. Maunde Thompson, the Palaeographical Society, and first made classical palaeography an exact science. He was the editor of four volumes of facsimiles of Anglo-Saxon charters from 679 to the Conquest, The Speeches in ike Trial of Warren Hastings (1859-1861), and a number of other interesting historic documents.

Edward Singleton Holden (November 5, 1846 – March 16, 1914) was an American astronomer. He was trained in West Point in the class of 1870. In 1873 he became professor of mathematics at the US Naval Observatory, where he made a favorable impression on Simon Newcomb. He was director of Washburn Observatory at the University of Wisconsin from 1881 to 1885. He was elected a member of the American National Academy of Sciences in 1885. He was president of the University of California from 1885 until 1888, and the first director of the Lick Observatory from 1888 until the end of 1897. He resigned as a result of internal dissent over his management among his subordinates. In 1901 he became the librarian of the US Military Academy at West Point, where he remained until his death. His cousin, George Phillips Bond, was director of Harvard College Observatory. He discovered a total of 22 NGC objects during his work at Washburn Observatory. He authored many books, including science books intended for children. For example the book Real Things In Nature. A Reading Book of Science for American Boys and Girls published in 1916. Craters on Mars and the Moon were named in his honor.

Eratosthenes of Cyrene Eratosthenes of Cyrene (c. 276 BC Cyrene – c. 194 BC Alexandria), a friend of Archimedes of Syracuse, lived in Alexandria. He was born in Cyrene, a place in Libya which is called today Shahhat. He worked on geometry and prime numbers. He was a director of the great Library of Alexandria. He is best remembered for his prime number sieve which, in modified form, is still an important tool in number theory research. Eratosthenes measured the tilt of the Earth's axis with great accuracy and compiled a star catalogue containing 675 stars (now lost); he suggested that a leap day be added every fourth year and tried to construct an accurately-dated history. He became blind in his old age and is said to have committed suicide by starvation, like Democrit. Eratosthenes came to Alexandria from Athens to be the chief librarian of Ptolemy Euergetes. He was not merely an astronomer and a geographer, but a poet and grammarian as well. His contemporaries jestingly called him Beta the Second, because he was said through the universality of his attainments to be "a second Plato" in philosophy, "a second Thales" in astronomy, and so on throughout the list. For the same reason he was called a Pentathlos which means and athlete in five disciplines. We know indirect what he did by Strabo and Cleomedes who wrote 150-200 years later about Eratosthenes.

It is believed that Eratosthenes invented an important modification of the gnomon which was elaborated afterwards by Hipparchus and called an *armillary sphere.* This consists essentially of a small gnomon, or perpendicular post, attached to a plane representing the Earth's equator and a hemisphere in imitation of the Earth's surface. With the aid of this, the shadow cast by the sun could be very accurately measured. It involves no new principle. Every perpendicular post or object of any kind placed in the sunlight casts a shadow from which the angles now in question could be roughly measured. The armillary sphere made angle measurements extremely accurate.

Eratosthenes invented, probably around 205 BC, a very beautiful method to measure the circumference of the Earth. Details of his method he published in a work *On the measurement of the Earth* which unfortunately was lost. We know indirect about his method from other authors, mainly Cleomedes and Theon of Smyrna. He noted that, on the summer solstice, the sun casts no shadow in Syene but he knew that it casts a shadow in Alexandria. He reasoned that the change in angle of the shadow was caused by the spherical shape of the Earth (Aristotle and others knew this earlier) and that it would be possible from this angle to obtain the circumference of the Earth..

The *scaphe dial*, probably the oldest form of sundials. *Scaphe* (Greek boat) a bowl-shaped cup within which the hour-lines are marked. At the time of summer solstice the shadow is shortest and falls exactly on the bottom line. In the following time the shadow grows again until it reaches the top line at the time of winter solstice. The days are divided into *temporal hours*. Their length is not fixed but instead the time between sunrise and sunset is divided into 12 intervals of equal length. Klaus Kohl provides a possible method used by Eratosthenes with the scaphe to determine the circumference, avoiding the measurement of angles.

The Earth's orbit around the Sun is very nearly circular, and it defines a plane in space called the *ecliptic plane.* With respect to the perpendicular to the ecliptic plane (which points to orbital north), the Earth's axis is tilted at an angle of 23.5°: When the Earth's north pole is tilted directly towards the Sun, the latter is highest in the sky (in the northern hemisphere), which is what we called the summer solstice and when the north pole is tilted directly away from the Sun, the latter is lowest in the sky (in the northern hemisphere), which is the winter solstice. The intermediate positions are the vernal and autumnal equinoxes.

He was also a mathematician, geographer and astronomer with (probably) Chaldean origins. He was born in Cyrene (now Shahhat, Libya) and died in Ptolemaic Alexandria. He is noted for devising a system of latitude and longitude and computing the size of the Earth. Eratosthenes studied at Alexandria and for some years in Athens. In 236 BC he was appointed by Ptolemy III Euergetes I as librarian of the Alexandrian library. He made several important contributions to mathematics and science, and was a good friend to Archimedes. Around 255 BC he invented the armillary sphere, which was widely used until the invention of the orrery in the 18th century. He calculated the earth's circumference circa 240 BC, using trigonometry and knowledge of the angle of elevation of the Sun at noon in Alexandria and Syene (now Aswan, Egypt). The calculation is based on the assumption that the Earth is spherical and that the Sun is so far away that its rays can be taken as parallel.

Eratosthenes' method was used by Posidonius about 150 years later. Circa 200 BC Eratosthenes is thought to have coined or to have adopted the word geography, the descriptive study of the Earth. Eratosthenes was known under the name â, because he supposedly proved himself to be the second in the world in many fields. He was also reputedly known for his haughty character. In 195 BC he became blind and a year later he starved himself to death.

Fabricius, Johann Albert see Johann Albert Fabricius

Francis Hayman (1708 - 2 February 1776) was an English painter and illustrator who became one of the founding members of the Royal Academy in 1768 and later its first librarian. Born in Exeter, Devon, Hayman begun his artistic career as a scene painter in London's Drury Lane theatres (where he also appeared in minor roles) before establishing a studio in St Martin's Lane. A versatile artist influenced by the French Rococo style, he achieved some note during the 1740s through decorative paintings executed for Vauxhall Pleasure Gardens in London, but could also turn his hand to portraits, landscapes, and scenes from history and literature. Combining some of these, he contributing 31 pictures to a 1744 edition of Shakespeare's plays by Sir Thomas Hanmer, and later portrayed many leading contemporary actors in Shakespearean roles, including David Garrick as Richard III (1760). He also illustrated the novels of Samuel Richardson. He was an able teacher. His pupils included Mason Chamberlin, Nathaniel Dance-Holland and Lemuel Francis Abbott and he was also a strong influence on Thomas Gainsborough

Franklin, Benjamin see Benjamin Franklin

Friedrich Sylburg (1536 - February 17, 1596), was a German classical scholar. The son of a farmer, he was born at Wetter near Marburg. He studied at Marburg, Jena, Geneva, and, lastly, Paris, where his teacher was Henry Estienne (Stephanus), to whose great Greek Thesaurus Sylburg afterwards made important contributions. Returning to Germany, he held educational posts at Neuhaus near Wörms and at Lich near Giessen, where he edited a useful edition of the Institutiones in graecam linguam (1580) of Nicolaus Clenardus (Cleynaerts). In 1583 he resigned his post at Lich and moved to Frankfurt to act as corrector and editor of Greek texts for the enterprising publisher Johann Wechel. To his Frankfurt period belong the editions of Pausanias, Herodotus, Dionysius Halicarnassensis (one of his best pieces of work, highly praised by Carsten Niebuhr), Aristotle, the Greek and Latin sources for the history of the Roman emperors and the IlepJ owras of Apollonius Dyscolus. In 1591 he moved to Heidelberg, where he became librarian to the elector palatine. The Wechel series was continued by Hieronymus Commelinus of Heidelberg, for whom Sylburg edited Clement of Alexander, Justin Martyr, the Etymologicum magnum, the Scriptores de re rustica, the Greek gnomic poets, Xenophon, Nonnus and other works. All Sylburg's editions show great critical power and indefatigable industry; the latter may well have caused his death.

Fuat Seizgin Born in the first quarter of the 20th century. Fuat Seizgin is one of the most prominent historian od science and technology of the Muslim world. He is Professor and Director of the Institute for the History of Arab-Islamic Science at the Johann Wolfgang Goete University, Frankfurt. Sezgin is the white-haired, genteel octogenarian explaining the exhibits to visitors. As he does, he easily switches between Turkish, Arabic, German, and English. The professor is one of the world's leading authorities on Islam's Golden Age of Science, which he says extended from the 8th to the 16th centuries. He is also one of that period's most prolific chroniclers.

Sezgin has spent 55 years writing. Islam's Golden Age of Science finally ended as the stability and wealth of the Muslim world was shaken by rival powers. European states controlled the Mediterranean trade routes by the 14th century, and the Mongol invasions of the 13th to 15th centuries disrupted trade with China. State patronage of science gave way to military affairs. Still, Muslim science never disappeared. Sezgin says Portuguese and Spanish navigators used the knowledge they gained from Muslim cartographers while Iberia was under Arab domination to launch their own voyages of discovery.

Sezgin mostly writes in German. The first volume of his book on the Muslim cartographers has just been translated into English and will be published next month. He hopes the translation will help his work reach a broader audience, both in the West and the Muslim world.

Gabriel Naudé (February 2, 1600 - July 10, 1653) was a French librarian and scholar. He was born in Paris. He studied medicine at Paris and Padua, and became physician to Louis XIII. In 1629 he became librarian to Cardinal Bagni at Rome, and on Bagni's death in 1641 librarian to Cardinal Barberini. At the desire of Richelieu he began a wearisome controversy with the Benedictines, denying Gerson's authorship of De Imitatione Christi. Richelieu intended to make Naudé his librarian, and on his death Naudé accepted a similar offer on the part of Mazarin, and for the next ten years devoted himsel to bringing together from all parts of Europe the noble assemblage of books known as the Bibliothéque Mazarine. Mazarin's library was sold by the parlement of Paris during the trouble of the Fronde, and Queen Christina invited Naudé to Stockholm. He was not happy in Sweden, and on Mazarin's appeal that he should re-form his scattered library Naudé returned at once. But his health was broken, and he died on the journey at Abbeville on the 10th of July 1653.

Naudé was no mere bookworm; his books show traces of the critical spirit which made him a worthy colleague of the humorists and scholars who prepared the way for the better known writers of the "siècle de Louis XIV" Including works edited by him, a list of ninety-two pieces is given in the Naudaeana. The chief are Le Marfore, ou discours contre les libelles (Paris, 1620), very rare, reprinted 1868; Instruction a la France sur la vérité de l'histoire des Frères de la Roze-Croix (1623, 1624), displaying their impostures; Apologie pour tous les grands personnages faussement soupconnez de magie (1625, 1652, 1669, 1712), Pythagoras, Socrates, Thomas Aquinas and Solomon are among those defended; Advis pour dresser une bibliothèque (1627, 1644, 1676; translated by J. Evelyn, 1661), full of sound and liberal views on librarianship; Addition a l'histoire de Louys XI (1630), this includes an account of the origin of printing; Bibliographia politica (Venice, 1633, etc.; in French, 1642); De studio hiberali syntagma (1632, 1654), a practical treatise found in most collections of directions for studies; De studio militari syntagma (1637), esteemed in its day; Considérations politiques sur les coups d'êtat.

Gaius Suetonius Tranquillus (75-160), commonly known simply as Suetonius, was a Roman writer. Suetonius was an administrator working as a secretary to the emperor Hadrian, prior to his disemployment by Hadrian. He is remembered chiefly as the author of "The Lives of the First Twelve Caesars" (*De vita Caesarum*), history of Roman leaders, which has been the source for many works on Roman history and is generally regarded as about as impartial as a historian of ancient times could be. This does not mean, however, that he did not have his favorites such as Caesar Augustus, whom he preferred vastly over such emperors as Nero and Gaius Caligula. Suetonius was also rather fond of alleged lewd details from the lives of those about whom he wrote. Many of these episodes, often sexual in nature, are likely derived from rumors going about at the time of Suetonius or in the records available to him in his erstwhile position in the administration of Hadrian. Thus potentially representing 2nd century attitudes regarding prior emperors and the imperial office. In very few cases did Suetonius cite his sources; one such example is when he was accentuating the fact that Caesar Augustus's detractors were often his enemies, such as Marcus Antonius, who is cited as a dubious source for some negative rumors regarding Caesar Augustus in the fourth chapter of Suetonius's biography thereof.

Gary Price is an electronic librarian, well-known for his technical knowledge, founding resourceshelf.com, and originating Price's List of Lists, "a database of ranked listings of companies, people and resources freely available on the Internet", which is now maintained by others. A former reference librarian at George Washington University, this native of the Chicago area holds a masters of library and information science degree from Wayne State University and a bachelors of arts degree from the University of Kansas. With Chris Sherman, Price co-authored the book The Invisible Web.

In 2002, the Special Libraries Association [4] (http://www.sla.org/) gave him the Innovations in Technology Award. He received the Special Libraries Association News Division's Peter, count Griffenfeldt (Peder Schumacher) (August 24, 1635 - March 12, 1699), was a Danish statesman. Born at Copenhagen into a wealthy trading family connected with the leading civic, clerical and learned circles in the Danish capital, he was prepared for university (at the age of ten) by Jens Vorde. Vorde praises his extraordinary gifts, his mastery of the classical languages and his unnerving diligence.

Gasanova, Giacomo see Giacomo Casanova

George Watterston (October 23, 1783-February 4, 1854) was the third United States Librarian of Congress, serving from 1815 to 1829. Watterson, the son of a builder from Jedburgh, Scotland, was born on board a ship in New York Harbor. When Watterson was eight, his family moved to Washington D.C., his father attracted by the ongoing construction in the capital. Watterson became a lawyer, first practicing in Hagerstown, Maryland, later partnered with Thomas Law in Washington. He became a man of letters, publishing his first novel, The Lawyer, or Man As He Ought Not to Be, in 1808. Many of his works contained unflattering portrayals of his profession.

In 1813, he became editor of the Washington City Gazette. During the War of 1812, Watterson participated in the failed defence of Washington D.C. The British burned the capitol, including the Library of Congress, which was then housed in the US Capitol Building. After war's end, Watterson was appointed by President James Madison as Librarian of Congress, the third person to hold the position and the first with that as his sole responsibility. (Previous Librarians also served as the Clerk of the United States House of Representatives). The Library was replenished by purchasing the collection of former President Thomas Jefferson and Watterson organized it based on Jefferson's basic classification scheme. Watterson was a Whig and active in politics. He opposed the election of President Andrew Jackson and upon Jackson's election was replaced. Watterson fruitlessly sought reinstatement for years. After his dismissal, he became editor of the National Journal and published books on many subjects, including biographies and works on agriculture. He was instrumental in the campaign to construct the Washington Monument and was secretary of the Washington National Monument Society.

Gesner, Johann Matthias see Johann Matthias Gesner

Giacomo Casanova (April 5, 1725 - June 4, 1798). Famous 18th century Italian adventurer whose name has become synonymous with seduction. Casanova's extraordinary life carried him across the breadth of Europe in all kinds of scandalous adventures which he memorialized in his "Histoire de Ma Vie"—perhaps the most fascinating source for the social history of The Enlightenment. During his travels Casanova made and lost fortunes and encountered many famous personalities such as the pope Clement XIII (1760), Voltaire (1760), Rousseau, and Mozart (1787), who wasn't famous at that time.

Born in Venice to a family of actors, Casanova started his career in Padua where he studied for the priesthood. His licentious behaviour there resulted in expulsion whence he travelled to Rome to become the secretary to a cardinal. More scandals followed and he moved on to Venice where he made his way by defrauding wealthy socialites with occult tricks a la Cagliostro. The Inquisition in Venice convicted him of witchcraft in 1755 and he was led across the Bridge of Sighs and imprisoned. He escaped and fled to France where he sensationalized the exploit by a pamphlet that made him into a minor celebrity. In Paris he used the name Jacques Casanova and styled himself the "Chevalier de Seingalt". There he made a fortune by starting a lottery. This success was not to last and his restless genius led him to other countries and adventures. Impecunious at the end he retired in 1785 to become the librarian to the Count of Waldstein in the castle of Dux, Bohemia (now Duchcov, Czech Republic) where he died aged 73. Casanova (and the archetype that he has come represent) have appeared in a significant number of both regular and "adult" movies. The first was the 1918 Hungarian movie of that name by Alfréd Deésy in which the director also played the title role. One well known representation was in 1976 by Donald Sutherland in Il Casanova di Federico Fellini.

Gosse, Edmund William see Edmund William Gosse

Henri Marie La Fontaine (April 22, 1854-May 14, 1943) was born in Brussels. A professor of international law, a senator in the Belgian legislature for thirty-six years, a renowned bibliographer, a man of wide-ranging cultural achievements, he was noted, most of all, for his fervent and total internationalism.

La Fontaine was a member of the Belgian delegation to the Paris Peace Conference in 1919 and a delegate to the First Assembly of the League of Nations in 1920-1921. To those deliberations he brought his uncompromising internationalism. For example, during a plenary meeting that was considering Article 16 of the Covenant - the article which provided that members of the League must unite in diplomatic pressure, sanctions, or, if necessary, armed force to prevent a resort to aggressive war in breach of the Covenant - he spoke against an amendment releasing from commitment those countries which deemed themselves endangered should they take part in sanctions, saying: «Belgium thinks that however great the peril which a country might have to undergo under the system which we seek to establish here, that country ought to do its duty. It was thus that Belgium understood her obligations in 1914... We fully admit that, in circumstances of this nature, powerful countries may take certain measures, but in our opinion it would be impossible, on the pretext that they would suffer more than others, for some countries to hold aloof from the sacred task of defending justice, even at the peril of their own existence. ‹Fais ce que dois, advienne que pourra.

La Fontaine entered the organized peace movement when Hodgson Pratt, the British pacifist, came to Belgium in the early 1880's to establish a branch of his International Arbitration and Peace Association. Becoming the secretary-general of the Société belge de l'arbitrage et de la paix in 1889, La Fontaine thereafter participated actively in virtually all of the peace congresses held in the next twenty-five years. In 1907, he succeeded Fredrik Bajer (one of the two Nobel Peace laureates for 1908) as president of the International Peace Bureau (winner of the 1910 Peace Prize), an organization he helped to found and whose titular head he remained until his death

La Fontaine became a member of the Interparliamentary Union as soon as he attained eligibility by virtue of being elected to a national legislature. To La Fontaine the Union was an embryo world parliament, the precursor of a world government. An enthusiastic member, he was chairman of its Juridical Committee prior to World War I and a member of two of its important commissions - that on preparation of a model world parliament and that on drafting a model treaty of arbitration.

In the two decades between 1894 and 1915, La Fontaine's literary efforts were prodigious, with much of his more important work associated with internationalism.

The *Manuel des lois de la paix: Code de l'arbritrage* (1894) was approved by the International Peace Congress held at Antwerp. Published in 1902, the immense volume, *Pasicrisie internationale: Histoire documentaire des arbitrages internationaux, 1794-1900*, is a source book of 368 documents on arbitration, including agreements, rules of procedure, and case decisions, printed in whole or in part in their original languages. A complementary work, *Histoire sommaire et chronologique des arbitrages internationaux, 1794-1900*, provides commentary on *Pasicrisie*. His exhaustive and carefully edited *Bibliographie de la paix et de l'arbitrage international*, containing 2,222 entries, appeared in 1904. *The Great Solution: Magnissima Charta* (1916) offers a set of principles for organized international relations, not for a «World State which he considered many years away, and sketches a constitution embodying the necessary institutions that would fit the times while preventing future wars. In International Judicature (1915) he outlines the essentials for a supreme court of the world. Not that he was very optimistic at this time.

In the period before World War I, La Fontaine inaugurated an ambitious bibliographical scheme. In 1895, in collaboration with Paul Otlet, he established the Institut international de bibliographie. This House of Documentation, as it came to be called, was a vast informational retrieval scheme, in which he proposed to file, index, and provide information for retrieval on anything of note published anywhere in the world. With the help of a subsidy from the Belgian government, he went some distance in bringing his plan into reality, for the House developed a methodology of universal classification and produced some reference works, particularly bibliographies of social sciences and peace.

From the work of the Institute came the idea for the Union of International Associations, which he founded with Paul Otlet in 1907, and, as secretary-general, directed thereafter. Still located in Brussels, the Union was granted consultative status with the Economic and Social Council of the United Nations in 1951 and with UNESCO in 1952. As the «only centre in the world devoted to documentation, research and promotion of international organizations, particularly the voluntary (nongovernmental) variety and as the publisher of *The Yearbook of International Organizations*, the first of which appeared in 1909, and of a host of reference works of proceedings, documents, bibliographies, directories, and calendars of meetings of international organizations, it carries on in a sophisticated manner the embryonic conceptions of its founder.

La Fontaine's talents and energy led him to explore many interests. A mountaineer, he wrote about climbing, compiled an international bibliography of «Alpinism», and served as president of the Club alpin belge. He translated portions of Wagner's operas, published essays on American libraries and the status of American women, founded the review *La Vie internationale*, lectured to adult education classes on modern movements in the arts, served on the Brussels City Council from 1904 to 1908, and even, in his young manhood, produced a volume of poetry.

Herbert Putnam (September 20, 1861-August 14, 1955) was an American librarian. He was born in New York City, where his father George Palmer Putnam was a noted publisher. He graduated from Harvard in 1883, studied law at Columbia, and was admitted to the bar in 1886. He was librarian at the Minneapolis Athenaeum, 1884-1887, and the Minneapolis Public Library, 1887-1891. He practised law in Boston, 1892-1895, and was librarian of the Boston Public Library, 1895-1899 where he did much to improve that library's collection of photographs. He was appointed elected president of the American Library Association in 1898 and again in 1904, and was appointed Librarian of Congress in 1899 by President William McKinley. He was the first experienced librarian to hold the post. He held the post until 1939 when he retired with the title of librarian emeritus to be succeeded by the poet Archibald MacLeish. Early during his administration, Putnam introduced a new system of classifying books, that continues to this day as the Library of Congress classification. He also established an interlibrary loan system, and expanded the Library of Congress's role and relationships with other libraries, through the provision of centralized services. He became an overseer of Harvard in 1902. He died in Woods Hole, Massachusetts.

Hypatia of Alexandria (b. 370 d. 415) was a neo-Platonic philosopher, mathematician, and teacher who lived in Alexandria, then a Greek settlement. Several works are attributed to her by later sources, including commentaries on Diophantus's *Arithmetica*, on Apollonius's *Conics* and on Ptolemy's works, but none have survived. Letters to her by her pupil Synesius give an idea of her intellectual milieu. She was murdered in March 415 by a Christian mob, led by a cleric named Peter, for reasons which are still debated. She was the daughter of Theon, the last fellow of the Museum of Alexandria, which was adjacent to or included the main Library of Alexandria. Hypatia did not teach in the Museum, but received her pupils in her own private home. Theophilus, the patriarch of Alexandria, had destroyed some "pagan" temples in the city in 391, which may have included the Museum and certainly included the Serapeum (a temple and "daughter library" to the Great Library). In 391, Emperor Theodosius had published an edict which prohibited visiting pagan temples, and Christians in the entire Roman Empire had embarked on an intense campaign to destroy pagan places of worship. Hypatia clearly lived during a power struggle between pagans and tolerant Christians on the one side, and dogmatic Christians who demanded the final destruction of paganism on the other. Hypatia herself was a pagan, but was respected by many Christians, and exalted by some (though by no means all) later Christian authors as a symbol of virtue, often portrayed as a lifelong virgin. These later accounts should not be seen as strict historical records, though, as they often contradict each other. Some insights into the power struggle of the time are granted by the letters written by Synesius of Cyrene, Bishop of Ptolomais, to Hypatia, whom he loved and respected as a teacher. In one of them, he complains about dogmatic thinkers: "Their philosophy consists in a very simple formula, that of calling God to witness, as Plato did, whenever they deny anything or whenever they assert anything. A shadow would surpass these men in uttering anything to the point; but their pretensions are extraordinary." In this letter, he also tells Hypatia that "the same men" had accused him for storing copies of "unrevised copies" of books in his library. This indicates that books were rewritten to suit the prevailing Christian dogma, which may also relate to the difficulty of finding accurate contemporary information about Hypatia's life and death.

Theories range from a local, spontaneous Christian uprising tolerated by the Christian patriarch Cyril of Alexandria over a conflict between Cyril and the more tolerant prefect Orestes to a conspiracy supported by the Emperor himself. Another point of view holds that Hypatia was part of a "rebellion" and her murder unfortunate, but inevitable. With no iron hooks available, Hypatia's death seems to match the prescribed punishment for witchcraft precisely. She may have been the first famous "witch", as was noted by many church-critical authors. In spite of Cyril's probable involvement in, or at least toleration of, her murder, he was later declared a saint. Some authors have used Hypatia's death as a symbol of the repression of reasoned paganism by irrational religion. Included among these authors was the astronomer Carl Sagan, who provided a vivid account of her death and the burning of the Library of Alexandria in his popular science book *Cosmos*.

Imtiaz Ali Khan Arshi Imtiaz Ali Khan was born at Rampur in India on 8 th December 1904. His ancestors were from Afghanistan. Migrating to India, they settled down in Rampur, and served under Faizullah Khan, the Nawab of Rampur as Risaldars. His grandfather was a soldier and a learned teacher of theology. His father served as a Veterinary doctor and was in-charge of the stables of the State of Rampur. Imtiaz Ali Khan and his family were Sunni Muslims. He married Hajira Begum in the year 1933 and had nine children from this marriage.Earlier, he had lost his mother Chammi Begum at the age of three years. He was brought up under the care of his father and stepmother. He commenced his education at the age of five and completed it in the year 1924 in Rampur securing his Honors in Arabic studies. In the next year, he studied the Persian language and passed the course at the end of the academic year of 1925, from Punjab University, Lahore. Later in his career, he acquired knowledge of English, German, and Hindi languages. His teacher Maulana Syed Ahmad Hazrawi was a simple, honest, and a truthful man. He was deeply religious and this had a profound influence in molding the character of Imtiaz Ali Khan. His education had armed him with a complete mastery over the Arabic, Urdu, Persian, and English languages, which would greatly help him in his later years as a writer. He had studied History and Islamic theology and he continued to supplement his knowledge with other studies until the end of his life.

After serving in Nadwatul Ulàma, Lucknow for three months, Imtiaz Ali Khan tried his hand in various business ventures, which were unsuccessful. He finally settled down in Raza Library, at Rampur as its Librarian and Director on 31 July 1932. Apart from running the administration of the library, he passed his time in writing articles and books. He would attend seminars, conferences, functions, where he would be invited to deliver lectures touring different parts of India and abroad.From 1946-49, he became a Principal, in People's College, in Rampur.

He was also a member of a delegation of Indologists to USSR in the year 1958. He was made President of All India Islamic Studies Conference in 1966-67. He attended two seminars in Afghanistan as a representative of India in the years 1967-68.He was a prolific writer and published thirty-seven books. Eleven books were written in Arabic, one book in English, six in Persian, and nineteen in the Urdu language. His books covered a variety of subjects, such as poetry, literature, lexicography, grammar, biographies, travelogues, History, and translations. He also wrote a commentary on the Holy Qur'an, which he called as Tafsir- ul- Qur'an Sawri. In addition, he wrote many articles that touched on many subjects including criticism, philosophy, and scholasticism etc.He occasionally composed poetry and published it under a pen name. He first wrote under the name of Taj and then as Arshi.

He won fame as an author of international repute, He never wrote on any topic until he had with him all the needed books for references on any given subject. His style of writing earned him a number of honors and awards. Prominent awards included the Sahitya Akademi Award (1961), President's Certificate of Honor (1972), and U.P Government's Special Literary Prize (1974). He served the Raza Library as a Director, until his death on 25 th February 1981.

Ina Coolbrith (born Josephine Donna Smith) (March 10, 1841-1928) was a poet and writer, and a prominent and beloved figure in the San Francisco literary community. She was a friend of Samuel Clemens, Bret Harte, Charles Warren Stoddard, and Joaquin Miller, and contributed articles to the influential magazine, the *Overland Monthly*. In 1873 she became librarian at the Oakland Free Library, and, in 1895, befriended and mentored the young Jack London. Jack London called her his "literary mother." In 1915 she was named Poet Laureate of California.

Isaac Casaubon (February 18, 1559 - July 1, 1614) was a classical scholar, first in France then later in England, regarded by many at the time as the most learned in Europe. He was born in Geneva to French refugee parents. The family returned to France with the publication of the Edict of Saint-Germain in 1562, and settled at Crest in Dauphiné, where Arnaud Casaubon, Isaac's father, became minister of a Huguenot congregation. Till he was nineteen, Isaac had no other instruction than what could be given him by his father during the years of civil war. Arnaud was away from home whole years together in the Calvinist camp, or the family were flying to the hills to hide from the fanatical bands of armed Catholics who patrolled the country. Thus it was in a cave in the mountains of Dauphiné, after the massacre of St Bartholomew, that Isaac received his first lesson in Greek, the textbook being Isocrates ad Demonicum. At nineteen Isaac was sent to the Academy of Geneva, where he read Greek under Francis Portus, a native of Crete. Portus died in 1581, having recommended Casaubon, then only twenty-two, as his successor. He remained at Geneva as professor of Greek till 1596. Here he married twice, his second wife being Florence, daughter of the scholar-printer, Henri Estienne.

He was never insensible to the attractions of teaching, and his lectures at Montpellier were followed not only by the students, but by men of mature age and position. But the love of knowledge was gradually growing in him, and he began to see the editing of Greek books as a more suitable job for him than teaching. At Geneva he had produced some notes on Diogenes Laertius, Theocritus and the New Testament, the last undertaken at his father's request. His debut as an editor had been a complete Strabo (1587), of which he was so ashamed afterwards that he apologized to Scaliger for it. This was followed by the text of Polyaenus, an. editio princeps, 1589; a text of Aristotle, 1590; and a few notes contributed to Estienne's editions of

Dionysius of Halicarnassus and Pliny's *Epistolae*. His edition of Theophrastus's *Characteres* (1592), is the first example of that peculiar style of illustrative commentary, at once apposite and profuse, which distinguishes Casaubon among annotators. At the time of his removal to Montpellier he was engaged upon what is the capital work of his life, his edition of, and commentary on, Athenaeus. In 1598 Casaubon was at Lyons, superintending the passage of his Athenaeus through the press, for which he had been unable to find facilities at Montpellier. Here he lived in the house of Méric de Vicq, *surintendant de la justice*, a liberal-minded Catholic. In the suite of de Vicq, Casaubon made a flying visit to Paris, and was presented to King Henry IV of France. The king said something about employing Casaubon's services in the "restoration" of the fallen University of Paris. Full of hope, he returned to Montpellier. In January 1599, he received a summons to return to Paris.

Casaubon remained in Paris till 1610. These ten years were the brightest period of his life. He had attained the reputation of being, after Scaliger, the most learned man of the age, in an age in which learning formed the sole standard of literary merit. He had enough to live on. He had such facilities for religious worship as a Huguenot could have, though he had to go out of the city to Hablon, and afterwards to Charenton, for them. When the assassination of Henry IV gave full rein to the Ultramontane party at court, Duperron became more importunate, and even menacing. It was now that Casaubon began to pay attention to overtures from the bishops and the court of England. In October 1610 he came to England in the suite of the ambassador, Lord Wotton of Marley (brother of Casaubon's early friend), an official invitation having been sent him by Richard Bancroft, Archbishop of Canterbury. He had the most flattering reception from King James I, who was perpetually sending for him to discuss theological matters. The English bishops were equally delighted to find that the great French scholar was a ready-made Anglican, who had arrived, by independent study of the Fathers, at the very *via media* between Puritanism and Romanism which was becoming the fashion in the English Church.

Casaubon, though a layman, was collated to a prebendal stall in Canterbury, and a pension of £300 a year was assigned him from the exchequer. Nor were these merely paper figures. When Sir Julius Caesar made a difficulty about payment, James sent a note in his own hand: "Chanceler of my excheker, In 1613 he was taken to Oxford by Sir Henry Savile, where, amid the homage and feasting of which he was the object, his principal interest was for the manuscript treasures of the Bodleian Library. He declined the honorary degree which was offered him. Besides the editions of ancient authors which have been mentioned, Casaubon published with commentaries Persius, Suetonius, the Scriptores Historiae Augustae.

The edition of Polybius, on which he had spent vast labour, he left unfinished. His most ambitious work was his revision of the text of the *Deipnosophistae* of Athenaeus, with commentary. The *Exercitationes in Baronium* are but a fragment of the massive criticism which he contemplated; it failed in bringing before the reader the uncritical character of Baronius's history, and had only a moderate success, even among the Protestants. His correspondence (in Latin) was finally collected by Van Almeloveen (Rotterdam, 1709), who prefixed to the letters a careful life of Isaac Casaubon. But this learned Dutch editor was acquainted with Casaubon's diary only in extract. This diary, *Ephemerides*, of which the MS. is preserved in the chapter library of Canterbury, was printed in 1850 by the Clarendon Press. It forms the most valuable record we possess of the daily life of a scholar, or man of letters, of the 16th century. His son Méric Casaubon was also a classical scholar.

James Douglas Pearson Professor J. D. (Jim) Pearson was born in 1911. He was a great literary figure in the field of oriental studies mainly the Index Islamicus. He is the founder of *Index Islamicus* , and one of the most eminent, and pioneering, librarians and bibliographers in the field of Islamic studies. Born in December 1911, he grew up and was educated in humble circumstances in Cambridge. First employed in Cambridge University Library at the age of 16 as a book-fetcher, he developed a taste for, and skill in, "exotic" languages, and was awarded a scholarship (for Hebrew) at St John's College. After studying also Arabic and Persian at Pembroke College, he graduated in 1936. He was then employed in the Oriental Section of the Library until 1941, when he was enlisted for war service until 1945. He worked again in Cambridge University Library as an Assistant Under-Librarian from 1945 until 1950.

In 1950 he was appointed Librarian of the School of Oriental and African Studies (SOAS) in London, and from then until 1972 oversaw the drastic expansion and development of the SOAS Library in what were probably the most important years of its history. In the mid-1950s, he decided that, in addition to maintaining the normal catalogue of books, it would be useful also to compile a catalogue of the articles contained in the Library's periodicals and other collective volumes. He reasoned that, in Islamic studies especially, a very important part of the scholarly literature is produced in this form, and that this material is of lasting importance to researchers. If left uncatalogued, much of it, especially in the less obvious sources, would tend to be overlooked, and work would be duplicated. With a team of helpers at SOAS, he eventually compiled a register of more than 25,000 articles in this field, published in the fifty years from 1906 to 1955. Although conceived initially as a catalogue, rather than a bibliography, the holdings of libraries other than SOAS came to be included, and so the obvious next step was to arrange the list in classified form, and to publish it, for the benefit of scholars world-wide. Thus emerged the first *Index Islamicus* , published in 1958, containing details of 26,076 articles.

The volume was well received, and soon found its way onto the reference shelves of nearly all libraries with interests in Islamic and Middle Eastern studies. Pearson was therefore encouraged to continue the project, and a series of supplements was produced. In 1977 he started to issue the bibliography also in quarterly parts, and to record monographs as well as articles, so that the character of a comprehensive bibliography was then assumed. The work became an internationally recognised research tool, and did more than anything to establish Pearson's reputation as a bibliographical scholar

He was also responsible for a number of other reference tools and surveys, most notably *Oriental Manuscripts in Europe and North America* (1971), the *World Bibliographies of African* and *Oriental Bibliographies* (1975), the Supplement to Creswell's *Bibliography of the Architecture, Arts and Crafts of Islam* for 1972-80 (1984) and the series of comprehensive surveys of British archives relating to Asia, Africa and the Middle East (1965-94). He was still working on a further volume (on the Middle East) in this series at the time of his death.

In 1972 he was appointed Senior Fellow, and subsequently Professor of Bibliography with reference to Asia and Africa in the University of London. He retired from this post in 1979 and moved back to his native Cambridge, while still working on *Index Islamicus* . In 1982, after a quarter of a century of devoted work on it, he finally retired from the editorship, and handed over responsibility for its continuation to Cambridge University Library. He continued, however, to devote himself to other bibliographical projects until shortly before his death.

Apart from his own work as librarian and

bibliographer, he was active in encouraging and inspiring colleagues elsewhere in Britain and other countries to follow his lead. In 1967 he took the initiative in establishing the Middle East Libraries Committee (MELCOM)-now MELCOM (UK)-which brought together most British librarians in this field, and gave birth to a long series of major and minor bibliographies and research tools, in several of which Pearson himself actively participated. He was closely involved also in the beginnings of a European dimension to this activity in 1979, resulting eventually in the formation of MELCOM International. An enthusiastic and assiduous traveller, he visited many colleagues, Orientalists and scholars throughout the world, including especially those in MELA. He became well known for his genial conviviality, as well as his practical advice. He died on Friday, 1 August 1997, at the age of 85 when he suffered a stroke. He will be greatly missed and mourned by a wide international circle of friends, companions and collaborators, and by all those who have benefited from his bibliographical legacy.

James Hadley Billington (born June 1, 1929) James Billington was sworn in as the Librarian of Congress on in 1987 as the 13th person to hold the position since the Library was established in 1800. Participants in the ceremony included the congressional leadership, President Ronald Reagan who had nominated Billington, and Chief Justice William H. Rehnquist, who administered the oath on the Library's 1782 Aiken Bible.

Dr. Billington has championed the Library's American Memory National Digital Library (NDL) Program, which makes freely available on-line over 8.5 million American historical items from the collections of the Library and other research institutions. These unique American Memory materials and the Library's other Internet services, which include THOMAS (a congressional database), the on-line "card catalog," exhibitions, information from the U.S. Copyright Office, and a Web site for children and families called America's Library, handled more than 2.6 billion transactions last year. Dr. Billington created the Library's first national private-sector advisory group, the James Madison Council, whose members have supported the NDL Program, many other Library outreach programs, and acquisitions for the Library's collections. In 2000, the Library's bicentennial year, Madison Council Chairman John W. Kluge made the largest monetary donation in the Library's history: $60 million to create within the Library a center for advanced scholars and a Nobel-level prize for lifetime achievement in the humanities or social sciences. Born in Bryn Mawr, Pennsylvania, Dr. Billington was educated in the public schools of the Philadelphia area. He was class valedictorian at both Lower Merion High School and Princeton University, where he graduated with highest honors in 1950. Three years later, he earned his doctorate from Balliol College, Oxford, where he was a Rhodes Scholar. Following service with the U.S. Army and in the Office of National Estimates, he taught history at Harvard University from 1957 to 1962 and subsequently at Princeton University, where he was a professor of history from 1964 to 1974.

From 1973 until his appointment in 1987, Dr. Billington was director of the Woodrow Wilson International Center for Scholars, the nation's official memorial in Washington to America's 28th president. As director, he founded the Kennan Institute for Advanced Russian Studies at the Center and seven other new programs as well as the Wilson Quarterly. Dr. Billington is the author of Mikhailovsky and Russian Populism (1956), The Icon and the Axe (1966), Fire in the Minds of Men (1980), Russia Transformed: Breakthrough to Hope, August 1991 (1992) and The Face of Russia (1998), the companion book to the three-part television series of the same name, which he wrote and narrated for the Public Broadcasting Service. The Icon and the Axe, Fire in the Minds of Men and The Face of Russia have been translated and published in a variety of languages. Dr. Billington has accompanied ten congressional delegations to Russia and the former Soviet Union. In June 1988 he accompanied President Ronald Reagan to the Soviet Summit in Moscow. He is the founder of the Open World Program and Chairman of the Board of Trustees of the Open World Leadership Center. The Open World Program is a nonpartisan initiative of the U.S. Congress that has brought 6,265 emerging young Russian political leaders to communities throughout America.

Dr. Billington has received 33 honorary degrees, as well as the Woodrow Wilson Award from Princeton University (1992), the UCLA Medal (1999), and the Pushkin Medal of the International Association of the Teachers of Russian Language and Culture (2000). Most recently he was awarded honorary doctorates from the University of Tbilisi in Georgia (1999) and the Moscow State University for the Humanities (2001). He received an honorary doctorate from the University of Oxford in November 2002. Dr. Billington is an elected member of the Russian Academy of Sciences, and has been decorated as Chevalier and again as a Commander of the Order of Arts and Letters of France, as Commander of the National Order of the Southern Cross of Brazil, awarded the Order of Merit of Italy, and a Knight Commander's Cross of the Order of Merit by the Federal Republic of Germany. He has also been awarded the Gwanghwa Medal by the Republic of Korea, and the Chingiz Aitmatov Gold Medal by the Kyrgyz Republic. Dr. Billington was a longtime member of the editorial advisory boards of Foreign Affairs and of Theology Today, and a member of the Board of Foreign Scholarships (1971-76; Chairman, 1973-1975), which has executive responsibility for academic exchanges worldwide under the Fulbright-Hays Act. He is on the Board of the John F. Kennedy Center for the Performing Arts and is a member of the American Philosophical Society and of the American Academy of Arts and Sciences. Dr. Billington is married to the former Marjorie Anne Brennan. They have four children: Dr. Susan Billington Harper, Anne Billington Fischer, the Rev. James Hadley Billington Jr., and Thomas Keator Billington, and 11 grandchildren

James, Thomas see Thomas James

Jan Gruter (or Gruytere; Latinized Janus Gruterus) (December 3, 1560 - September 20, 1627), was a critic and scholar of the Netherlands. He was Dutch on his father's side and English on his mother's, and was born at Antwerp. To avoid religious persecution his parents came to England while he was a child; and for some years he studied at Cambridge, after which he went to Leiden, where he graduated with an M.A. In 1586 he was appointed professor of history at the University of Wittenberg, but as he refused to subscribe the formula concordiae he lost his position. From 1589 to 1592 he taught at Rostock, after which he went to Heidelberg, where in 1602 he was appointed librarian to the university. Gruter's chief works were his Inscriptiones antiquae totius orbis Romani (2 vols., Heidelberg, 1603), and Lampas, sive fax artium liberalium (7 vols., Frankfort, 1602-1634).

Johann Albert Fabricius (November 11, 1668 - April 30, 1736), was a German classical scholar and bibliographer. He was born at Leipzig. He studied under JG Herrichen, and afterwards at Quedlinburg under Samuel Schmid. It was in Schmid's library, as he afterwards said, that he found the two books, F Barth's Adversaria and DG Morhof's Polyhistor Literarius, which suggested to him the idea of his Bibliothecæ, the works on which his great reputation was founded. Having returned to Leipzig in 1686, he published anonymously (two years later) his first work, Scriptorum recentiorum decas, an attack on ten writers of the day. His Decas Decadum, sive plagiariorum et pseudonymorum centuria (1689) is the only one of his works to which he signs the name Faber. He then applied himself to the study of medicine, which, however, he relinquished for that of theology; and having gone to Hamburg in 1693, he proposed to travel abroad, when the unexpected tidings that the expense of his education had absorbed his whole patrimony, and even left him in debt to his trustee, forced him to abandon his project. He therefore remained at Hamburg in the capacity of librarian to JF Mayer.

In 1696 he accompanied his patron to Sweden; and on his return to Hamburg, not long afterwards, he becamea candidate for the chair of logic and philosophy. The suffrages being equally divided between Fabricius and Sebastian Edzardus, one of his opponents, the appointment was decided by lot in favour of Edzardus; but in 1699 Fabricius succeeded Vincent Placcius in the chair of rhetoric and ethics, a post which he held till his death, refusing invitations to Greifswald, Kiel, Giessen and Wittenberg. He died at Hamburg. Fabricius is credited with 128 books, but very many of them were only books which he had edited. One of the most famed and laborious of these is the Bibliotheca Latina (1697, republished in an improved and amended form by JA Ernesti, 1773). The divisions of the compilation are—the writers to the age of Tiberius; thence to that of the Antonines; and thirdly, to the decay of the language; a fourth gives fragments from old authors, and chapters on early Christian literature. A supplementary work was Bibliotheca Latina mediae et infimae Aetatis (1734-1736; supplementary volume by C Schottgen, 1746; ed. Mansi, 1754). His chef-d'oeuvre, however, is the Bibliotheca Graeca (1705-1728, revised and continued by GC Harles, 1790—1812), a work which has justly been denominated maximus antiquae eruditionis thesaurus. Its divisions are marked off by Homer, Plato, Jesus, Constantine, and the capture of Constantinople in 1453, while a sixth section is devoted to canon law, jurisprudence and medicine. Of his remaining works we may mention: Bibliotheca Antiquaria, an account of the writers whose works illustrated Hebrew, Greek, Roman and Christian antiquities (1713); Centifolium Lutheranum, a Lutheran bibliography (1728); Bibliotheca Ecclesiastica (1718). His Codex Apocryphus (1703) is still considered indispensable as an authority on apocryphal Christian literature. The details of the life of Fabricius are to be found in De Vita et Scriptis J.A. Fabricii Commentarius, by his son-in-law, HS Reimarus, the well-known editor of Dio Cassius, published at Hamburg, 1737; see also C.F. Bähr in Ersch and Gruber's Allgemeine Encyclopaedie, and JE Sandys, Hist. Class. Schol. iii. (1908).

Johann Matthias Gesner (April 9, 1691 - August 3, 1761), was a German classical scholar and schoolmaster. He was born at Roth an der Rednitz near Ansbach. He studied at the University of Jena, and in 1714 published a work on the Philopatiis ascribed to Lucian. In 1715 he became librarian and vice-principal at Weimar, Germany, where he became good friends with Johann Sebastian Bach in 1729 rector of the gymnasium at Ansbach, and in 1730 rector of the Thomas school at Leipzig. On the foundation of the University of Göttingen he became professor of rhetoric (1734) and subsequently librarian. He died at Göttingen. His special merit lies in the attention he devoted to the explanation and illustration of the subject matter of the classical authors.

John Gould Stephenson (March 1, 1828-November 12, 1882) was the fifth United States Librarian of Congress, serving from 1861 to 1864. Stephenson was born in Lancaster, New Hampshire. After training at the New Hampshire Medical Institution and the Castleton Medical College, he moved to Terre Haute, Indiana. Active in Republican Party politics, President Abraham Lincoln appointed him to the post of Librarian of Congress, replacing John Silva Meehan. The historical record is unclear why a physician sought appointment to this post. Stephenson spent most of his time serving as a Colonel in the Union Army during the Civil War, first with the 19th Indiana Regiment and later with the Army of the Potomac, participating in the Battles of Fitzhugh Crossing, Chancellorsville, and Gettysburg. His most significant act was appointing Ainsworth Rand Spofford as Chief Assistant Librarian. Spofford would later become Librarian himself and was responsible for the transition of the Library from Congressional resource to national institution. Following his resignation in 1864, Stephenson held several political jobs, including medical reviewer at the Pension Office.

John James Beckley (August 4, 1757-April 8, 1807) was the first U.S. Librarian of Congress, serving from 1802 to 1807. Born in England, at age 11 he was sent to Virginia to work as a scribe for a mercantile firm. He was a political ally of President Thomas Jefferson and Jefferson appointed Beckley to the dual post of Clerk of the United States House of Representatives and Librarian of Congress. (The posts were not separated until 1815.) His son Alfred Beckley founded the town of Beckley, West Virginia and named it in honor of his father.

John Russell Young (November 20, 1840-January 17, 1899) an American journalist, author, diplomat, and the seventh Librarian of Congress, serving from 1897 to 1899. Young was born in County Tyrone, Ireland, but as a young child his family emigrated to Philadelphia. He entered the newspaper business as a proofreader at age 15. As a reporter for the Philadelphia Press, he distinguished himself with his coverage of the Battle of Bull Run. By 1862 he was managing editor of the Press and another newspaper. In 1865 he moved to New York. He began writing for 's New York Tribune and became managing editor of that paper. He also began working for the government, undertaking missions to Europe for the US Department of State and the US Department of the Treasury.

In 1872, he joined the New York Herald and reported for them from Europe. Young was invited to accompany

President Ulysses S. Grant on Grant's famous 1877-1879 world tour, chronicled in Young's book Around the World with General Grant. Young impressed Grant, especially in China where Young struck up a friendship with Li Hongzhang. Grant persuaded President Chester A. Arthur to appoint Young minister to China in 1882. In this position he distinguished himself by mediating and settling disputes between the US and China and France and China. In 1885 he resumed working for the Herald in Europe. In 1890 he returned to Philadelphia.

In 1897 President William McKinley appointed him Librarian of Congress, the first Librarian confirmed by Congress. During his tenure, the Library began moving from its original home in the US Capitol Building to its own structure, an accomplishment largely the responsibility of his predecessor, Ainsworth Rand Spofford. Spofford served as Chief Assistant Librarian under Young. Young held the post of Librarian until his death. His brother was Congressman James Rankin Young.

John Silva Meehan (February 6, 1790-April 24, 1863) was the fourth United States Librarian of Congress, serving from 1829 to 1861. Meehan was a Democratic printer and publisher appointed Librarian of Congress by President Andrew Jackson, replacing in the post the Whig activist George Watterston, who opposed Jackson. However, Meehan's tenure was a conservative one and he and his Congressional supporters advocated limits on the size of the Library. Many of the Library's functions were transferred to other government agencies. When a fire destroyed 35,000 volumes in 1851, including two-thirds of the materials originally provided by President Thomas Jefferson, the money provided by Congress for restoration was used solely for replacing lost materials and not for expansion. Meehan did provide a small collection of periodicals for Congressional perusal which, under later Librarians, became the periodicals division. Meehan served under nine presidents. Despite Congressional opposition,

President Abraham Lincoln replaced Meehan with a Republican supporter, John G. Stephenson.

Jorge Luis Borges (August 24, 1899 – June 14, 1986) was an Argentine writer who is considered to be one of the foremost writers of the 20th century. A poet and an essayist, Borges is generally best-known for his short stories. Borges was born in Buenos Aires. His father, Jorge Guillermo Borges, was a lawyer and a psychology teacher, who also had literary aspirations ("he tried to become a writer and failed in the attempt," Borges once said. "He composed some very good sonnets"). Borges's mother, Leonor Acevedo Suárez, was a translator. His father's family was part Italian, Spanish, Portuguese, and British; his mother's Spanish, Catalan, and possibly Portuguese. At his home, both Spanish and English were spoken, so from earliest childhood Borges was effectively bilingual, and learned to read in English before Spanish. He grew up in the suburban neighborhood of Palermo in a large house with an extensive library. Borges's name in full was Jorge Francisco Isidoro Luis Borges Acevedo, but he never used the entire name.

Jorge Guillermo Borges was forced into early retirement from the legal profession owing to the same failing eyesight that would eventually afflict his son, and in 1914, the family moved to Geneva, where Borges senior was treated by a Geneva eye specialist while Borges and his sister Norah (born 1902) attended school. Borges's first collection of poetry was *Fervor de Buenos Aires* (1923). He contributed to the avant-garde review *Martín Fierro* (whose "art for art's sake" approach contrasted to that of the more politically-involved Boedo group), co-founded the journals *Prisma* (1921 - 1922, a broadsheet distributed largely by pasting copies to walls in Buenos Aires) and *Proa* (1922 - 1926). He was, from the first issue, a regular contributor to *Sur*, founded in 1931, by Victoria Ocampo, which became Argentina's most important literary journal. Ocampo herself introduced Borges to Adolfo Bioy Casares, who was to become Borges's frequent collaborator and Ocampo's brother-in-law, and another well-known figure of Argentine literature.

Borges's father died in 1938, a great blow because the two were very close. At New Year's 1939, Borges suffered a severe head wound in an accident; during treatment for that wound, he nearly died of blood poisoning. While recovering from the accident, he began writing in a style he became famous for, and his first collection of short stories, *El jardín de senderos que se bifurcan* (*The Garden of Forking Paths*) appeared in 1941.

Starting in 1937, Borges began working at the Miguel Cané branch of the Buenos Aires Municipal Library as a first assistant. When Juan Perón came to power in 1946 he was effectively fired, being "promoted" to the position of "Poultry and Rabbit Inspector" for the Buenos Aires municipal market (from which he immediately resigned). His offenses against the Peronistas up to that time had apparently consisted of little more than adding his signature to pro-democratic petitions, but shortly after his resignation he addressed the Argentine Society of Letters saying, in his characteristic style, "Dictatorships foster oppression, dictatorships foster servitude, dictatorships foster cruelty; more abominable is the fact that they foster idiocy." Left without a job, his vision beginning to fade, and unable to fully support himself as a writer, Borges began a new career as a public lecturer. Despite a certain amount of political persecution, he was reasonably successful, and became an increasingly public figure, obtaining appointments as President (1950 - 1953) of the Argentine Society of Writers and as Professor of English and American Literature (1950 - 1955) at the Argentine Association of English Culture. His short story Emma Zunz was turned into a film (under the name of Días de odio, which in English became Days of Wrath) in 1954 by Argentine director Leopoldo Torre Nilsson. Around this time, Borges also began writing screenplays.

Justin Winsor (January 2, 1831-October 22, 1897) was a prominent American writer, librarian, and historian. He was born in Boston, Massachusetts, and graduated from the Boston Latin School. He entered Harvard, but left early to study in Paris and Heidelberg. He did finally receive his degree in 1853. He died in Cambridge, Massachusetts. Justin Winsor published his first book, A History of the Town of Duxbury, during his first year at Harvard. He contributed to many periodicals, and, in addition to editing many smaller works, he edited some of the most important historical works of the 19th century. Among them; Reader's Handbook of American History (1879), The Memorial History of Boston (4 vols., 1880-81) and the Narrative and Critical History of America (8 vols., 1884-89). The latter was the standard history reference for most of the next century. He served as Trustee of the Boston Public Library, 1867-1868, and Superintendent, 1868-1877. In 1877 he was appointed Librarian of Harvard University and served there until his death. He was a founder of the American Library Association and of the Library Journal. He served as president of the ALA from 1876 through 1885. The Library History Round Table of that organization awards the Justin Winsor Prize, established in 1978, for exceptional library history essays. Justin Winsor was a founding member of the American Historical Association and served as the president during the 1886-1887 term. The Justin Winsor Prize was the first prize established by the AHA and was awarded from 1896 through 1930 and from 1936 through 1938.

Kaul, H.K. Dr. H. K. Kaul (Hari Krishen Kaul) was born in 1941 in Srinagar, Kashmir. After completing his graduation, he worked as a researcher in Yoga at the Lakshmibai College of Physical Education, Gwalior, Madhaya Pradesh. for one year in 1965. Subsequently he took his Bachelors Degree in Library Science from Rajasthan University in 1967 and Masters in Library Science from the University of Bombay in 1992 securing

First Class First. Later he completed his Ph. D. in Library and Information Science in 1999 from the University of Pune.

Dr. Kaul joined the India International Centre Library in 1967 and later in 1972 he took charge of the Library. In the1970s Dr. Kaul organised national level exhibitions on *India Through the Eyes of European Artists; Travels in India* and *Customs of India*. Along with the exhibitions Dr. Kaul organised Workshops for Asian and African Writers as the Project Director. These projects were sponsored by the Ministry of Education, Government of India.

In January 1988 Dr. Kaul was responsible for initiating the establishment of Delhi Library Network (DELNET). He became the Founding Director of DELNET. As DELNET became a national network of libraries, its name was slightly modified as DELNET – Developing Library Network. DELNET has 200 institutions as its members in 20 States in India and five countries outside India. DELNET became the first operational library network in India and has now become a major library network in South Asia.

Dr. Kaul has authored, edited and written more than 30 books, almost one book per year ever since his first book entitled *Sri Aurobindo: A Descriptive Bibliography* was published in 1972. He has contributed on themes such as Bibliographical Works, Library Networking, Literature, Library Science, Historical and Travel Literature and Yoga. His important titles include *Early Writings on India* (1975); *Travels in South Asia* (1975); *Travellers' India* (1979); *Historic Delhi* (1985); *Library Networks : An Indian Experience* (1992); *Firdaus in Flames* (An epic poem on Kashmir 1995); *Library Resource Sharing and Networks* (1999) including edited volumes of *Library and Information Networking* and edited volumes of *Poetry India*.

Dr. Kaul had been the Project Director of various

projects sponsored by the Government of India. He has been a member of various important national Committees and Commissions appointed by the Government of India including Indian National Commission for UNESCO; Expert Group for Strengthening the Library System in India; Networking Group on Libraries and Informatics, Ninth Five Year Plan; Advisory Board, National Library; Raja Rammohan Roy Library Board; Delhi Public Library Board etc.

A widely travelled person in India and abroad for various professional assignments, Dr. Kaul received the D. N. Marshall Felicitation Prize (1992); Senior Fellowship of the Department of Culture, Government of India (1997-1999); Best Librarian Award of DBPA (1999) and Punjab Librarian Award (2000).

Kaula, Prithvi Nath Professor Prithvi Nath Kaula is a living legendary figure in library and information science. He was born at Srinagar in India in 1924 where he studied and started his service career as Librarian, DAV College, Srinagar in 1944. After three years of service he shifted to Pillani as Chief Librarian, Birla Central Library where he stayed for a short time. Prof. Kaula worked with many libraries till 1958.

In 1958, he was appointed as Reader, Department of Library Science of the Delhi University after which he joined the Banaras Hindu University as University Librarian and Head of the Department of Library Science. He was actively involved in the University administration as Head of the Department and Dean, Faculty of Arts.

Prof Kaula has been associated with a large number of library and information science institutions of the country and abroad in various capacities such as Professor Emeritus, Kashi Vidyapeeth and Lucknow University, visiting Professor in 36 universities of India and more than 24 foreign universities, UNESCO expert, Regional Centre in Western Hemisphere, Havana, Cuba, 67-68. life member,

Indian Library Association, Indian Association of Special Libraries and Information Centres, Delhi Library Association, U.P. Library Association, President, Indian Association of Teachers of Library and Information Science from 1973-1985, Federation of Indian Library Associations 66-83.

The contribution of Professor Kaula has been recognized at the International level and he has been associated with many international bodies in the field of library and information science. He has been an expert member of the National and international bodies like FID, IFLA,ISO,UNRSCO, National Library, Kolkata, Review Committee, UGC, ISO, Bureau for Promotion of Urdu, Library Science Terminology Committee, Raja Ram Mohan Roy Foundation., National Policy on Library and Information Science, Chairmain, Panel on Library and Information Science

Professor Kaula has to his credit a large number of publications. From the beginning of his career in library science, he remained active in publication work. He was Managing Editor of Annals Bulletin and Granthalaya of the Indian Library Association, Editor, Sarada, 53-55, Library Herald, 58-61; Herald of Library Science since 62, Granthalaya Vijnana, since 1970, International Information Communication and Education since 1982, Progress in Library and Information Science, 79-83. He has authored about five dozen books, 43 bibliographies, over 300 technical papers, 400 book reviews and over 2 dozen development plans.

Professor Kaula has been honoured by International Festschrift Committee in 1974 and 1982, awarded Prof Mundi Benet Medal from Brazilian Academy of Humanities, 1975, Indian Library Movement Award, 1974, Plaque from International Bibliographic Centre, Cambridge, Deutsche Bucheri Medal, 81, International Roll of Honour, Plaque, 82, Gold Medal of Honour, 87. He has established Kaula Endowment for Library and information

Science in 1975. Recently, Professor Kaula has been awarded with the prestigious award of Padams Shree by the Government of India in recognition of the great contribution. He has made to library and information science.

Kenneth MacLean Glazier, Sr. (September 21, 1912 - November 11, 1989) was a Canadian minister and librarian. He was minister of Glenview Presbyterian Church in Toronto before working at the Hoover Institution at Stanford University and eventually serving as chief librarian of the University of Calgary Library. While at the University of Calgary he founded the Kenneth M. Glazier Collection of the papers of Canadian authors, including those of Hugh MacLennan and Mordecai Richler. He also funded the Kenneth Maclean Glazier Scholarship for the study of Canadian literature at the university. He himself was the author of Africa South of the Sahara: A Select & Annotated Bibliography, 1964-1968. He was also Secretary of the Liberal Party in Alberta. He died of a heart attack in Calgary. It is important to distinguish him from his son Kenneth MacLean Glazier, Jr., a California attorney, who usually goes by "Kenneth M. Glazier" or "Kenneth MacLean Glazier."

Khuda Bakhsh Khan Born at Chapra in India on 2nd August 1842, Khuda Bakhsh was brought up under the guidance of his father who dedicated his life for the betterment of humanity. Educated at Patna and Calcutta he started his professional career as Peshkar. In 1880 he was appointed the Government Pleader of Patna and in 1881 the title of Khan Bahadur was conferred upon him for his social service. He was elevated to the post of Chief Justice of Nizam's Court Hyderabad for a period of three years in 1895.

He was also honoured with another title in 1903. In spite of having all these titles and honours he was a very simple man with determination and vision. The library was his life-long achievement for which he was committed and devoted. He spent whatever he earned on its growth and as a result he was penniless. He had to borrow money for his medical treatment. The Government of Bengal made him a generous grant of Rs. 8,000 to liquidate his debts. He died on 3rd August 1908 at the age of 66, and was buried in the premises of the Library.

La Fontaine, Hanri see Henri La Fonraine

Larkin, Philip see Philip Larkin

Larry Page is one of the founders of Google internet search engine. Larry Page has a Bachelor of Science in engineering, with a concentration on computer engineering, from the University of Michigan and a Masters from Stanford University. He is a graduate of East Lansing High School. Page has a Bachelor of Science degree in computer engineering from the University of Michigan and a Masters degree from Stanford University.

Larry Page is the son of Carl Vincent Page, a professor of computer science at Michigan State University and Gloria Page, a computer programming teacher. While a student in the Ph.D. program in computer science at Stanford University, Page met Sergey Brin. Together they developed and ran the Google search engine, which began operating in 1998. Google is based on patented PageRank technology, which relies on the structure of links between web sites to determine the ranking of an individual site. Page is still "on leave" from the Ph.D. program.

Page ran Google as co-president with Brin until 2001, when they hired Eric Schmidt to become Chairman and CEO of Google. Page now runs Google as a triumvirate along with Brin and Schmidt. Page and co-founder Sergey Brin are estimated to be worth $11 billion apiece. The two have recently purchased the very large passenger plane Boeing 767 for their private use.

Laura Welch Bush (born Laura Lane Welch November 4, 1946) is the wife of President George W. Bush and serves as First Lady of the United States. Laura Lane

Welch was born in Midland, Texas, the only child of Harold and Jenna Welch. She was a very popular student at school and attended the same high school as Tommy Franks. After graduating, she became a schoolteacher at Longfellow Elementary School in Dallas Independent School District until 1969. She then taught at John F. Kennedy Elementary School, a Houston Independent School District school in Houston, until 1972. Bush earned a Master of Science degree in Library Science in 1973 from the University Texas in Austin. She is the second First Lady (after Hillary Clinton) to hold a post graduate degree. After that, she worked at the Kashmere Gardens Branch at the Houston Public Library, until 1974, when she moved back to Austin. She was a librarian at an Austin Independent School District school, Dawson Elementary School, until 1977. She met George W. Bush in 1977 at the home of mutual friends and married him on November 5 of that year. In 1981, she gave birth to twin daughters, Barbara and Jenna, now graduated from college.

Laura became the first lady of Texas when her husband George was elected as the Governor of Texas and served as first lady of that state from 1995 to 2000. After the outcome of the 2000 Presidential Election was finally resolved in December 2000, George Bush resigned as Texas Governor to prepare for his inauguration as President of the United States in January 2001; Laura then became the First Lady of the United States. As First Lady of the United States, she has championed education causes and women's health issues, and launched the first National Book Festival. She also worked for women's and children's causes while she was the First Lady of Texas, when she established the Adopt-a-Caseworker Program and the Rainbow Room program. Bush has taken a decidedly less prominent role in policy-making than her predecessors. Following the September 11, 2001 attacks Bush took an interest in mitigating the emotional effects of the attacks on children, which were disturbing particularly as the images were repeatedly replayed on TV. Many schools closed early, especially those with children whose parents worked in Washington, D.C. and NYC. The following day, after consulting with many experts, Bush commented to parents that it was not good for children to be exposed to the numerous replays of the incidents, and that parents should consider turning off the television. She also composed open letters which were distributed by state education officials. A "Dear Students" letter went to middle and high school students. In November 2001, she became the first person other than a president to deliver the weekly presidential radio address. She used the opportunity to discuss the plight of women in Afghanistan during the U.S. invasion of Afghanistan. In May 2002, she made a speech to the people of Afghanistan through Radio Liberty, a radio station in Prague, Czech Republic.

Lawrence Quincy Mumford (December 11, 1903 - August 15, 1982) was a U.S. librarian. He was the Librarian of Congress between 1954 and 1974. Nominated by President Dwight D. Eisenhower, Mumford is the only librarian by academic training (a B.S. in library science) to ever serve as Librarian of Congress. Mumford, a graduate of Columbia University, was director of the Cleveland Public Library and president of the American Library Association.

Leibniz,Gottfried Wilhelm von (July 1, 1646 in Leipzig - November 14, 1716 in Hannover) was a German philosopher, scientist, mathematician, diplomat, librarian, and lawyer of Sorb descent. Leibniz is credited with the term "function" (1694), which he used to describe a quantity related to a curve; such as a curve's slope or a specific point of said curve. Leibniz is generally, with Newton, jointly credited for the development of modern calculus; in particular, for his development of the integral and the product rule. He was born in Leipzig. Intellectually precocious, he went up to the University of Leipzig at the age of fifteen to read law, obtaining his baccalaureate in

1663. In 1666 the University declined to confer the degree of doctor of law upon him, owing to his youth, and he went instead to the University of Altdorf, where his dissertation gained him not only the doctorate, but the offer of a professorship.

Leibniz constructed the first mechanical calculator capable of multiplication and division. He also developed the modern form of the binary numeral system, used in digital computers. Some find it interesting to consider what might have resulted if Leibniz had combined his findings in binary arithmetic with those developments he made in mechanical calculation. Although there is some question of original authorship, Leibniz is credited along with Isaac Newton with inventing the infinitesimal calculus in the 1670s. According to his notes, a critical breakthrough in his work here occurred on November 11, 1675, when he demonstrated integral calculus for the first time to find the area under the y=x function. He introduced several notations used in calculus to this day, for instance the integral sign ? representing an elongated S from the Latin word summa and the d used for differentials from the Latin word differentia. Leibniz thought symbols to be very important for the understanding of things. He also tried to develop an alphabet of human thought, in which he tried to represent all fundamental concepts using symbols and combined these symbols to represent more complex thoughts. Leibniz never finished this.

Leibniz is believed to be the first person to suggest that the concept of feedback was useful for explaining many phenomena in many different fields of study. With regard to the first principle, the number of simple ideas is much greater than Leibniz thought; and, with regard to the second principle, logic considers three operations which are now known as logical multiplication, logical addition, and negation instead of only one. Characters were, with Leibniz any written signs, and "real" characters were those which as in the Chinese ideography represent ideas directly, and not the words for them. Among real characters, some simply serve to represent ideas, and some serve for reasoning. Egyptian and Chinese hieroglyphics and the symbols of astronomers and chemists belong to the first category, but Leibniz declared them to be imperfect, and desired the second category of characters for what he called his universal characteristic. It was not in the form of an algebra that Leibniz first conceived his characteristic, probably because he was then a novice in mathematics, but in the form of a universal language or script. It was in 1676 that he first dreamed of a kind of algebra of thought, and it was the algebraic notation which then served as model for the characteristic. Leibniz attached so much importance to the invention of proper symbols that he attributed to this alone the whole of his discoveries in mathematics.

Leiteritz, Margaret see Margaret Leiteritz

Li Dazhao (1888 - 1927) was a Chinese intellectual who cofounded the Communist Party of China with Chen Duxiu in 1921. Li was born in Hebei province to a peasant family. From 1913 to 1917 Li studied political economy at Waseda University in Japan before returning to China in 1918. As head librarian at the Peking University Library, he was among the first of the Chinese intellectuals who supported the Bolshevik government in the Soviet Union. Mao Zedong was an assistant librarian during Li's tenure at the library and Li was one of Mao's earliest and most prominent influences.

By many accounts, Li was a nationalist and believed that the peasantry in China were to play an important role in China's revolution. As with many intellectuals of his time, the roots of Li's revolutionary thinking were actually mostly in Kropotkin's communist anarchism, but after the events of the May Fourth Movement and the failures of the anarchistic experiments of many intellectuials, like his compatriots, he turned more towards Marxism. Under the leadership of Li and Chen, the CPC developed a close relationship with the Comintern. At the direction of the

Comintern, Li and Chen were inducted into the Kuomintang in 1922. Li was elected to the KMT's Central Executive Committee in 1924. Tensions between the Comintern, the KMT, and the CPC presented opportunities for political intrigue and opportunism. With the outbreak of the Chinese Civil War, Li was captured during a raid on the Soviet embassy in Guangdong and, with nineteen others, he was executed by strangulation on the orders of the Manchurian general Chang Tso-lin in April 1927.

Ludovico Antonio Muratori (1672 - 1750) was an Italian historian, notable as a leading scholar of his age, and for his discovery of the Muratorian fragment, the earliest known list of New Testament books. Born at Vignola and ordained a priest, he spent much of his career as archivist and librarian at the ducal library in Modena, where he died. He edited the Rerum Italicarum scriptores (28 vol., 1723 – 1751) and Antiquitates Italicae medii aevii (6 vol., 1738–1742), both of which are important collections of sources, and wrote a history of Italy (1744 - 1749) in 12 volumes. In 1950, Italy issued a postage stamp honoring him on the 200th anniversary of his death.

Ludwig Bechstein (November 24, 1801 - May 14, 1860) was a German writer and collector of folk fairy tales. He was born in Weimar, the illegitimate child of Johanna Carolina Dorothea Bechstein and Hubert Dupontreau, a French emigrant who disappeared even before the birth of the child, and Ludwig thus grew up his first nine years in very poor economic conditions. His situation improved only when his uncle Johann Matthäus Bechstein, a renowned naturalist and forester living in Meiningen in the district of Schmalkalden-Meiningen in Thuringia, adopted him in 1810. He was sent to school, and in 1818, started an apprenticeship as an pharmacist. From 1829 to 1831 he studied philosophy and literature in Leipzig and Munich thanks to a stipendiate granted by Duke Bernhard II of Sachsen-Meiningen, who hired him subsequently as a librarian. This life-time post provided Bechstein with a continuous income, while leaving him a lot of freedom to pursue his own interests and writing. Bechstein published many works and was a successful author of his time. He published several collections of folk tales, but also romances, poems, and novels.

Luther H. Evans (October 13, 1902-December 23, 1981) was an American political scientist and public administrator. Evans was born in Sayersville, Bastrop County, Texas. He organized and directed the Historical Records Survey for the Works Project Administration. After this, he was appointed by Librarian of Congress Archibald MacLeish as head of the Legislative Reference Service and later Chief Assistant Librarian of Congress. After MacLeish resigned, president Harry S. Truman appointed Evans as his successor, a position he held from 1945 to 1953. During his tenure, Evans opposed censorship of the library's holdings, and greatly expanded the library's collection. Well versed in international relations, he also returned a number of manuscripts to their countries of origin. He also served with various US delegations during the forming of UNESCO. In 1953 he resigned from the Library to accept a position as UNESCO's third director-general. He died in San Antonio, Texas

Lynne Brindley, is Chief Executive of the British Library since 2000. She was a member of the Lord Chancellor's Advisory Committee on Public Records from 1992 - 98, and has served with many other committees concerned with information services as well as advisory bodies for UNESCO and Stanford University. She was elected a Freeman of the City of London in 1989.

Major Robert Odell Owens (born June 28, 1936) is a New York politician. Owens was born in Collierville, Tennessee. He has a bachelor's degree from Morehouse College and a master of science degree from Atlanta University. Owens was a librarian before entering politics. He was elected to the New York state senate in 1974 as a Democrat. In 1982, he was elected to the House of

Represenatives replacing the retiring Shirley Chisholm. One of his achievements in the House was the passage of the Americans with Disabilities Act. Although Owens won the Democratic primary with just 45% of the vote, he was re-elected in 2004 with 94% of the vote. He plans to retire from the House at the end of his term in 2007.

Mangla, P.B. Professor P. B. Mangla is one of the great librarians of our time. He was born in July 1936 and received his education in India and abroad. Prof. Mangal was appointed lecturer in History, Government College, Nabha in 1958 but the next year he opted to teach library science in the University of Delhi. He was elevated to the post of Reader in the same institution in 1966 and worked as the Dean of the Faculty of Arts and Prof. and Head of the Department of Library Science in the University. Prof. Mangla has worked with international organizations such as the UNESCO expert, Guyana, 1978-80. He was the National lecrurer, University Grants Commission, 1984-86.

Professor Mangla has been associated with many professional bodies championing the cause of library and information science in the country and abroad. He was president of the Indian Library Association from 1981 to 83, Chairman, Board of Research and Stidies (Humanities) 1979-87. Governing Body, Deshbanndhu College, 1990-94. He was Vice President of the International Federation of Library Associations from 1987-1991. Special Advisor, IFLA Standing Committee for Asia and Oceana since 1987, Library Consultant, Reserve Bank of India, Mumbai since 1992.

Professor Mangla has been on the Editorial Boards of a number of reputed publications including Education for Information, International Journal of Reviews in Library and Information Science (Chicago), Chairman, Board of Editors, Journal of Library and Information Science. He has also been awarded for his excellent work by Shiromani Award in 1991 and Lifetime Achievement Award by Punjab Library Association 1n 1997.

Mao Zedong (December 26, 1893—September 9, 1976) was the chairman of the Communist Party of China from 1935 until his death. During the 1911 Revolution he served in the Hunan provincial army. In the 1910s, Mao returned to school, where he became an advocate of physical fitness and collective action. After graduation from Hunan Normal School in 1918, Mao travelled with his high-school teacher and future father-in-law, Professor Yang Changji to Beijing during the May Fourth Movement, when Yang lectured at *Peking University*. From Yang's recommendations, he worked under Li Dazhao, the head of the university library and attended speeches by Chen Duxiu. While working for the Peking University library as an assistant librarian, Mao acquired a taste for books, something he was to retain in later years. Also in Beijing, he married his first wife, Yang Kaihui, a Peking University student and the daughter of Mao's high-school teacher. At age 27, Mao attended the First Congress of the Communist Party of China in Shanghai in July 1921. Two years later he was elected to the Central Committee of the party at the Third Congress.

Mao was removed from his important positions and replaced by individuals (including Zhou Enlai) who appeared loyal to the orthodox line advocated by Moscow and represented within the CPC by a group known as the 28 Bolsheviks. Chiang Kai-shek, who had earlier assumed nominal control of China due in part to the Northern Expedition, was determined to eliminate the Communists. To evade the KMT forces, the Communists engaged in the "Long March", a retreat from Jiangxi in the southeast to Shaanxi in the northwest of China. It was during this 9600-km, year-long journey that Mao emerged as the top Communist leader, aided by the Zunyi Conference and the defection of Zhou Enlai to Mao's side. From his base in Yan'an, Mao led the Communist resistance against the

Japanese in the Sino-Japanese War (1937-1945). Mao further consolidated power over the Communist Party in 1942 by launching the Cheng Feng, or "Rectification" campaign against rival CPC members such as Wang Ming, Wang Shiwei, and Ding Ling. Also while in Yan'an, Mao divorced He Zizhen and married the actress Lan Ping, who would become known as Jiang Qing. During the Sino-Japanese War, Mao Zedong's strategies were opposed by both Chiang Kai-shek and the United States.

From 1954 to 1959, Mao was the Chairman of the PRC. He took up residence in Zhongnanhai, a compound next to the Forbidden City in Beijing, and there he decreed the construction of an indoor swimming pool and other buildings. Mao often did his work either in bed or by the side of the pool during his chairmanship, according to Dr. Li Zhisui, who claimed to be his physician. (Li's book, In 1958, Mao launched the Great Leap Forward, a plan intended as an alternative model for economic growth which contradicted the Soviet model which ended in 1960, after food shortages affected both the Chairman's home town and Zhongnanhai itself. Both inside and outside China, the Great Leap Forward is now regarded as a disastrous policy contributing to the deaths of millions of people. The Revolution led to the destruction of much of China's cultural heritage and the imprisonment of a huge number of Chinese intellectuals, amongst other social chaos. It was during this period that Mao chose Lin Biao to become his successor. Lin Biao attempted a military coup in 1971, resulting in Lin's death from a plane crash. Mao lost trust in many of the top CPC figures.

The Cultural Revolution and its great negative impact on China as a whole made it near-universally regarded as a complete disaster. In 1969, Mao declared the Cultural Revolution to be over, although the official history of the People's Republic of China marks the end of the Cultural Revolution in 1976 with Mao's death. In the last years of his life, Mao was faced with declining health due to either Parkinson's disease or, according to Li Zhisui, motor neurone disease, as well as lung ailments due to smoking, and heart trouble, and remained passive as various factions within the Communist Party mobilized for the power struggle anticipated after his death.

Margaret Leiteritz, (born 1907), was a German painter. In the 1960s and early 1970s, Leiteritz produced her 'painted diagrams', which drew heavily from the scientific articles and books in her care. She was a professional Librarian before becoming a painter. Many of her works were strongly influenced by chemical engineering, and especially the field's graphs which depicted physical properties of substances. Leiteritz's paintings typically reworked a mundane graph using large expanses of color and a bold abstract theme, into a dynamic painting. Other works are reminiscent of a Bunsen burner flame, or a DNA gel. One of her most famous paintings, "Crossing at the Left Border" (1966; oil on linen) appeared on the cover of the catalogue for an art exhibition in Chicago in 1969. This painting is known to have been inspired by a specific graph appearing in an otherwise unremarkable paper of the American Institute of Chemical Engineering Journal. Her work has much in common with that of Klee.

Marianne Moore (November 15, 1887 - February 5, 1972) was a Modernist American poet and writer. Marianne Moore was born in Kirkwood, Missouri, outside of St. Louis, the daughter of a construction engineer and inventor, John Milton Moore, and his wife, Mary Warner. She grew up in the household of her grandfather, a Presbyterian pastor, her father having been committed to a mental hospital before her birth. In 1905, Marianne Moore entered Bryn Mawr College in Pennsylvania, and graduated four years later. A few years on, she began to teach courses at the United States Industrial Indian School, Carlisle, and continued until 1915, when Moore began to professionally publish poetry. Her most famous poem is perhaps the one entitled, appropriately, "Poetry," in which she hopes for poets who can produce "imaginary gardens with real toads in them." In part because of her extensive European travels before the first World War, Moore came to the attention, and received the respect of, poets as diverse as Wallace Stevens, William Carlos Williams, H.D., T. S. Eliot, and Ezra Pound. From 1925 until 1929, Moore served as editor of the literary and cultural journal the Dial. This continued her role, similar to that of Pound, as a patron of poetry, encouraging promising young poets, including Elizabeth Bishop and Allen Ginsberg, and publishing, as well as refining poetic technique, early work. In 1933, Moore was awarded the Helen Haire Levinson Prize from Poetry. Her Collected Poems of 1951 is perhaps her most rewarded work; it earned the poet the Pulitzer Prize, the National Book Award, and the Bollingen Prize. After being awarded these prizes, she began to be a kind of minor celebrity, at least in New York literary circles. Moore often served as unofficial hostess for the Mayor. She attended boxing matches, baseball games and other public events, dressed in what became her signature garb, a tricorn hat and a black cape.

Moore corresponded for a time with W.H. Auden and Ezra Pound during the latter's incarceration. In 1955, the Ford Motor Company asked Moore to help them name a new model then in development. Moore submitted a list of suggestions that included "The Intelligent Whale," "The Utopian Turtletop," "The Pastelogram," and "The Mongoose Civique." The Company decided not to use any of Moore's suggestions and instead named the car the Edsel. The model, having lost Ford $250 million, was discontinued in 1959. Not too long after throwing the first pitch and opening the 1968 season in Yankee Stadium, Moore suffered a stroke. She suffered a series of subsequent strokes thereafter, and died, unmarried, in 1972.

McLeish, Archibald see Archibald MacLeish

Mcluhan, Marshall (1911-1980) The University of Toronto professor of literature and culture who became famous for his innovative theories about how methods of communication influence society. In 1963, his analysis of the effect of movable type on the culture of 15th century Europe (The Gutenberg Galaxy: The Making of Typographic Man) won the Governor-General's award for critical writing. In 1964, Mcluhan gained considerable attention in the popular press for Understanding Media: The Extensions of Man in which he argued that the communication media used by humans are extensions of the physical senses which, by their very nature, introduce changes in the way societies function and in human consciousness, apart from the content they convey. His assertion that "the medium is the message" eventually became "the medium is the massage

McLuhanism' is a term sometimes used to refer to his notion that 'the medium is the message', which had at least four apparent meanings: a) that the medium shapes its content (i.e. that the nature of any medium has implications for the kinds of experience which can be best handled with it); b) that using a medium is important in itself (e.g. watching television or reading books are experiences in themselves regardless of explicit content); c) that the 'message' of a medium is the 'impact' it has on society; d) that the 'message' of a medium is its transformation of the perceptual habits of its users. McLuhan was a technological determinist who adopted the 'hard determinist' stance that communication technologies such as television, radio, printing and writing profoundly transformed both society and 'the human psyche'. The technologies (or media) which he discussed reflected his very broad definition of 'media'. This stance (sometimes known more specifically as 'media determinism') can be seen as an application of extreme Whorfianism to the nature of media in general. Just as Whorf argued that different languages shape our perception and thinking differently, McLuhan argued that all media do this. Clearly for McLuhan, the medium was far from neutral. See also:

Form and content, Medium, Non-neutrality of medium, Linguistic determinism, Technological determinism, Whorfianism

Melville Dewey Melville Louis Kossuth Dewey was born at Adams Center, New York, on December 10, 1851. In 1874 Dewey graduated from Amherst College, Amherst, Massachusetts where he became acting librarian. This is where he worked as a student assistant.

He was the inventor of the Dewey Decimal Classification system for library classification, Dewey was born Melville Louis Kossuth Dewey in Adams Center, New York in the United States. He attended Amherst College, graduating in 1874. It was while working as an assistant librarian at Amherst from 1874 until 1877 that Dewey devised his decimal system. He moved to Boston where he founded and edited The Library Journal, which became an influential factor in the development of libraries in America, and in the reform of their administration.

In 1883 Dewey became librarian of Columbia College, and in the following year founded there the Columbia School of Library Economy, the first institution for the instruction of librarians ever organized. This school, which was very successful, was removed to Albany, New York in 1890, where it was reestablished as the New York State Library School under his direction; from 1888 to 1906 he was director of the New York State Library and from 1888 to 1900 was secretary of the University of the State of New York, completely reorganizing the state library, which he made one of the most efficient in America, and establishing the system of state travelling libraries and picture collections. He was an advocate of English language spelling reform and is responsible for, among other things, the "American" spelling of the word Catalog (as opposed to the British Catalogue). He changed his own name from Melville Louis Kossuth Dewey to simply Melvil Dui. He is also credited with the invention of the vertical office file.

Dewey was a great enthusiast of nature, one-time owner of a lodge in the Adirondack Mountains, which he named the Adirondak Loj.

Dewey also helped establish the American Library Association (ALA) in 1876; he was secretary of ALA from 1876 to 1890 and president during the 1890/1891 and 1892/1893 terms. He co-founded (1877) and edited Library Journal. He was a promoter of library standards and formed a company to sell library supplies, which eventually became the Library Bureau. He was a pioneer in library education. In 1883, Dewey became the librarian of Columbia College (now Columbia University) in New York City. While there, he founded the first ever library school. In December 1889, he became the director of the New York State Library at Albany, retiring from that position in 1906.

Dewey considered himself to be a reformer and among his other reform passions were short-hand, the use of bicycles, and simplified spelling. He figured that three years could be saved if the English language was simplified. This was largely unsuccessful. However, he continued to use simplified spelling, he even cut his first name to Melvil and his last name to Dui.

Dewey died from a stroke on December 26, 1931. He is still primarily known for the Dewey Decimal Classification, the most widely used library classification scheme in the world.

Michael Lorenzen One of the leaders of the Library Instruction movement in the United States, Michael Lorenzen was born in 1970 in Bowling Green, Ohio. He graduated with BA in philosophy in 1992 from Bowling Green State University, a Master of Library Science degree from Kent State University in 1993, a Master of Education degree in 1996 from Ohio University, and an Educational Specialist degree from Michigan State University in 2002. First employed at Ohio University, Michael Lorenzen became prominent in the library instruction field while employed as the Library Instruction Coordinator at Michigan State University from 1996-2003. While there, he published over 20 articles on library instruction and information literacy. He also was the main figure in the creation of the Tales from the MSU Stacks (http://tales.lib.msu.edu) tutorial which won several national awards. Currently, Michael Lorenzen is Head of Reference at Central Michigan University. Writings of Michael Lorenzen have been on library instruction, information literacy, and active learning. They have appeared in journals such as Library Journal, Illinois Libraries, Journal of Library Management, LOEX News, and Research Strategies. He was formerly the Executive Editor of Academic Exchange Quarterly.

Nancy Pearl (born 1945?) is a book reviewer and was, until August 2004, a Seattle public librarian. Her prolific reading and her knowledge of books and literature first made her locally famous in Seattle, Washington, where she regularly appears on public radio recommending books. She then achieved broader fame with her book Book Lust. She founded the pioneering and much-imitated "If All Seattle Read The Same Book" project. She has had her face on American Library Association posters, has received numerous awards, and may be the only librarian in the United States to be the model for an action figure. A tribute band called 'The Nancy Pearls' gave their debut bluegrass performance on the Mitchell Library rooftop (Sydney, Australia) on 17 December 2004. It was a resounding success.

Newbery, John (1713-1767) The English writer, publisher, printer, and bookseller who first recognized the potential commercial market for books written specifically for children. Newbery began publishing works for children in 1744 with A Little Pretty Pocket-Book, containing rhyming fables and rules of conduct, followed by the didactic favorites The History of Little Goody Two-Shoes (1765) which may have been written by his friend Oliver

Goldsmith. Illustrated in color, the titles in his inexpensive Juvenile Library series were very popular in England. He also published the first children's encyclopedia, The Circle of the Sciences in seven volumes (1745-48), and the first children's periodical, The Lilliputian Magazine (1751). Newbery's contribution to children's literature is commemorated in the Newbery Medal, awarded annually since 1922 to the most distinguished children's book by an American author published in the United States during the preceding year.

Patrick Magruder (1768-December 24, 1819) was the second U.S. Librarian of Congress, serving from 1807 to 1815. Magruder was born at "Locust Grove", his family's estate near Rockville in Montgomery County, Maryland. Magruder attended Princeton College and became a lawyer. In 1805, he was elected to the Ninth United States Congress from Maryland. After the death of John J. Beckley, President Jefferson appointed Magruder to the dual post of Clerk of the United States House of Representatives and Librarian of Congress. (The posts were not separated until 1815.) During the War of 1812, the British burned Washington D.C., including the Library of Congress, which was then housed in the US Capitol Building. After a investigation by Congress into the destruction of the Library and the use of Library funds, Magruder resigned. He was buried on his family's ancestral estate, "Sweden," near Petersburg in Dinwiddie County, Virginia.

Paul Otlet Paul Otlet was born in Brussels, Belgium, in 1868. His monumental book *Traité de documentation.* (Brussels, 1934) was both central and symbolic in the development of information science then called "Documentation" in the first half of this century. In addition, it reminds us of something that has been too widely forgotten: That this field did have a lively existence in the early decades of this century and a sophistication concerning theory and information technology that now commonly surprises people.

Paul Otlet was the most central figure in the development of Documentation. He struggled tirelessly for decades with the central technical, theoretical, and organizational aspects of a problem central to society: How to make recorded knowledge available to those who need it. He thought deeply and wrote endlessly as he designed, developed, and initiated ambitious solutions at his Institute in Brussels.

Towards the end of working life he summarized his ideas in two large books of synthesis, the *Traité de documentation* in 1934 and *Monde: Essai d'universalisme* in 1935. In recent years there has been a renewed interest in Otlet's work. In 1989 the *Traité,* so long out of print, was in reprinted. In 1990 his biographer, Prof W. Boyd Rayward, of the University of New South Wales, published an annotated English translation of a selection of Otlet's best writings: Otlet, Paul. *International Organization and Dissemination of Knowledge: Selected Essays.* (FID 684). Amsterdam: Elsevier, 1990. Now Otlet's ideas and writings are again an active ingredient in information science, having historical interest and also a contemporary interest in relation, for example, to the nature of documents and of hypertext. It is now a century since Otlet and LaFontaine began their ambitious program which continues as the International Federation for Information and Documentation FID. (Adapted from the Preface to the Spanish edition of Otlet's *Traité*). Otlet and LaFontaine were also active in the founding of the Union of International Associations.

Otlet's archives and museum is now available again at Rue des Passages 15, B-7000 Mons,in Mons, Belgium, as The Mundaneum, which has started to publish research based on these archives, notably *Cent ans de l'Office International de Bibliographie : 1895 - 1995 ; les premisses du Mundaneum.* - Mons : Editions Mundaneum, 1995.

Philip Larkin (August 9, 1922–December 2, 1985) was an English poet, novelist and jazz critic. Larkin was born to Sydney and Eva Larkin in Coventry, a provincial city in the English Midlands. He was educated at King Henry VIII School in Coventry and St. John's College, Oxford. Soon after graduating from Oxford he applied for, and won, the position of Librarian at Wellington, Shropshire, in late 1943. In 1946, he became Assistant Librarian at the University College, Leicester; in March 1955, he became Librarian at the University of Hull. He remained in this position for most of the rest of his life. He never married.

Larkin's early work shows the influence of Yeats, but his later poetic identity was influenced mainly by Thomas Hardy. He is well-known for his use of slang and coarse language in his poetry, partly balanced by a similarly antique word choice. With fine use of enjambement and rhyme, his poetry is highly structured, but never rigid. Death was a recurring theme and subject of his poetry, Aubade being the best example of this. The Less Deceived, published in 1955, marked Larkin as an up-and-coming poet. He was for a time associated with The Movement. 1964's The Whitsun Weddings confirmed his reputation. The title poem is a masterful depiction of the sights from a train one Whitsun; though this description does the poem little justice. In 1972 he wrote the oft-quoted "Going, Going", a poem which reveals his increasing streak of romantic fatalism in his view of England in his later years - prophesising a complete destruction of the countryside and of a certain idealised idea of national togetherness and identity, it ends with the doom-laden statement "I just think it will happen, soon". High Windows, his last book, was released in 1974; for some critics it represents a falling-off from his previous two books into acrid self-parody (at its worst in a bitter poem like "Homage to a Government"); yet it contains a number of his most-loved poems, including the title-poem, "This Be The Verse" and "The Explosion".

Larkin was an major contributor to the re-evaluation of the poetry of Thomas Hardy, which had been unjustly ignored in comparison to his work as a novelist. Hardy received the longest selection in Larkin's idiosyncratic and controversial anthology, The Oxford Book of Twentieth-Century English Verse (1973). Larkin was by contrast a notable critic of modernism in contemporary art and literature; his skepticism is at its most nuanced and illuminating in Required Writing, a collection of his book-reviews and essays; it is at its most enflamed and polemical in his introduction to his collected jazz reviews, All What Jazz. On the death of John Betjeman, Larkin was offered the post of Poet Laureate, but declined, feeling that his poetic muse had permanently deserted him. However, he remains one of Britain's most popular poets; two of his poems, This Be The Verse and An Arundel Tomb, featuring in the "Nation's Top 100 Poems" as voted for by television viewers. Larkin's posthumous reputation has taken a hit with the publication of Andrew Motion's Philip Larkin: A Writer's Life and an edition of his letters, which revealed in detail his obsessions with pornography, his racism, his increasingly extreme shift to the political right wing, and his habitual venom and spleen. Such revelations do not alter the quality and sheer memorability of his best verse.

Pierre François le Courayer (November 17, 1681 - October 17, 1776), was a French Catholic theological writer. He was born at Rouen. While canon regular and librarian of the abbey of St Genevieve at Paris, he conducted a correspondence with Archbishop William Wake on the subject of episcopal succession in England, which supplied him with material for his work, Dissertation sur la validité des ordinations des Anglais et sur la succession des évéques de l'Eglise anglicane, avec les preuves justificatives des fails avancés, an attempt to prove that there has been no break in the line of ordination from the apostles to the English clergy. His opinions exposed him to a prosecution, and with the help of Francis Atterbury, then in exile in Paris, he took refuge in England, where he was presented by the University of Oxford with a doctor's degree. In 1736 he published a French translation of Paolo Sarpi's History of the Council of Trent, and dedicated it to Queen Caroline, from whom he received a pension of £200 a year. Besides this he translated Sleidan's History of the Reformation, and wrote several theological works. He died in London, and was buried in the cloisters of Westminster Abbey. In his will, dated two years before his death, he declared himself still a member of the Roman Catholic Church, although dissenting from many of its opinions.

Raj Reddy Dr. Raj Reddy is the Herbert A. Simon University Professor of Computer Science and Robotics in the School of Computer Science at Carnegie Mellon University. From 1960-63, Dr. Reddy worked as an Applied Science Representative for IBM Corp., in Australia. He began his academic career as an Assistant Professor at Stanford in 1966. He joined the Carnegie Mellon faculty as an Associate Professor of Computer Science in 1969. He became a Full Professor in 1973, and a University Professor in 1984. He served as the founding Director of the Robotics Institute from 1979 to 1991 and as the Dean of School of Computer Science from 1991 to 1999.

Dr. Reddy's research interests include the study of human-computer interaction and artificial intelligence. His current research projects include Million Book Digital Library Project; PCtvt: 5-in-1 PC architectures for rural environments (PC, TV, PVR, Video Phone, Audio Phone all in one) for use by illiterate people; 100x100 Networks connecting 100 million homes with 100 mbps+ connectivity (with Prof Hui Zhang and others); RADAR - Webmaster Agent subsystem; MAX: Mobile Autonomous Robot Platform (with Dr Khalid Ali and Ajinkya Bhave); Learning by Doing (at Carnegie Mellon West)

His professional honors include: Fellow of the Institute of Electrical and Electronics Engineers, Fellow of the Acoustical Society of America, Fellow of the American Association for Artificial Intelligence, Member of the National Academy of Engineering and Member of the

American Academy of Arts and Sciences. He was president of the American Association for Artificial Intelligence from 1987 to 89. He is a recipient of the IBM Research Ralph Gomory Fellow Award in 1991. He is the recipient of Okawa Prize in 2004.

Dr. Reddy was awarded the Legion of Honor by President Mitterand of France in 1984 and Padma Bhushan by President of India in 2001. He was awarded the ACM Turing Award in 1994. He served as co-chair of the President's Information Technology Advisory Committee (PITAC) from 1999 to 2001. He has been awarded honorary doctorates (Doctor of Science Honoris Causa) from SV University in India, Universite Henri-Poincare in France, University of New South Wales in Australia, Jawaharlal Nehru Technological University in India, University of Massachusetts in USA, University of Warwick in England, Anna University in India and the Indian Institute for Information Technology (Allahabad) . He serves on the Board of Governors of Peres Institute for Peace in Israel.

Ranganathan, Shiyali Ramamrita (August 9, 1892, Shiyali, Tamil Nadu - September 27, 1972, Bangalore) was an innovative mathematician and librarian from India. His most notable contributions to the field were his five laws of library science and the development of the first major analytico-synthetic classification system, the Colon classification. He is considered to be the father of library science in India. Ranganathan, born on 9 August 1892, came from a moderate background in British-ruled India. He was born in the rural village of Shiyali (also known as Sirkazhi), in the state of Tamil Nadu in South India. Ranganathan began his professional life as a mathematician; he earned B.A. and M.A. degrees in mathematics from Madras Christian College in his home province, and then went on to earn a teaching licensure. His lifelong goal was to teach mathematics, and he was successively a member of the mathematics faculties at universities in Mangalore, Coimbatore and Madras (all within the span of five years).

As a mathematics professor, he published a handful of papers, most on mathematics history, and his career as an educator was somewhat hindered by a handicap of stammering (a difficulty Ranganathan gradually overcame in his professional life). In 1923, the University of Madras created the post of University Librarian to oversee their poorly organized collection. Among the 900 applicants for the position, none had any formal training in librarianship, and Ranganathan's handful of papers satisfied the search committee's requirement that the candidate should have a research background. His sole knowledge of librarianship came from an Encyclopædia Britannica article he read days before the interview.

Ranganathan was initially reluctant to pursue the position (he had forgotten about his application by the time he was called for an interview there) and did little to boost his bid through the Indian tradition of lobbying the selection committee. To his own surprise, he received the appointment and accepted the position in January of 1924. At first, Ranganathan found the solitude of the position was intolerable. After a matter of weeks, complaining of total boredom, he went back to the university administration to beg for his teaching position back. A deal was struck that Ranganthan would travel to London, to study contemporary Western practices in librarianship, and that, if he returned and still rejected librarianship as a career, the mathematics lectureship would be his again. Ranganathan travelled to University College London, which at that time housed the only graduate degree program in library science in Britain. At University College, he earned marks only slightly above average, but his mathematical mind latched onto the problem of classification. a subject typically taught by rote in library programs of the time. As an outsider, he focused on what he perceived to be flaws with the popular decimal classification, and began to explore new possibilities on his own. He began drafting the system that was ultimately to become the Colon Classification while in England, and refined it as he returned home, even going so far as to reorder the ship's library on the voyage back to India.

Ranganathan returned with a powerful passion for libraries and librarianship and a vision of its importance for the Indian nation He returned to and held the position of University Librarian at the University of Madras for twenty years. During that time, he helped to found the Madras Library Association, and lobbied actively for the establishment of free public libraries throughout India and for the creation of a comprehensive national library. Ranganthan was considered by many to be a workaholic. During his two decades in Madras, he consistently worked 13-hour days, seven days a week, without taking a vacation for the entire time. Although he married in November 1928, he returned to work the afternoon following the marriage ceremony. He and his wife Sarada had only one son, a few years later, but they stayed married until Ranganathan's death. The first few years of Ranganathan's tenure at Madras were years of deliberation and analysis as he tackled the problems of library administration and classification. It was during this period that he produced what have come to be known as his two greatest legacies: his five laws of library science (1931) and the Colon Classification system (1933).

After two decades of serving as librarian at Madras — a post he had intended to keep until his retirement, Ranganathan retired from his position after conflicts with a new university vice-chancellor became intolerable. At the age of 54, he submitted his resignation and, after a brief bout with depression, accepted a professorship in library science at Hindu University in Banaras, his last formal academic position, in August 1945. There, he cataloged the university's collection; by the time he left four years later, he had classified over 100,000 items personally.

Ranganathan headed the Indian Library Association from 1944 to 1953, but was never a particularly adept administrator, and left amid controversy when the Delhi Public Library chose to use the Dewey Decimal Classification system instead of his own Colon Classification. He held an honorary professorship at Delhi University from 1949 to 1955 and helped build that institution's library science programs with S. Das Gupta, a former student of his. Ranganathan briefly moved to Zurich, Switzerland, from 1955 to 1957, when his son married a European girl; the unorthodox relationship did not sit well with Ranganathan, although his time in Zurich allowed him to expand his contacts within the European library community, where he gained a significant following. However, he soon returned to India and settled in the city of Bangalore, where he would spend the rest of his life. While in Zurich, though, he endowed a professorship at Madras University in honor of his wife of thirty years, largely as an ironic gesture in retaliation for the persecution he suffered for many years at the hands of that university's administration. Ranganathan's final major achievement was the establishment of the Documentation Research and Training Centre in Bangalore in 1962, where he served as honorary director for five years.

In 1965, he was honored by the Indian government for his contributions to the field with the title of "National Research Professor." In the final years of his life, Ranganathan finally succumbed to ill health, and was largely confined to his bed. On 27 September 1972, he died of complications from bronchitis. Upon the centenary of his birth in 1992, several autobiographical volumes and collections of essays on Ranganathan's influence were published in his honor. Ranganathan's autobiography, published serially during his life, is titled A Librarian Looks Back.

Sanford Berman (b. October 6, 1933) is an outspoken, radical librarian who promoted alternative viewpoints in librarianship, opposed library oppression and acted as a valuable one-man information conduit to other librarians around the world. Berman was born in Chicago, Illinois. He attended University of California at Los Angeles, where he earned a B.A. in Political Science with minors in Sociology, Anthropology and English, and received the Phi Beta Kappa from the national scholastic honour society. After acquiring an M.S. in Library Science from the Catholic University of America in Washington, D.C., Berman began work as a librarian. He worked for the U.S. Army Special Services Libraries, West Germany (1962-1966) ; Schiller College, Kleiningerheim, West Germany (1966-1967) ; University of California at Los Angeles Research Library (1967-1968) ; University of Zambia Library, Lusaka, Zambia (1968-1970) ; Makerere Institute of Social Research, Makerere University Library, Kampala, Uganda (1971-1972) ; and Hennepin County Library, Minnesota (1973-1999).

Schumacher Sanford Berman (August 24, 1635 - March 12, 1699), was a Danish statesman. Born at Copenhagen into a wealthy trading family connected with the leading civic, clerical and learned circles in the Danish capital, he was prepared for university (at the age of ten) by Jens Vorde. In 1663 he was appointed the royal librarian. A romantic friendship with the king's bastard, Count Ulric Frederick Gyldenlove, consolidated his position. In 1665 Schumacher obtained his first political post as the king's secretary, and the same year composed the memorable Kongelov. He was now a personage at court, where he won many over by his amiability and gaiety; and in political matters also his influence was beginning to be felt.

On the death of Frederick III (February 9, 1670) Schumacher was the most trusted of all the royal counsellors. He alone was aware of the existence of the new throne of walrus ivory embellished with three silver life-size lions, and of the new regalia, both of which treasures he had, by the king's command, concealed in a vault beneath the royal castle. Frederick III had also confided to him a sealed packet containing the Kongelov, which was to be delivered to his successor alone. Schumacher had been recommended to his son by Frederick III on his death-bed. "Make him a great man, but do it slowly," said Frederick, who thoroughly understood the characters of his son and of his minister. Christian V was, moreover, deeply impressed by the confidence which his father had ever shown to Schumacher.

Sergey Brin Sergey Mihailovich Brin (born August 21, 1973) is an American entrepreneur. Bom in Russia, Brin studied computer science and mathematics before co-founding Google with Larry Page. Brin is the President of Technology at Google and has a net worth estimated at $12.9 Billion, making him the 26th richest person in the world.

Sergey was born in Moscow, Russia, the son of a Jewish mathematician and economist. In 1979, when Sergey was five, his family emigrated to the U.S. (for freedom from anti-Semitism, according to the book "The Google Story" [1]) where Sergey's father began to work as a professor of mathematics at the University of Maryland, College Park, where he continues to teach today. Sergey's mother currently works as a specialist at NASA.

Sergey attributes his success to many factors. Growing up during the microcomputer revolution, he had an interest in computers from early in his childhood. He received his first computer, a Commodore 64, as a present from his father on his ninth birthday. Sergey's natural talent for mathematics and computing was apparent during his first years of schooling. In the first grade, Sergey surprised a teacher by submitting a project in the form of a printout, at a time before computers were commonplace in the home. Sergey, and Google co-founder Lawrence E. Page have both given credit for their success

Sergey attended grade school in the U.S. at Paint Branch Montessori School in Adelphi, Maryland, but he received further education at home; his father nurtured his interest in mathematics and his family helped him retain his Russian language skills. In September 1990, after high school, Sergey enrolled in the University of Maryland, College Park to study Computer Science and Mathematics, where he received his Bachelors of Science in May 1993 with high honors. After graduating from Maryland, Sergey received a graduate fellowship from the National Science Foundation, which allowed him to study for his masters degree in Computer Science at Stanford University. Sergey received his masters degree in August 1995 ahead of schedule in the process of his Ph.D. studies. Though still enrolled in the Stanford doctoral program, Sergey has suspended his Ph.D. studies indefinitely while he is working at Google.

Sergey expressed interest in the Internet very early on in his studies at Stanford. He authored and co-authored various papers on data-mining and pattern extraction. He also wrote software to ease the process of putting scientific papers often written in TeX, a text processing language, into HTML form, as well as a website for film ratings.

The defining moment for Sergey, however, was when he met future co-president of Google, Larry Page. Sergey was assigned to show Larry around the university on a weekend tour. Reportedly, they did not get on well to begin with, arguing about every topic they discussed, and even throwing a few pies at each other. However, they soon found a common interest: retrieving relevant information from large data sets. Together, the pair authored what is widely considered their seminal contribution, a paper entitled "The Anatomy of a Large-Scale Hypertextual Web Search Engine". The paper has since gone on to become the tenth most accessed scientific paper at Stanford University. Despite his success, Sergey has remained relatively unknown to the public eye. He is not known to be lavish with his wealth and drives an inexpensive car the Toyota Prius. According to his father, Sergey still rents a two-bedroom flat.

Seymour Lubetzky (April 28, 1898-April 5, 2003) A cataloging theorist and a prominent librarian, Seymour Lubetzky was 104 years of age when he died on April 5, 2003. Born in Belarus as Shmaryahu Lubetzky, he worked for years at the Library of Congress. Lubetzky also taught at UCLA's School of Library Service. Lubetzky's theory of cataloging went far beyond the Dewey Decimal System. He divised a colorful yet tactful way of identifying but ordering books where even the most simple person could find it. Lubetzky was fluent in six languages, and was also immortalized in two books himself, entitled "Seymour Lubetzky: Writings on the Classical Art of Cataloging" and "Future of Cataloging: The Lubetzky Symposium". Just before his 104th birthday, the American Library Association awarded Lubetzky its highest honor, an honorary lifetime membership.

Shiyali Ramamrita Ranganathan see Ranganathan, Shyali Ramamrita

Thomas James (c. 1573 - August, 1629) was an English librarian, first librarian of the Bodleian Library, Oxford. He was born at Newport, Isle of Wight, and educated at Winchester and New College, Oxford, where he became a fellow in 1593. In 1602, his wide knowledge of books, together with his skill in deciphering manuscripts and detecting literary forgeries, secured him the post of librarian to the library newly founded by Sir Thomas Bodley at Oxford. At the same time he was made rector of St Aldate's, Oxford. In 1605 he compiled a classified catalogue of the books in the Bodleian Library, but in 1620 substituted for it an alphabetical catalogue. The arrangement in 1610, whereby the Stationers' Company undertook to supply the Bodleian Library with every book published, was James's suggestion. Ill health compelled him to resign his post in 1620, and he died at Oxford in August 1629.

Thomas Louis Berger (born July 20, 1924) is a U.S. novelist. Born in Cincinnati, Ohio, Berger was in Europe with the U.S. army, and then studied at the University of Cincinnati and at Columbia University. He worked as a librarian and a journalist before publishing his first novel, Crazy in Berlin, in 1958.

Wallace Breem (1926–1990) was a British librarian and author, the Librarian and Keeper of Manuscripts of the Inner Temple Law Library at his death, but perhaps more widely known for his historical novels, including the classic Eagle in the Snow (1970). At the age of 18, Breem entered the Indian Army's Officers Training School, and in 1945 was commissioned as an officer of the Corps of Guides, an elite Cavalry detachment of the North West Frontier Force. After Partition in 1947, Breem returned to England and held a variety of jobs which included labourer in a tannery, assistant to a veterinary surgeon, and rent-collector in the East End of London. He eventually joined the library staff of the Inner Temple in London, in 1950. Breem was a founder member of the British and Irish Association of Law Librarians (BIALL (http://www.biall.org.uk)), and at various times held the offices of Secretary, Treasurer, Chairman, Vice-President, and President in that organization. In 1990, BIALL inaugurated the Wallace Breem award in his memory.

Wilhelm Lexis (1837 – 1914) was an eminent German economist and social scientist and a founder of the interdisciplinary study of insurance. Born in Eschweiler as the son of a physician, Lexis obtained a Ph.D. in Physics from the University of Heidelberg, where he was an assistant of the famous Chemist Robert Bunsen. He then worked as a Gymnasium teacher, librarian, and journalist, until in 1872 he became, until 1874, extraordinary professor at the newly-refounded German-language

Imperial University of Straßburg. In 1874-1876, he taught at the University of Tartu, then at the University of Freiburg im Breisgau, since 1884 at the University of Breslau, and from 1887 at the University of Göttingen, which was his final appointment. He died in Göttingen. Although the author of an Allgemeine Volkswirtschaftslehre (general economics book) (1910) and certainly a distinguished economist, even a pioneer of Law and Economics thinking and of the study of consumption and crises, Lexis is today primarily known as a statistician, and maybe particularly as a demographer. He is also one of the founding fathers of the interdisciplinary, professional study of insurance.

Lexis was closely affiliated with academic policy makers in Prussia and one of Friedrich Althoff's experts and the editor of important works on German higher education, most famously the six-volume Das Unterrichtswesen im Deutschen Reich, compiled for the St. Louis World's Fair of that year and still the key reference work for that time. Lexis' theoretical works on social science epistemology are largely forgotten but very relevant today. Being unable to read and write, he relied on his mother, with whom he had always been personally close, and who began to work with him as his personal secretary.

William Henry Bliss Bliss was bora 26 April 1835 in Newton St Loe, Somerset. He was the son of Rev. William Bliss and Jane Monck (born Jane Bridges). Bliss was the grandson of Dr. John Bliss M.D., a physician who specialised in the treatment of gout. The family owned a tweed factory at Chipping Norton, Oxfordshire.

He was educated at Winchester from 1847 to 1852. He then went up to Magdalen College Oxford where he received a Bachelor of Arts in 1859 and a Master of Arts in 1863. In 1868 he was awarded a BCL. In 1854, he edited The Parson. On 4 May 1959 he married Mary Jane Wray, daughter of Rev. Cyril Wray of St. Martin's, Liverpool. Over twenty years they were to have eleven children.

Bliss suffered from a stammer. He therefore spent more than the usual time as a deacon. He was finally ordained by the Church of England in 1865. He served as Curate of Honington for four years from 1858, then moved to St James, Plymouth until 1865 and took the Vicarage of North Hincksey on the outskirts of Oxford in 1866. In 1867 Bliss published his first major work, The Canons of the First Four General Councils, in Greek and English. It warranted a second edition in 1869.

Bliss appeared to have very good prospects within the established church. He was the son of a clergyman, was blessed with a good education and had very useful contacts. He was being published. However, at Oxford he came into contact with the Oxford Movement. This group of High Churchmen originally attempted to show that the Church of England was a direct descendant of the Church established bythe apostles. Many members of the group converted to Catholicism, including John Cardinal Newman, (as he would become). Bliss became curate to his uncle James at Plymouth. His uncle was a leading Anglo-Catholic.

Bliss was increasingly turning towards Catholic theology and doubting the historical legitimacy of the Church of England. In 1869 he followed Newman into the Roman Catholic faith. He then secured the position of Keeper of Periodicals at the Bodleian Library in Oxford.

In 1877 the Public Records Office asked Bliss to go to Rome to do research in the Vatican Archives on its behalf. He accepted the offer and spent most of his time searching the mediaeval Papal Registers in order to find all the dealings between the Papacy and Great Britain and Ireland. This job required Bliss to spend nine months of each year in Rome and this became Bliss' habit until he died at the Via Delphini in 1911. His wife raised the children in England and remained an Anglican. At first the Papal bureaucrats were suspicious of an Englishmen. He won them over and by 1886 he was the English Tutor to Victor Emmanuel, heir to the Italian crown. He enjoyed cordial relations with the Italian Royal family.

In the Vatican Bliss produced a series called the Calendar of The Entries in the Papal Registers Relating to British Isles Volumes I and II. These were entirely Bliss" work. He edited volumes III, IV and V with collaborators.

William Jones Willian Jones was born in London on 28th September 1746. His father died when William was only three years old, but his mother aroused boundless curiosity in him. At a tender age of twenty he became adept in French, Italian, Spanish, Portuguese, Greek, Latin and English. His knowledge of Arabic and Persian made King Christian VII of Denmark assign him the translation of "Tariq-i-Nadiri" into French He was made a fellow of the Royal Society in 1772 and in the following year, a member of the prestigious Literary Club of Dr. Johnson

Jones arrived in India in September 1783 a judge in the Supreme Court in Calcutta. He realized that India had much to offer to the world in the sciences and the arts, and that the discovery of her rich past and culture could not be achieved by himself. He discussed with his colleagues and established the "Asiatic Society" on 15th January 1784, and this was a revolutionary event in the world of letters. It marked the restoration of ancient learning in and about India. Jones realized that it was the East, which held the secrets of early history and civilization of man; and that unless the East was know, the history of man could not be written.

Jones invented the system of transliteration and translated the Laws of Manu (Manusmriti) into English. He was the first westerner to study and write a paper on Indian Classical Music, the first person to put forward a plan for classification of Indian plants and animals. He was instrumental for compilation of books on Botany,

Zoology, Astronomy and Philosophy. He declared that the Sanskrit language is of wonderful structure, more perfect than Greek, more copious than the Latin and thus laid foundation for birth of Science of Linguistics. Thereafter, many western universities began founding chairs in Sanskrit. He translated Kalidasa's "Abhiknana Shakuntala" and "Ritu Samhara," and Jayadeva's "Gita Govinda" into English. This lead to study of Indian dramatic literature and mythology. Further he also encouraged study of Indian chronology. On 27th April 1794 he passed away because of an inflammation of liver. He was only forty eight years old, and a great progress in the study of India was untimely curtailed.